Codes of Ethics in Tourism

ASPECTS OF TOURISM
Series Editors: Professor Chris Cooper, *University of Queensland, Australia*
Dr C. Michael Hall, *University of Canterbury, Christchurch, New Zealand*
Dr Dallen Timothy, *Arizona State University, Tempe, USA*

Aspects of Tourism is an innovative, multifaceted series which will comprise authoritative reference handbooks on global tourism regions, research volumes, texts and monographs. It is designed to provide readers with the latest thinking on tourism world-wide and in so doing will push back the frontiers of tourism knowledge. The series will also introduce a new generation of international tourism authors, writing on leading edge topics. The volumes will be readable and user-friendly, providing accessible sources for further research. The list will be underpinned by an annual authoritative tourism research volume. Books in the series will be commissioned that probe the relationship between tourism and cognate subject areas such as strategy, development, retailing, sport and environmental studies. The publisher and series editors welcome proposals from writers with projects on these topics.

Other Books in the Series
Tourism Marketing: A Collaborative Approach
    Alan Fyall and Brian Garrod
Music and Tourism: On the Road Again
    Chris Gibson and John Connell
Tourism Development: Issues for a Vulnerable Industry
    Julio Aramberri and Richard Butler (eds)
Nature-based Tourism in Peripheral Areas: Development or Disaster?
    C. Michael Hall and Stephen Boyd (eds)
Tourism, Recreation and Climate Change
    C. Michael Hall and James Higham (eds)
Shopping Tourism, Retailing and Leisure
    Dallen J. Timothy
Wildlife Tourism
    David Newsome, Ross Dowling and Susan Moore
Film-Induced Tourism
    Sue Beeton
Rural Tourism and Sustainable Business
    Derek Hall, Irene Kirkpatrick and Morag Mitchell (eds)
The Tourism Area Life Cycle, Vol.1: Applications and Modifications
    Richard W. Butler (ed.)
The Tourism Area Life Cycle, Vol.2: Conceptual and Theoretical Issues
    Richard W. Butler (ed.)
Tourist Behaviour: Themes and Conceptual Schemes
    Philip L. Pearce
Tourism Ethics
    David A. Fennell
North America: A Tourism Handbook
    David A. Fennell (ed.)
Lake Tourism: An Integrated Approach to Lacustrine Tourism Systems
    C.Michael Hall and Tuija Härkönen (eds)

For more details of these or any other of our publications, please contact:
Channel View Publications, Frankfurt Lodge, Clevedon Hall,
Victoria Road, Clevedon, BS21 7HH, England
http://www.channelviewpublications.com

ASPECTS OF TOURISM 33
Series Editors: Chris Cooper (*University of Queensland, Australia*),
C. Michael Hall (*University of Canterbury New Zealand*)
and Dallen Timothy (*Arizona State University, USA*)

Codes of Ethics in Tourism
Practice, Theory, Synthesis

David A. Fennell and David C. Malloy

CHANNEL VIEW PUBLICATIONS
Clevedon • Buffalo • Toronto

Library of Congress Cataloging in Publication Data
Fennell, David A.
Codes of Ethics in Tourism: Practice, Theory, Synthesis/David A. Fennell and David C. Malloy.
Aspects of Tourism: 33
Includes bibliographical references and index.
1. Tourism–Moral and ethical aspects. I. Malloy, David Cruise. II. Title. III. Series.
G155.A1F368 2007
174'.991–dc22   2007004440

British Library Cataloguing in Publication Data
A catalogue entry for this book is available from the British Library.

ISBN-13: 978-1-84541-061-2 (hbk)
ISBN-13: 978-1-84541-060-5 (pbk)

Channel View Publications
An imprint of Multilingual Matters Ltd

UK: Frankfurt Lodge, Clevedon Hall, Victoria Road, Clevedon BS21 7HH.
USA: 2250 Military Road, Tonawanda, NY 14150, USA.
Canada: 5201 Dufferin Street, North York, Ontario, Canada M3H 5T8.

The policy of Multilingual Matters/Channel View Publications is to use papers that are natural, renewable and recyclable products, made from wood grown in sustainable forests. In the manufacturing process of our books, and to further support our policy, preference is given to printers that have FSC and PEFC Chain of Custody certification. The FSC and/or PEFC logos will appear on those books where full certification has been granted to the printer concerned.

Typeset by Wordworks Ltd.
Printed and bound in Great Britain by the Cromwell Press Ltd.

Dedication

from David Fennell – to his children, Sam, Jessie and Lauren
and to his wife, Julie.

from David Malloy – to his travelling companion and bliss,
Valerie Loy Sluth
and to his brother, Brian,
who opened the door to adventure.

Contents

Part 4: Synthesis

Part 1

Context

Chapter 1

Preface

Setting the Stage: Epistemology and Morality

Thinking and ethical behaviour may be a case of the chicken and egg or a game of cat and mouse – which comes first or who is chasing whom? It may be then open to debate whether the following should be the first or the last section in this text. We have chosen, for better or worse, to set the stage for codes of ethics by providing the reader with a brief discussion on thinking because, ultimately, we believe that the purpose of a code is to make individuals consider their actions in a philosophical manner. Specifically, we have chosen two powerful constructs developed by the German philosopher, Martin Heidegger. The implications of these two philosophical tools for the way we perceive and, as a result – perhaps – the way we behave, are significant and worthy of our attention.

A Discourse on Thinking

In his text entitled *Discourse on Thinking*, Heidegger (1966:45) states that we are in a 'flight from thinking'. He suggests also that we of the developed world, in which science is our guide and our god, would vehemently deny this assertion. We, the children of logic, research and empiricism, of efficiency, effectiveness and productivity, believe we are better thinkers in this day and age than any of the generations before us. Heidegger would agree that we are not in a flight from this kind of teleological or *calculative* thinking, as the evidence in terms of technological advances is overwhelming. Rather, our flight is from the meaning we *ought* to draw from our behaviour (i.e. *meditative* or reflective thinking).

Heidegger argues that not only are we 'in flight from thinking' but we are also without foundation in our thinking – our rootedness. Science may well be argued to be the foundation of our penchant for calculative thinking, but do we overlook that which underpins science? In other words, for what reason or meaning do we invest implicitly in science? Well, generally speaking we don't know the answer to this question and rarely do we ask for clarification. Such flights from introspection are legion when one considers other aspects of our daily existence. For example, our own basic happiness is profoundly misunderstood and elusive.

Calculative thinking

This kind of thinking involves much of what we take for granted in terms

3

of logical and linear processing of information. Calculative thinking is the engine that drives planning, organising, computation, consequence, and the practical affairs of science, state, economics, and even tourism. People, animals, nature and the planet in general are perceived through the lens of calculative thought as resources for our consumption – they are valued for functionality. Calculative thought provides us with the intellectual means by which we are best able to exploit these resources. Thus mountains are valued for the skiing opportunities they provide, as well as for the raw materials that can be extracted from them – the mountains (and nature in general) are ours for the taking.

Meditative thinking

We are in flight from meditative thinking. Why? Well, it is perceived to be more difficult and less functional in an immediate sense than calculative thinking. Its difficulty, according to Heidegger, lies in its under use. Because we've been nurtured on the calculative process, the meditative skill is rather foreign to us – analogous perhaps to learning a new language.

Meditative or reflective thinking seeks to understand the meaning behind action. Its purpose is to enhance or to 'open the possibilities' of an individual's appreciation of the bigger picture (i.e. the horizon against which an object exists). By looking at an object's functionality without seeing its existence as part of a broader perspective is to fail to understand the object comprehensively – e.g. similar to *Zen and the Art of ...* (Pirsig, 1975). If I travel to the mountain and can appreciate its natural majesty (as well as its functionality), then my subsequent behaviour is better informed than had it been driven by calculation and exploitation.

The essential point here is that because we can create, extract, organise, and structure does not imply that we ought to if the implications of its use are unknown – a mindset articulated through the precautionary principle (see Fennell & Ebert, 2004). A classic example of this can be seen in the development of the nuclear bomb during the Second World War. Robert Oppenheimer, the so-called 'father of the A-bomb', became a vocal critic of the nuclear weaponry, presumably after he had realised its horrific potential for death and destruction. One might assume that he had been thinking in a calculative frame of mind as he developed the science behind the actual construction of the bomb in his laboratory. We might further assume that his calculative thinking gave way to meditative thinking once he witnessed the actual force of a nuclear blast in July 1945 at Los Alamos, New Mexico. It leaves one to speculate: if Oppenheimer had the skill of meditative thinking prior to his involvement in this project, would he have agreed to assist the American military in the first place?

Thinking and ethical behaviour

While it may be a significant leap of faith to suggest that what and how we think necessarily results in behaviour, leap we must. Calculative thinking is outcome driven as is the ethical school of thought known as consequentialism (to be discussed in detail in Chapter 4). In this school of thought, possible outcomes are calculated and the most efficient and effective option that will achieve the greatest good for the greatest number will be selected. This manner of ethical thinking is commonplace to most of us as it employs rational decision-making and democratic principles. However, can the calculation of the best outcome cloud the decision-maker's broader perspective? For example, it could be argued using consequential rationale that tourists should be allowed to come into physical contact with various rare fauna (e.g. penguins in Antarctica) regardless of the stress and potential damage this may create. The broader perspective missed by this activity is the backdrop of ecological sensitivity, the 'rights' of animals, etc.

Meditative thinking, on the other hand, implies the search for meaning. Thus our actions and our perceptions are judged against the backdrop of the broader horizon than the immediate context of frenetic activity. Ethical conduct is juxtaposed with notions of duty based upon tradition, culture and universality (i.e. deontology) or, as Heidegger would term, auto-chthony or rootedness. Therefore it is not the outcome of one's actions that is the criterion for goodness but rather the principle upon which the action or perception was based.

So, in my travels to the Antarctic, I assess the philosophical principles of ecotourism prior to my contact with flora or fauna. Against these concepts or this philosophical horizon, I select a behaviour and frame my perception of the ecology in which I am about to participate and I act. I then evaluate my action against these principles (i.e. view my action against the horizon of philosophical concepts) and judge the extent to which I have blended my calculative or discovery behaviour and my introspection of meaning.

The point

What we're attempting to convey here is that behaviour in the tourism context can occur without thought for its broader implication – this may in fact be the norm. Calculative thinking is short term, lacks grounding, and can have potentially serious and negative outcomes. On the other hand, behaviour that is logically grounded in philosophical rationale (i.e. well constructed codes of ethics) is much more apt to bring about positive outcomes for all stakeholders. This is the premise from which this book is written. Our intent is to provide the tools necessary to develop codes of ethics in tourism that will become the meditative horizon for tourist and practitioner behaviour.

The Problem

One of the realities of the present times is that we find ourselves enmeshed in a web of technology, communications and an international business agenda that has added significantly to the removal of borders and the virtual annihilation of time and distance (Hobsbawm, 1994). This has lead to an increasing intersection of cultures and economies that have contributed more to global homogenisation than heterogeneity. One of a growing number of problems with globalisation, the phenomenon that is barely 20 years old, is that while those who need money the least continue to prosper, a large percentage of the world's population still lives in relative poverty (Saul, 2005). For those companies that continue to rely on the resources and labour of the less fortunate, there is increasing pressure to make good in the face of mounting criticism – criticism that continues to come fast and furious in the face of public awareness vehicles (e.g. media) that deliver brand-damaging information at a rate never before seen (Mamic, 2004). In emphasising this point, one need only reflect on the repercussions to the senior directors of Enron and WorldCom at the turn of the century

One of the tangible outcomes that has emerged from the forces shaping globalisation over the last couple of decades is the emergence of corporate social responsibility, riding parallel with so many recent ethical transgressions, forcing multinationals (through investors, consumers and unions), to be more accountable in their practices. The face of this corporate conscientiousness is the code of ethics, what Barenberg (2004) calls a 'new form of workplace regulation', that sets forth workplace rights and standards and has become fully integrated into global production and supply chains. Although his terminology is largely heuristic, the parallels with other forms of standards (e.g. technical standards) are strikingly similar through the development of elaborate systems for planning, implementation, monitoring and revision of norms.

As one of the world's largest industries, involving millions of international and domestic travellers, tourism necessitates formal or informal interaction with a number of others with whom we don't regularly mix. These interactions are largely premised on profit and self-fulfilment – deemed the 'priority of pure profit' by Knowles *et al.* (1999) in reference to UK tour operators. While travel to new places allows for personal growth and satisfaction, especially from the tourist's vantage point, the underlying mechanisms that catalyse tourism (e.g. competition for resources, self-interest and profit) are often premised on the rational decision-making process inherent in calculative thinking. The impacts are most noticeable, at least by virtue of what is written in the tourism literature, on the lesser developed countries (LDCs) where corrective attention is greatly needed

(Ahmed *et al.*, 1994). The World Bank estimates that less than 45% of the money that tourists spend on vacation actually stays in local communities, with the figure as low as 10% in some of the LDCs (Amaro, 1999). These figures in translation mean that, 'It should be amply clear ... that today's form of tourism is highly exploitative and socially damaging. It is manifestly unethical and unjust to foist it on traditional communities' (D'Sa, 1999: 65–66).

By all accounts such interactions are going to be far more numerous. *Travel Wire News* reported in early November of 2004, on information for the World Tourism Organisation (now known as the United Nations World Tourism Organisation, or UNWTO), that tourism grew by about 10% in 2004, corresponding to an estimated 65 to 70 million more arrivals (*Travel Wire News*, 2004). This is attributed to three relatively weak years preceding 2004 and the pent-up demand from the global events of 2001 through to the SARS outbreak of 2003. The record growth is comparable to 20 years ago, when the early 1980s were marked by a weak economy due to the second global oil crisis. Such is the magnitude of the tourism industry that continues to demonstrate a vibrant resiliency over the long term. Travel is now very much part of the fabric of life, both recreationally and commercially, especially for those in the Western world.

As a privileged and accepted aspect of our lives – privileged in the sense that many in the world simply cannot afford to travel – there is a certain prestige and entitlement that comes packaged with travel. As Wheat (1999) contends, because we so look forward to our yearly two-week holiday and the hedonistic trappings that go along with it, the last thing we want hanging around our necks is ethics. For example, with regard to sex tourism, including the propensity to sunbathe naked on the beaches of Eastern societies, Seabrook and Burchill (1994) write that, like money and fun, it is so desirable as an end in the West that it has emerged as the holy trinity at the heart of consumerism. While such tourists bare it all in the sun, they are said to be displaying not just their nudity but also a form of cultural bareness that strips away all but their senses, the authors note, which must be constantly stimulated and distracted. To show shock or revulsion at this hedonism can only be the sign of archaic prudishness, antiquated moralism and the denial of reality.

Przeclawski (1996) has suggested that freedom has always been an important constituent of tourism. Travellers are free from the bonds of work and home, they can go wherever they wish, they can do as they please in these places, and can be free to cast off the moral cloak that regulates their behaviour in everyday life. However, according to Przeclawski, this freedom is the freedom 'from' something rather than the freedom 'for'. We should not take this distinction lightly, because it may very well be the key to overcoming the divisiveness that exists between two camps: those who see ethics and codes of ethics as a pious hope, and those who see them as a Trojan Horse (to borrow a familiar phrase). The 'ethics as Trojan Horse' group is represented by Wheeller (1994) and Butcher (2003); the latter feels that that the current trend towards the moralisation of tourism restricts our ability to enjoy the time we have away from the pressures at home. The moral authority of tourism is undeserved, because it is no more and no less a form of sustainable tourism than mass tourism, which is a popular criticism on the basis of extensive travel by air and little in the way of economic development in the hands of the people who need it most.

However, like the case of international business above, there is little denying what appears to be a wave of ethics and responsibility pervading the tourism industry, where operators and tourists alike appear to be clamouring for richer experiences. This finding is reported by Goodwin and Francis (2003) in their summary of the work of the UK-based organisation Tearfund group which found that, generally, ethical tourism adds value to tourism packages. It was also discovered that those operators seen to be more ethical gain a competitive advantage in the marketplace by securing long-term relationships. More specifically, according to the report 63% of respondents reported wanting information on at least one ethical issue at the destination; 52% said they would rather book a holiday with an operator if they had a code of ethics in 2001, compared to 45% who said this in 1999 (Goodwin & Francis, 2003). In the words of Weeden (2001), ethical tourism is now an established part of the tourism industry landscape, especially from the consumer demand standpoint, where tourists are starting to make decisions on the basis of the ethical credentials of operators on issues related to tour operator-host community relations, treatment of employees, product marketing, and operators' actions and attitudes towards the natural environment.

With this brief introduction in mind, part of the stimulus for writing this book is timing. We feel that with the burgeoning interest in tourism ethics, and given the importance of codes of ethics to industry in general, the time is right for an intensive look at the theory and practice of codes of ethics in tourism. This will entail looking at what has been done to date in tourism, but also (and arguably just as important) the theoretical work on codes of ethics that comes to us from outside of tourism – noting the importance of working between disciplines for the purpose of blending philosophies and techniques, as observed by Echtner and Jamal (1997). The other stimulus comes on the back of one of the earliest and most comprehensive analyses of codes of ethics in existence by Mason and Mowforth (1996: 166), who concluded that, 'We feel that the one issue that stands out above all others is the need for further investigation into the use, value, design, uptake and distribution of codes of conduct'. In the words of Burns (1999), we can no longer shrug-off the chaos brought on by mass tourism as a matter of 'what consumers want', 'the lack of proper planning regulations', 'it isn't a level playing field', or 'it's a cut throat business'. If we are to assume greater responsibility in tourism, it will be through the recognition that ethics has worked in other fields of endeavour. Taken a step further, if we are to use ethics in tourism, in whatever form it comes packaged, it cannot be employed on a reactive basis. Such attempts usually come about in the absence of a cohesive and unified philosophy that is otherwise greatly needed to offset potential impacts down the road (Davis, 1999). As noted above, we hope to address this philosophical deficiency in our presentation of codes of ethics.

In surveying the vast literature on ethics and codes of ethics both inside and outside of tourism, we are thus working from the premise that codes have long become an accepted and expected means of communicating to target groups in affecting their behaviour (Brookes, 1991). Well over a decade after the work of Brookes, the relevancy of codes of ethics has only strengthened and will continue to gather momentum, we suspect, as tourism continues to be challenged by a growing base of social, economic and ecological issues.

What follows

Part 2 of this book, Calculative Thinking, is structured around the examination of codes of ethics both inside and outside tourism. Chapter 1 contrasts codes of ethics with other organisational expressions of ethics, including credos, missions, principles and value statements. This is followed by a brief history of codes of ethics and various definitions of codes. Chapter 2 surveys the enlarging base of literature on ethics and codes of ethics in tourism, with a focus on differentiating between voluntary and non-voluntary mechanisms. This chapter also includes a discussion of codes of ethics 'for whom' and 'by whom', tourism policy, regulation, best practice, benchmarking and certification. The purpose of including these related concepts is to demonstrate the link that exists between codes of ethics and other mechanisms in striving for sustainability in tourism. Chapter 3 examines code development and compliance. In the case of the former, codes are examined on the basis of development in general as well as development in practice. The broad concept of compliance is articulated as implementation, monitoring, compliance and non-compliance, reporting, auditing and enforcement, as consistent with the business literature. The chapter concludes with a look at the pros and cons of codes.

Part 3 of the book, Meditative Thinking, is comprised of just one chapter (Chapter 4). It begins with a discussion of the basis of human nature and the evolution of ethics as a backdrop for an understanding of why we are moral beings; this is followed by an illustration of the three historical and predominant ways of looking at moral issues: teleology, deontology and existentialism. Moral development and values are also examined in the context of these ethical traditions, along with a brief history of applied ethics with an emphasis on environmental ethics and moral standing.

Part 4, Synthesis, looks at codes-in-action from the perspective of theory and practice (Chapter 5). Particular attention is paid to commitment to codes of ethics, behaviour and decision-making, organisational culture and individual conditions. The chapter continues with a broad look at codes of ethics through integrative social contract theory and its application to the United Nations World Tourism Organisation's global code of ethics for tourism. The final chapter of the book focuses on a way forward for tourism codes of ethics. One of the main conclusions is that ethical theory is rarely considered in tourism scholarship, and further that better interaction between educational systems and industry needs to take place in generating a more ethical industry.

Part 2

Calculative Thinking

Chapter 1

Organisational Expressions of Ethics

Introduction

In this chapter, credos, missions, principles, values and codes are discussed as overt expressions of an organisation's philosophy. These statements indicate to internal and external participants and observers what the organisation stands for, believes in and strives to accomplish, and how its members should behave in the pursuit of these lofty ideals. These expressions of philosophy have significant roles to play in explicating the meaningfulness of work within the organisation as opposed to its utility. The distinction between these expressions often lies in the extent to which they stress aspirational, educational, or regulatory intent. It is important for organisational leaders to fully understand the content and form of these expressions in order to provide the most effective way in which to develop, modify, communicate, and reinforce them. In this section we discuss organisational expressions of philosophy and their impact on organisational life (see Glossary for these and other related terms). Credos, missions, principles and values are discussed in brief, with an expanded discourse on codes of ethics, including code of ethics defined and the rationale for a code.

Credo (Vision statement)

The term 'credo' has its root in the Latin verb *credere*, which translates to the English imperative, to believe. Therefore, a credo is a general statement of belief (e.g. the Christian Nicene Credo, which begins each statement with '*we believe* ...'). In the organisational context, the credo signifies in what the organisation believes. Perhaps the most cited corporate credo is that of the Johnson & Johnson drug company, who employed this philosophical expression in their rationale to pull their product, Tylenol, from the shelves in 1982 in response to incidents of tampering They did so in spite of legal/financial counsel not to pull the product at the cost of millions of dollars to the company. Here is an excerpt from their credo:

Johnson & Johnson
We believe our first responsibility is to the doctors, nurses and patients,
to mothers and fathers and all others who use our products and services.
In meeting their needs everything we do must be of high quality.
We must constantly strive to reduce our costs

13

in order to maintain reasonable prices.
Customers' orders must be serviced promptly and accurately.
Our suppliers and distributors must have an opportunity
to make a fair profit. (http://www.jnj.com/our_company/our_credo/; accessed 05.12.06

The credo is a general statement and is designed to be wide-ranging (it is sometimes referred to as a 'vision' statement), and is less a statement of regulation or education, than a statement of aspiration. The International Institute for Peace Through Tourism (IIPTT) and the Sierra Club provide us with other examples of an aspirational credo:

IIPTT

Grateful for the opportunity to travel and experience the world and because peace begins with the individual, I affirm my personal responsibility and commitment to:
Journey with an open mind and gentle heart,
Accept with grace and gratitude the diversity I encounter,
Revere and protect the natural environment which sustains all life,
Appreciate all cultures I discover,
Respect and thank my hosts for their welcome,
Offer my hand in friendship to everyone I meet,
Support travel services that share these views and act upon them and,
By my spirit, words and actions, encourage others to travel the world in
   peace. (http://www.iipt.org/credo.html; accessed 05.12.06)

Sierra Club[1]

To explore, enjoy, and protect the wild places of the earth;
To practice and promote the responsible use of the earth's ecosystems and resources;
To educate and enlist humanity to protect and restore the quality of the natural and human environment; and to use all lawful means to carry out these objectives. (www.sierraclub.org; accessed 05.12.06)

Cynically, credos may be perceived to be unenforceable platitudes that are statements with which no one would or could disagree. This may be true; however, the point of a credo is to provide an ideal in which one can have faith, and the details are worked out in other more specific documents, such as mission statements and codes of ethics.

Mission statement

A mission statement, like a credo, is designed to be aspirational, though it tends to be more specific to the purpose of the organisation. For example, 'The Tourism Division's Mission is to enrich the quality of life and improve the economy of Arkansas by generating travel and enhancing the image of the State' (http://www.adptfoi.com/Tourism/mission.htm; accessed 14.07.04).

Consider as well the following: 'The Zimbabwe Tourism Authority (ZTA) works with various stakeholders to sustainably develop and promote Zimbabwe as a leading tourist destination through setting and monitoring high standards, market research and product development' (http://www.zimbabwetourism.co.zw/about/vision.htm; accessed 05.12.06).

Mission statements provide the public and the organisational member with a, usually brief, sense of organisational direction and intent. Bart (2002: 41) suggests that a mission statement 'is a formal written document intended to capture an organisation's unique and enduring purpose, practices, and core values'. Pearce and David (1987: 109) state that mission statements describe 'the fundamental purpose that sets a business apart from other firms of its type and identify the scope of businesses' operations in product and market terms'.

Statement of principles

Technically, principles imply truism, as in the principles of physics or geography. However, when stated in terms of the highly fluid and often irrational and unpredictable context of the organisation, principles, if taken too judiciously, can be reduced to the absurd. Frankfurt (2005: 34–35) argues that it 'is just this lack of connection to a concern with truth – this indifference to how things really are – that I regard as of the essence of bullshit'. Having said this, the notion of principles, taken in the most forgiving light, can provide the basic philosophical groundwork or foundation upon which other more specific statements can be generated. An outstanding example of this can be found in the Canadian Code of Ethics for Psychologists (Canadian Psychological Association, 1991). This document lists, in rank order of importance, four principles and numerous standards and value statements that accompany each.

Value statements

A value statement is an explicit declaration of what the organisation deems to be the conceptual basis of its overt behaviour. Discussed in much more detail in Chapter 5, a value can be defined as a 'concept of the desirable with a motivating force' (Hodgkinson, 1983: 36). In other words, our behaviour is the outward manifestation of what we, internally, find to be of worth. Therefore value statements are public insights into the motivational force behind the organisation's behaviour. As a consequence, the employee or consumer of the service or product presumably has a right to hold the organisation's actual behaviour to this set of value statements. If behaviour is not a reflection of its stated values, then clearly the organisation has provided stakeholders with statements of platitude and not of true core values. Here is an example of a value statement from the Carteret County Chamber of Commerce, North Carolina, USA (http://www.nccoast chamber. com/; accessed 18.12.06):

(1) encourage consumers to 'Shop Carteret First';
(2) advocate pro-business positions on local, state and federal issues;
(3) work to aggressively expand our region's economic base;
(4) work to attract more tourism, conference and meeting business;
(5) promote the county and its communities to regional, state and national audiences;
(6) forge strong partnerships with state and local elected and appointed officials;
(7) support those actions to retain and recognise our local military bases and installations;
(8) provide community and leadership training for new and emerging business leaders;
(9) create and promote tangible benefits and advantages for members;
(10) work for improvements to area highways serving the county.

While credos, missions and principles tend to be aspirational, usually by design (i.e. they send messages of broad philosophical/metaphysical goals), value statements generally send a message that is more pragmatic and accountable. This is perhaps the result of the intimate linkage between value *and* behaviour.

Codes of Ethics

The predominant expression of organisational philosophy comes in the form of the code of ethics. The other mediums that portray the ontological[2] profile of the organisation, while essential in understanding the true meaning of the workplace, may be overlooked in favour of the more functional code of ethics. While there appears to be no empirical evidence regarding the prevalence of other kinds of philosophical documents (e.g. credos), Wood and Rimmer (2003) report that the vast majority of companies in Europe, Australia, Canada, and the United States have a code.

The face of ethics in tourism, even well past the turn of the century, is still very strongly linked to codes of ethics. In a practical sense there are literally thousands of codes of ethics in tourism and outdoor recreation that are geared towards host communities, governments, service providers, individual firms, and tourists throughout the world. The vast majority of these are tied to specific activities. For example, an Internet search of hunting and fishing – two popular forms of nature-based tourism – can yield upwards of 5000 hits each; with many of these dealing specifically with codes of ethics for these activities (see Boxes 1.1, 1.2 and 1.3).

Box 1.1 The Federation of Fly Fishers' Code of Angling Ethics (Montana)

- Angling ethics begin with understanding and obeying laws and regulations associated with the fishery. Fly anglers understand that their conduct relative to laws and regulations reflects on all anglers. Angling ethics begin with and transcend laws and regulations governing angling and the resources that sustain the sport.
- The opportunity to participate in the sport of fly fishing is a privilege and a responsibility. Fly anglers respect private property and always ask permission before entering or fishing private property. They seek to understand and follow the local customs and practices associated with the fishery. They share the waters equally with others whether they are fishing or engaging in other outdoor activities.
- Fly fishers minimise their impact on the environment and fishery by adopting practices that do not degrade the quality of the banks, waters, and the overall watersheds upon which fisheries depend. These practices include avoiding the introduction of species not native to an ecosystem, and cleaning and drying fishing gear to prevent the inadvertent transport of invasive exotics that may threaten the integrity of an aquatic ecosystem. In simplest terms, fly anglers always leave the fishery better than when they found it.
- Fly anglers endeavour to conserve fisheries by understanding the importance of limiting their catch. 'Catch and release' is an important component of sustaining premium fisheries that are being over-harvested. Fly anglers release fish properly and with minimal harm. They promote the use of barbless hooks and angling practices that are more challenging but which help to sustain healthy fish populations.
- Fly anglers do not judge the methods of fellow anglers. Fly fishers share their knowledge of skills and techniques. They help others to understand that fly fishing contributes to sound fisheries conservation practices.
- Fly anglers treat fellow anglers as they would expect to be treated. They do not impose themselves on or otherwise interfere with other anglers. They wait a polite time, and then, if necessary, request permission to fish through. They may invite other anglers to fish through their positions. Fly fishers when entering an occupied run or area always move in behind other anglers, not in front of them whether in a boat or wading.
- Fly anglers when sharing the water allow fellow anglers ample room so as not to disturb anyone's fishing experience. They always fish in a manner that causesas little disturbance as practical to the water and fish. They take precautions to keep their shadow from falling across the water (walking a high bank). When fishing from watercraft fly anglers do not crowd other anglers or craft. They do not block entrances to bays or otherwise impede others. Fly anglers do not unnecessarily disturb the water by improperly lowering anchors or slapping the water with paddles or oars.
- Fly anglers always compliment other anglers and promote this Code of Angling Ethics to them whether they fish with a fly or not.

Source: www.fedflyfishers.org/codeofethics.htm. Accessed 19.10.04

Box 1.2 British Columbia Wildlife Federation Hunter Code of Ethics

- Ethical hunters respect the animals we hunt, and, when we hunt, we do so responsibly.
- Ethical hunters are students of nature – learning as much as possible about the game pursued, its habitat, habits and life cycle.
- Ethical hunters support the concept of 'fair chase'.
- Ethical hunters are skilled in the use of the tools of hunting. When we shoot, we do so accurately and safely.
- Ethical hunters are true conservationists who believe in the sustainable use of natural resources. Our interest in wildlife and the environment includes non-game and endangered species.

Source: http://www.bcwf.bc.ca/programs/core/hunethics.html. Accessed 10.10.04

Box 1.3 Boone and Crockett Club Hunter Ethics

- Fundamental to all hunting is the concept of conservation of natural resources. Hunting in today's world involves the regulated harvest of individual animals in a manner that conserves, protects, and perpetuates the hunted population. The hunter engages in a one-to-one relationship with the quarry and his or her hunting should be guided by a hierarchy of ethics related to hunting, which includes the following tenets:
- Obey all applicable laws and regulations.
- Respect the customs of the locale where the hunting occurs.
- Exercise a personal code of behaviour that reflects favourably on your abilities and sensibilities as a hunter.
- Attain and maintain the skills necessary to make the kill as certain and quick as possible.
- Behave in a way that will bring no dishonour to either the hunter, the hunted, or the environment.
- Recognise that these tenets are intended to enhance the hunter's experience of the relationship between predator and prey, which is one of the most fundamental relationships of humans and their environment.

Source: http://www.boone-crockett.org/huntingEthics/ethics_fairchase.asp?area = hunting Ethics. Accessed 10.10.04

A brief history

Codes of ethics, or close variations of such, have been in existence for millennia. For example, The Code of Hammurabi, named after the king who ruled over Babylon in the 18th century BC, may have been the first attempt to assemble a body of law under one common code. The 282 laws that comprise the code were engraved on an 8-foot high stone and placed in the town square for all to see. These laws regulated the organisation of society by striving to secure peace and justice through directives that were impartial, binding, and applicable to all (www.wwlia.org/hamm1.htm, accessed 1.09.05). The regulatory aspect of this code is clear, with precise lines of enforcement. For example, statement 3 of the code says that 'If any one bring an accusation of any crime before the elders, and does not prove what he has charged, he shall, if it be a capital offence charged, be put to death'.

In the 5th century BC, the Greek Hippocrates developed an oath pledging the medical field to the preservation of life and the service and well being of mankind (Veatch, 2003). Divided into two parts, the second part (the first was an oath of initiation) included directives on dietetics, surgery and pharmacology. Much later, during the 1790s, Thomas Percival (1740–1804) gained fame by developing a code of ethics for the medical field, in the Hippocratic tradition, in an effort to organise nurses, physicians and various levels of administrators, all of whom were in disarray as a result of a typhus and typhoid epidemic at his hospital in Manchester, England. Percival was able to mediate the dispute through his code, which sought to define the responsibilities of physicians in an effort to protect the rights of patients. But beyond this, Percival also sought to define the responsibilities of hospital administrators and trustees who, not unlike today, were often more concerned with financial realities of hospital management instead of patient and surgeon well being. Percival expanded his code of ethics into a book entitled *Medical Ethics*, published in 1803 (www.iit.edu/departments/csep/perspective/pers19_1fall99_2.html, accessed 15.10.04; Veatch, 2003)

Before the onset of the 20th century, personal honour or a code of gentlemanly honour thrived as the principal manner by which to maintain personal integrity and character, where character appears to have been the main guarantor of professional conduct (i.e. 'you have my word that the product will be made at the required time and at the required price'). The types of values inherent in the code of gentlemanly honour, were later resurrected through individual efforts. For example, Gene Autry's (1907–1998) *Cowboy Code* (Delta Airlines, 1998) of the 1940s was a simple credo for living a virtuous life based on courage, justice and courtesy. Cowboys were required to live by 10 basic principles, including: 'He must never go back on his word, or a trust confided in him', 'He must always tell the truth', 'He must not advocate or possess racially or religiously intolerant ideas', 'He must help people in distress', 'He must be a good worker' and 'He must respect women, parents, and his nation's laws'. In this way the cowboy collective was bound through the embodiment of a shared sense of responsibility that took on an element of chivalry that is rare in the present day.

The problem with a system that was tied to the integrity and honour of the *individual* is that it fails to more broadly apply at the level of the *institu-*

tion. Required was a concept of professional morality that transcended the individual to one that encompassed the group (the word 'profession' is Latin for 'bound by an oath'). Seen from this perspective, the changing social and political climate in Europe and North America was such that, as professional institutions increased in number and magnitude, there was a need to more broadly generalise a system that sought to codify the actions and behaviours of all who worked within a profession. This is confirmed by Stevens (1994), who traced the origin and impetus for ethical codes back to the Middle Ages in which common law held the master liable for the wrongdoing of his servants. The concept of *respondeat superior* or 'let the master answer' (http://dictionary.law.com/; accessed 05.12.06), places the organisation in a situation of rather significant responsibility for employee behaviour. As a result, it is in the organisation's best utilitarian interest to develop a means to aspire, educate, and regulate ethical conduct to avoid the damage and responsibility of reckless and unethical employees. In this regard, Kolk and Tulder (2002) note that wealthy businessmen like Carnegie in the early parts of the 20th century thought that business should be more than just profit making. This coincided with the realisation that governments, particularly in the US, were much too altruistic towards large corporations which had been subsuming power and compromising physical and social systems in the process. This realisation led to two related principles: the charity principle and the steward principle. The first is founded on the belief that the wealthy – individuals and later corporations – should be obligated to take care of the needs of the poor. The latter focused on the need to take care not only of one's company and its stakeholders, but also the social systems in which it was enmeshed.

Interest in the development of codes of ethics from the business perspective is said to have grown during the 1970s, when the social and ecological behaviour of large companies became increasingly controversial (Kolk & Tulder, 2002). Groups like the Organisation for Economic Cooperation and Development, the International Labour Organisation, and the United Nations first pioneered codes of ethics for multinational corporations. While some firms adopted their own codes, the vast majority resisted. During the 1980s, and after the realisation that mandatory codes of ethics were not manageable or feasible, the focus turned to voluntary codes of ethics (Chapter 2). The chief stimuli catalysing code development during the 1980s appears to be the neo-liberal policies of government which supported non-intervention and withdrawal, the subsequent internationalisation of markets, and the resulting regulatory void that created a climate of negative implications surrounding investment and production (Kolk & Tulder, 2002). Recognising the need for change, NGOs, church groups and trade unions initiated discussions on codes of ethics during this time, and individual companies like Levi Strauss, Shell, and Nike were active in developing codes for the purpose of managing their societal interactions (Kolk & Tulder, 2002). These events created the basis for the explosion of codes in business during the 1990s, and provided the impetus for deepening the discussion on the regulation of the activities of transnational corporations. The discourse surrounded three main issues, including: outsourcing of production facilities to developing countries; cooperation or implicit support of oppressive regimes, by virtue of the relationships established between developed and developing nations; and the ecological damage that has resulted from the activities of large corporations.

What is a code of ethics?

As might be expected, there are numerous definitions of codes of ethics, and many of these overlap with codes of practice, codes of conduct, value statements, etc. (Codes of ethics are more philosophical and value-based; while codes of conduct or practice are more technical and specific to the actions of an organisation or group in time and space. See the Glossary.) Essentially a code of ethics is a formal, written statement that functions as a *message* to internal and external stakeholders regarding how it wishes to be perceived and it is a *guide* for employees that identifies preferred modes of behaviour. It embodies how an organisation thinks about itself ethically. The following are examples of variation in definition:

A code of ethics is:

(1) messages through which corporations hope to shape employee behaviour and effect change through explicit statements of desired behaviour (Stevens, 1994: 64);

(2) a short set of ethical principles expressed in the imperative mode (L'Etang, 1992: 737);

(3) statements of the norms and beliefs of an organisation (McDonald & Zepp, 1989: 183);

(4) an attempt to purposively influence or control the ethical dimensions of members' organisational behaviour (Cassell *et al.*, 1997: 1080).

(5) a systematised set of standards and principles that defines ethical behaviour appropriate for a profession. The standards and principles are determined by moral values (Ray, 2000).

In tourism, theorists have argued that codes, as noted above, are designed to change the way visitors act – and further to reinforce good behaviour (Tribe *et al.*, 2000). Sharpley (1996) observes that, by being generic and voluntary for the most part, their main strength is flexibility; but they do depend on the willingness of individuals to embrace the code and accept responsibility for their own actions in the context of the human and ecological environments in which they interact. These characteristics can be seen in the work of Genot (1995: 169), who defines a code of ethics as a 'public statement of ethical, rather than legal, commitment to certain values and standards of behaviour'.

Rationale for a code

Ideally, a code of ethics serves three general purposes:

(1) to establish the moral values recognised by a company;
(2) to communicate the company's expectations to employees; and
(3) to demonstrate to employees and the public that the company in fact operates within specific ethical parameters. (Montoya & Richard, 1994: 713; see also Wood & Rimmer, 2003)

In this regard, Molander argues that:

> A well-written ethical code, reliably and fairly enforced, can eliminate unethical practices, relieve ethical dilemmas, and throughout the process demonstrate a firm's or industry's commitment to ethical conduct. If poorly designed and implemented, the code will not only be ineffectual but the code further reduce business's credibility with the general public and important opinion-forming institutions in the society. (Molander, 1987: 631)

L'Etang (1992) suggests that codes of ethics should provide the member with guidance based upon a Kantian rationale with no other ulterior motive. In other words, a code should not be written to enhance the reputation of the company, it should not be provided to members in order for them to feel better or more secure about their working environment, and it should not be written to avoid potential problems related to unethical conduct (i.e. *respondeat superior*). In fact it should not be written for any other reason than to assist members to come to the realisation that they ought to be ethical because it is a basic duty of humanity. If done for any other reason, it is not morally worthy (Kant, 1785/2001). Robert Bolt echoes this Kantian sentiment in the following excerpt from *A Man for All Seasons*:

> If we lived in a state where virtue was profitable, common sense would make us good, and greed would make us saintly. And we'd live like animals or angels in the happy land that needs no heroes. But since in fact we see avarice, anger, envy, pride, sloth, lust and stupidity commonly profit far beyond humility, charity, fortitude, justice and thought, and have to choose to be human at all ... why then perhaps we must stand fast a little – even at the risk of being heroes. (Bolt, 1974: 83–84)

Lofty ideals to be sure, however, the utilitarian goals mentioned earlier generally win the so-called *is* vs. *ought* battle, i.e. what happens in practice as opposed what should happen or empirical vs. theoretical (Starr, 1983). Perhaps the most genuine rationale of organisational codes of ethics may be to make an implicit and/or explicit impact on decision behaviour. (We discuss ethics and decision-making in detail in Chapter 5.)

The rationale for any code will generally fall into one or more of the following three possibilities: to aspire, to educate and to regulate. As mentioned earlier, credos and mission statements tend to be written to inspire and aspire. Codes of ethics can serve a similar role based upon how they are presented to the reader. If, as L' Etang (1992) suggests, codes are made up of statements in the imperative or command mode, then they may inspire the reader to do his or her duty in order to aspire to be a moral individual. On the other hand if the code of ethics is presented as a lengthy and complex array of what one should not do, then it may fail to motivate or guide the member toward higher moral levels.

Codes of ethics may be effective documents to educate the member if it provides him or her with new and relevant knowledge. If it is neither new nor relevant, then no transmission of knowledge occurs and the educational function fails. Furthermore, codes of ethics can in some cases be written to provide regulatory information to members (see Chapter 2). These documents are perhaps not so much codes of ethics as codes of conduct or standards of practice. The discourse can become rather convoluted in semantics at this point. We argue that this regulatory function is best addressed in codes of conduct/practice, and that the educational function be reserved for codes of ethics.

Earlier we noted that there has been a significant level of interest in codes of ethics from industry over the past decade. This interest has spawned the development of organisations like the Centre for the Study of Ethics in the Professions, Illinois Institute of Technology, which lists over 20 professions where codes of ethics are being used. Some of these include agriculture, construction, education, health care, law, media, real estate, religion, sports, and travel and transportation. We acknowledge the importance of ethics in these different areas when we try to imagine what professions like health care, law, and sport would be like without an ethical framework to follow in guiding policy and practice.

Buchholz (2004) observes that professionals, both psychologically and culturally, legitimise themselves through the code of ethics. They do this in two important ways. First, the code of ethics acts as a social contract, outlining group norms, values, expectations and responsibilities through a unique social utility. This means that we are professional by virtue of our unique role that we play in society. Secondly, the code articulates a form of altruism (which Buchholz defines as the public vow to serve all mankind) that motivates the profession. So we are responsible in our actions as professionals to other people (tourists) and to flora and fauna because of how we are mandated to behave in living up to the lofty goals of the profession (e.g. professional tour operators). Buchholz notes that this altruism is often misguided, as in cases where doctors and lawyers seem to be motivated more by money than medicine or law, but what matters to the collective is the projection of altruistic attitudes necessary for the profession to maintain its standing.

The aspects of professional legitimisation and social utility are discussed by Frankl (1989), who identifies a series of functions of codes of ethics for the purpose of providing professional guidance. These stem from both empirical work and his experience as the Director of the Professional Ethics program at the American Association for the Advancement of Science. Frankl lists the following eight functions:

(1) *Enabling document.* The code offers guidance to individuals and groups by simplifying the moral universe through a framework that allows for the evaluation of alternative courses of action.

(2) *Source of public evaluation.* The code serves as a basis for the public's expectations of professional performance, thus holding the unit more accountable for their actions.

(3) *Professional socialisation.* The code helps to foster pride in the profession along with strengthening identity and allegiance of the membership.

(4) *Enhance profession's reputation and public trust.* The adoption of a code of ethics allows the profession to gain the public's trust and to enhance its own status. This leads to confidence and respect as well as increased social and economic rewards.

(5) *Preserve entrenched professional biases.* Each profession has a dominant value that is in need of preservation through a code of ethics (e.g. for the health care profession, it is improved health care). The danger lies in elevating professional values such that they are incongruent with social values, or the group they are supposed to serve.

(6) *Deterrent to unethical behaviour.* Codes act to restrain unethical behaviour through the threat of sanctions, and by making it duty to report errant colleagues. This plants the seeds of a monitoring system that should be the responsibility of all in preserving the integrity of the group.

(7) *Support system.* The code should act as a source of support for professionals against the erosion of power and improper demands made by bureaucrats, clients, or unreasonable demands by employers.

(8) *Adjudication.* Codes have the added benefit of serving as a basis for adjudicating disputes between members of the profession, or between members and outsider and outsiders. The profession itself can adjudicate or courts or other authorities can legitimise the tenets of a professional code.

These aspects of a code of ethics, above, echo our previous claim that the code of ethics is a formal written document that functions as a message to different stakeholders about preferred modes of behaviour – how an organisation or other entity thinks about itself ethically. In an attempt to further conceptualise codes of ethics as an important ethical devise for the organisation, we include Veatch's (2003) philosophical hierarchy of codes of ethics (Figure 1.1), which is a continuum ranging between antinomianism and legalism and is based upon the extent to which a code is contextually or relativistically bound. The four aspects of his framework include:

- antinomianism – the position that ethical action is determined independent of law or rules;
- situationalism – the position that ethical action must be judged in each situation guided by, but not directly determined by, rules (this includes 'rules of thumb' and guidelines);
- rules of practice – the position that rules govern practices such that actions are normally judged by rules; and
- legalism – the position that ethical action consists in strict conformity to law or rules.

Veatch concludes that the extremes of this continuum, legalism and antinomianism, are almost never adhered to since there are always cases where there are exceptions to laws (legalism) and, further, that there is no case that is so unique that rules or rights could never be used to determine what one ought to do in a specific situation (antinomianism). The more plausible action would be to use either situationalism or rules of practice in searching for the right course of action. Rules of practice are different from situationalism in that exceptions to rules can be made only in very extraordinary cases. One can appreciate the importance of such a framework in the context of medicine, the field of study in which Veatch created this continuum. So the rule 'Always get consent before surgery' would be a rule of practice that is stringently binding on conduct. Working outside this rule opens the physician and hospital to liability if the patient, who was operated on without consent, holds specific religious beliefs about the practice

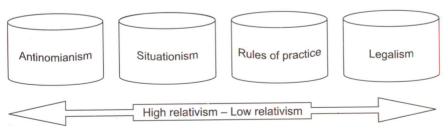

Figure 1.1 Philosophical framework

Adapted from Veatch (2003: 11)

of medicine and well being. Aspects of this continuum will be discussed in more detail in the following chapter with regard to differences between regulatory (non-voluntary) and voluntary codes of ethics.

Conclusion

This chapter has drawn comparisons and contrasts between codes of ethics and other expressions of ethics within the organisation, including credos, missions, principles and values. These statements indicate to internal and external participants what the organisation stands for, believes in and strives to accomplish, and how its members should behave in the pursuit of the articulated goals. The bulk of the chapter focused on codes of ethics from the historical standpoint, and included definitions of codes of ethics, the rationale for a code, and an examination of many different ethical positions within a philosophical hierarchy. This was deemed important in providing a foundation from which to examine codes in more detail in the next chapter (with exclusive reference to tourism), and also as a departure point from which to examine deeper theoretical notions around ethics that will be dealt with later in the book.

Notes

1. The Sierra Club lists this as a mission statement. However, in our categorisation scheme it is much more in line with the generalities and aspirational qualities of a credo.
2. Ontology refers to the essence of human endeavour. Thus ontological statements about an organisation would be focused on the essence of its ultimate purpose and aspiration

Chapter 2

Surveying the Tourism Landscape

Introduction

In this broadly-based chapter the tourism ethics literature is explored with the purpose of highlighting the nature and extent of work conducted to date. Research on tourism studies and ethics is barely a decade old, with only a very recent intensive examination of the subject, despite the proliferation of literally hundreds of codes of ethics that are both activity-specific and generic by origin. Before embarking on a survey of codes of ethics in tourism, some of the earliest works are summarised, dating back to the early 1990s. The discussion includes an examination of non-voluntary and voluntary approaches in tourism, the former being more authoritarian in nature, along with a section on who codes have been developed for and by whom. The final section of the chapter is designed to establish a link between codes of ethics as the forerunner to other more sophisticated tools for sustainability in tourism, including best practice, benchmarking, certification and ecolabels.

Ethics in Tourism

The interest and involvement in ethics by tourism scholars and decision makers may be a function of three different but related factors. First, it is likely that the alternative tourism and sustainable tourism paradigms contributed significantly to what has been an increasing effort to pull ethics into the mainstream of tourism, both practically and philosophically. Second, meetings like the Rio and AIEST (see Przeclawski, 1996) conferences, both in 1992, created the impetus for a more sustained approach to ethics. Lastly, the prevalence of codes of ethics developed in other commercial sectors during the 1980s and 1990s (see Chapter 1) spilled over into tourism as a logical extension of organisational accountability and competitive advantage mindsets. This final aspect has been corroborated by Harris and Jago (2001), who write that codes of ethics and certification programmes in tourism evolved out of the need to generate better-quality products for the purpose of gaining competitive advantage. What is evident by way of a review of literature is that ethics was virtually *terra incognita* up until the beginning of the 1990s (see Payne & Dimanche, 1996).

One of the earliest academic papers to discuss tourism and ethics came from Lea (1993), who surveyed the sociology and environment literature in reference to the Third World (see Wheeler 1994, 1995 for early work in hospitality). Lea identified three categories of ethical thought and action with reference to the place of ethics in tourism: (1) development ethics in the Third World; (2) social and physical impacts resulting from tourism; and (3) ethics related to the actions of individual travellers. He notes that a Christian-inspired origin to the anti-tourism movement has stereotyped the discourse in certain circles as somewhat of a diatribe or even a new form of missionary activity (see Chapter 1). While it is not the place here to speculate on the motivations of these groups in affecting change within the industry, Lea suggests that industry pundits attempted to downplay the ethical issues identified by these groups because of the religious overtones emanating from these sources.

The scant treatment of ethics in tourism from the 1990s onward is further demonstrated by the fact that neither ethics nor morality appears as a stand-alone entry in the *Encyclopedia of Tourism* (Jafari, 2000), one of the more recent comprehensive surveys of the tourism literature. Even codes of ethics are afforded a mere eight lines of text in this publication. The decade-older *Dictionary of Concepts in Recreation and Leisure Studies* (Smith, 1990) and *The Dictionary of Hospitality, Travel and Tourism* (Metelka, 1990) also fail to contain entries on either ethics or morality.

Examples of subsequent work on tourism and ethics include work on international tourism ethics (Ahmed *et al.*, 1994); Upchurch and Ruhland's (1995) study of Missouri lodging managers from the perspective of Victor and Cullen's (1988) ethical climate questionnaire; Hultsman's (1995) work on 'just' tourism; and Karwacki and Boyd's (1995) work on ethics and ecotourism. More recent work includes research by Tapper (2001), who found that UK operators were motivated to adopt ethical practices by the desire to address issues that were important to their client base (in maintaining a positive company image), and in order to differentiate themselves from the competition (in finding the right niche). Another recent piece of research is Ross's (2003) study of work-stress response perceptions among tourism and hospitality employees. Ross found that ethical dilemmas are continually brought about by visitor and staff interactions in the absence of the knowledge about how to effectively implement and operationalise trust in the workforce for the betterment of employees and the organisation on the whole. It is indeed a sign of the times, however, that research has included recent books by authors such as Butcher (2003), and more comprehensively by Smith and Duffy (2003), and Fennell (2006a).

The Emergence of Codes of Ethics in Tourism

The first code of ethics of a tourism and recreation nature appears to be the United Kingdom's Country Code originally launched in 1951, and designed to limit the amount of damage to the countryside and increase the level of respect between urban and rural inhabitants (www.country sideaccess.gov.uk/docs/history.pdf and www.countrysideaccess.gov.uk /countryside_code, accessed 02.11.04). This code was conceived during the 1930s and 1940s by three different groups: the Commons and Open Spaces Society, which produced a Country Code; the Council for the Protection of Rural England, which produced a Code of Courtesy; and the Ramblers Association, which developed a Rambler's Code. These were later amalgamated as a result of the National Parks and Access to the Countryside Act, giving way to the Country Code on the back of a series of consultations with a wide variety of interested parties. Increasing intensity of use through the 1950s, 60s and 70s compelled the Countryside Commission, formerly the National Parks Commission, to adopt the following set of guidelines developed in 1981:

(1) Enjoy the countryside and respect its life and work.
(2) Guard against all risk of fire.
(3) Fasten all gates.
(4) Keep your dogs under close control.
(5) Keep to public paths across farmland.
(6) Use gates and stiles to cross fences, hedge and walls.
(7) Leave livestock, crops and machinery alone.
(8) Take your litter home.
(9) Help to keep all water clean.
(10) Protect wildlife, plants and trees.
(11) Take special care on country roads.
(12) Make no unnecessary noise.

Heightened levels of pressure and changing circumstances (e.g. new forms of outdoor recreation and tourism) in association with the introduction of the public's new right of access to the countryside (Countryside Rights of Way Act of 2000) necessitated a change to the Country Code. The Countryside Code, launched in England on July 12, 2004 (and in 2005 in Wales) originated, again, through consultation with a vast number of stakeholder groups, and the articulation of values such as respect, protection and enjoyment. The newest incarnation has diversified, not in the number of specific guidelines, but rather in the detail afforded to each guideline and through a new section for land managers. The two main sections of the Countryside Code, one for the public and other for managers, are contained in Boxes 2.1 and 2.2.

Another early example of a code of ethics, more specifically oriented towards tourism, is one developed by the Ecumenical Coalition on Third World Tourism (ECTWT), an organisation founded in 1982 as an outcome of a workshop that took place in Manila in 1980 (http://home.pacific.

Box 2.1 For the public

- **Be safe – plan ahead and follow any signs**
  Even when going out locally, it's best to get the latest information about where and when you can go; for example, your rights to go onto some areas of open land may be restricted while work is carried out, for safety reasons or during breeding seasons. Follow advice and local signs, and be prepared for the unexpected.
- **Leave gates and property as you find them**
  Please respect the working life of the countryside, as our actions can affect people's livelihoods, or heritage, and the safety and welfare of animals and ourselves.
- **Protect plants and animals, and take your litter home**
  We have a responsibility to protect our countryside now and for future generations, so make sure you don't harm animals, birds, plants, or trees.
- **Keep dogs under close control**
  The countryside is a great place to exercise dogs, but it's every owner's duty to make sure their dog is not a danger or nuisance to farm animals, wildlife or other people.
- **Consider other people**
  Showing consideration and respect for other people makes the countryside a pleasant environment for everyone – at home, at work and at leisure.

net.hk/~contours/history.htm; accessed 04.12.02). This workshop was the first of its kind to analyse tourism from the perspective of the people of the Third World. There was consensus amongst all participating members that tourism, as it is practised in most parts of the Third World, has triggered more costs than benefits. The main objectives of ECTWT are to:

- focus on tourism and the effect it has on the lives of the people of the Third World;
- provide opportunities for local people affected by tourism to express their views and concerns;
- denounce unfair practices in tourism and encourage action to change them;
- promote good quality of tourist activity that is appropriate to the quest for a just, participatory and sustainable society;
- empower indigenous people and support them in their attempts to get a fair price in their participation in tourism;
- lobby against the violation of Human Rights related to tourism development projects at national and international level; and
- provide research and information on the impact of tourism.

The 11-point tourism code of ethics used by ECTWT is one that apparently evolved from the 1975 Christian Conference of Asia. It was derived from a report entitled 'Tourism, the Asian Dilemma (Edgell, 1999). So while

Box 2.2 For land managers

- **Know your rights, responsibilities and liabilities**
  Visitors are allowed to access land in different ways. For more guidance on how this affects you and what your rights, responsibilities and liabilities are, contact your local National Park authority.
  The Ordinance Survey's 1:25,000 maps show public rights of way and designated areas of open land. These maps are generally reliable but not 'definitive' so you will need to check the legal status of rights of way with your local authority.
  By law, you must keep rights of way clear and not obstruct people's entry onto access land – it's a criminal offence to discourage rights of public access with misleading signs.
  Trespassing is often unintentional – see Managing public access for advice on tackling trespass.

- **Make it easy for visitors to act responsibly**
  Keeping paths, boundaries, waymarks, signs, gates and stiles in good working order will help manage access over your land.
  Where there is public access through a boundary feature, such as a fence or hedge, use a gap if you can. If this isn't practical, use an accessible gate or, if absolutely necessary, a stile. When installing new gates and stiles, make sure you have the permission of the local authority.
  Encourage respect for your wishes by giving clear, polite guidance where it is needed. For example, telling visitors about your land management operations helps them to avoid getting in your way.
  Rubbish attracts other rubbish – by getting rid of items such as farm waste properly, you'll discourage fly tipping (dumping rubbish illegally) and encourage others to get rid of their rubbish responsibly.

- **Identify possible threats to visitors' safety**
  Your duty of care under the Occupiers' Liability Acts of 1957 and 1984 depends on the type of access right – so it's important to know what rights, if any, apply to your land. Contact the Country Land and Business Association or the national Farmers' Union for more guidance.
  Consider possible man-made and natural hazards on your land and draw any risks to the public's attention if they are not obvious.
  Avoid using electric fencing and other hazards close to areas that people visit, particularly alongside narrow paths and at the height of a child. The use of plain wire is strongly recommended in place of barbed wire.
  Animals likely to attack visitors should not be allowed to roam freely where the public has access – you may be liable for any resulting harm.

it appears that ECTWT was developed in 1982, the code has been in existence for at least another 7 years (see Lea, 1993, above in reference to the Christian-inspired origin of codes of ethics in tourism).

The importance of the 1980 Manila conference is highlighted in a United Nations Environment Programme report, which underscored the significance of social, cultural, environmental, economic, educational and political values required to set tourism on a more ethical path:

The protection, enhancement and improvement of various components of man's environment are among the fundamental conditions for the harmonious development of tourism. Similarly, rational management of tourism may contribute to a large extent to protecting and developing the physical environment and the cultural heritage as well as improving the quality of life ... tourism brings people closer together and creates an awareness of the diversity of ways of life, traditions and aspirations. (UNEP, 1995: 2–4)

The UNEP document also recognised the WTO's Tourism Bill of Rights, adopted by the general assembly at the Sofia, Bulgaria meeting in 1985. This Bill, said by the authors of the UNEP report to be a historic voluntary code of conduct for tourism, recognises the rights of tourists and local people, as well as the importance of tourism policies designed to protect cultural and ecological integrity from ill-formed development. Issues of rights and justice have only increased as items of importance in tourism more than 20 years later (see Glossary for a description of related terms).

One of the first nations to take an active lead in the development of codes of ethics for the tourist industry was Canada, through the National Round Table on the Environment and the Economy (NRTEE), in response to the 1987 Commission on the Environment and Development (*Our Common Future*). The development of codes of ethics by NRTEE in association with the Tourism Industry Association of Canada (TIAC, 1991) was an attempt to fulfil part of its mandate to generate sustainability in Canada through tourism. This involved a series of workshops and a Delphi study involving many key stakeholders in Canada's tourism industry (D'Amore, 1992). The key to the success of the resultant codes of ethics and guidelines for specific sectors was said to lie in the extent to which they would be implemented by the approximately 60,000 tourism-related organisations in Canada, and the millions of tourists who visit the country. This code of ethics was seen to be extremely progressive for the time, especially given the time it took for organisers to undertake workshops and include various stakeholder groups. As perhaps the first such undertaking of its kind at the time, it would be interesting to see how well this document is integrated into the tourism industry so many years later – see http://www.tiac-aitc.ca /english/welcome.asp (accessed 07.01.05) for a description of TIAC and its mandate.

At the international level, authors such as Ahmed *et al.* (1994) provided an early call to the international tourism community for the development of codes of ethics in tourism. These authors suggest that organisations like the World Tourism Organisation needed to be active in convening a conference on ethical issues in tourism, specifically with the hosts of less well-developed countries in mind. Even before this, however, Krohn *et al.* (1991) wrote that international organisations like the World Travel and Tourism Council and the WTO should take the lead in the development of a code of ethics for tourism marketers across the many sectors of tourism (cruise lines, hotels and motels, travel agencies, and so on). Such a mechanism was thought to be essential in punishing those who violate the ethical standards of the code. The sectoral approach for codes of ethics in tourism has also been championed by Payne and Dimanche (1996), who argued that the goals of the industry on the whole may be better accomplished in view of the unique differences between divisions.

Two of the most comprehensive treatises on codes of ethics in tourism to date can be found in reports that emerged at the same time. Mason and Mowforth's *Codes of Ethics in Tourism* and The United Nations Environment Programme (UNEP) Industry and Environment's *Environmental Codes of Conduct for Tourism* both came out in 1995, riding a wave of interest generated by the Rio Summit in 1992. The influence of Rio is reflected in the following quote on the cover of the UNEP document from Chapter 30 of Agenda 21, 'Business and Industry, including transnational corporations, should be encouraged to adopt and report on the implementation of codes of conduct promoting best environmental practice' (UNEP, 1995). The value of these reports lies in the inclusion of a number of codes of ethics that had been amassed at the time, along with sections on tourism-related organisations that were linked to codes of ethics, and a breakdown of codes of ethics as they applied to tourists, local communities and the tourism industry itself. Both reports also have sections that briefly touch on the monitoring of codes of ethics, while the UNEP report has a useful section on the implementation of codes (this will be examined more fully in Chapter 3). Both documents are also premised on the notion that voluntary codes of ethics are increasingly important as a tool for raising awareness about the deleterious social and ecological effects of tourism (see also Williams, 1993b).

Formal investigations of tourism codes of ethics have taken place only recently. For example, Stevens (1997) undertook a content analysis of hotel and management-company ethical codes in the US and found that the hotel industry does not have codes to the extent found in corporate America. Only 57% of hotels and 21% of management companies were found to have codes. Hotel codes discussed the legal advantages of acting morally, while management company codes held little regard for environmental issues (6%), or civic and community affairs (12%). A study by Stevens and Brownell (2000) found that communication of standards is essential if we are to have ethical tourism and hospitality businesses. In their work on employees of two hotels, the authors discovered that: (1) organisations were not doing enough in terms of transmitting information about ethics; and (2) ethical guidance of employees was actually coming from external sources such as family and friends rather than from sources from within the firm. Stevens and Brownell suggest that standards must be articulated foremost in an ethical code, and followed up by training, handbooks, manuals, policies and procedures, and, perhaps most importantly, through coaching and modelling of desired behaviour.

Other studies on codes of ethics in tourism include work by Garrod and Fennell (2004) on 58 whale-watching codes (based on codes compiled by Carlson, 2001). These authors discovered that 29.3% of codes were developed in North America, followed by 24.1% in Central and South America, and another 24.1% in Europe. Almost one-half of the codes were developed by government (46.6%), and most were put into operation during the mid- to late-1990s. Garrod and Fennell also found that 62.0% of the codes were of a voluntary nature compared with 38% that were regulatory (see next section for a discussion of non-voluntary and voluntary mechanisms). Just over 90% of the whale-watching codes of ethics (whale-watching being defined as viewing all types of cetaceans) were of a deontological or mostly deontological nature, whereas 8.5% were teleological or mostly teleological (see Chapter 4 and the Glossary for a description of these theories). These results compare with research conducted by Malloy and Fennell (1998a), who found that 77.2% of the guidelines in 40 codes of ethics were deontological, while 22.7% were teleological. Table 2.1 presents results generated by Garrod and Fennell according to permit requirement, control of pollution, restrictions on viewing pods and calves, the basis of rule, application of rule, and marine park protection (see also Hughes, 2001).

Non-Voluntary and Voluntary Mechanisms

Non-voluntary and voluntary approaches to tourism exist as two prominent management options designed to control the actions of tourism industry stakeholders. The implementation of one or both approaches in tourism is a function of more broadly based policy directives within a region and particular to specific activities and sectors. Tourism policy advanced quickly in post-World War II Europe where tourism was seen as a regional development tool to help in the rebuilding process after the war. The Organisation for Economic Cooperation and Development (OECD) emerged during this time and very quickly recognised the importance of establishing policy for tourism. The main purpose driving decision makers to implement tourism policy – as relevant then as it is now – is said to rest in the need to maximise tourist arrivals in an effort to improve the balance of payments through international tourism receipts (Edgell, 1999; see also Hall, 1994)

Even with this financial prime directive behind policy, theorists (Lickorish, 1991; Coccossis, 1996) suggest that there is a critical lack of

Table 2.1 Management and policy directives for whale watching

Management Characteristic	n = 58	%
Permit required		
No data	40	69.
No permit required	3	5.2
Permit required for all activities	8	13.8
Permit required for certain whale-watching activities	7	12.1
Control of pollution/rubbish		
No data	46	79.3
Controls stated	12	20.7
Restrictions on viewing pods with calves		
No data	28	48.3
Viewing not allowed	9	15.5
Viewing allowed	6	10.3
Viewing allowed, with conditions	15	25.9
Specific basis of rule		
Voluntary	36	62.0
Regulatory (statutory or non-voluntary	22	37.9
Application of rule		
No specific species	4	6.9
Whales only	23	39.7
Dolphins and porpoises only	8	13.8
Cetaceans in general	14	24.1
Marine fauna in general	9	15.5
Marine Park Protection		
Cetacean protection through marine park guidelines	16	27.6
No protection through park guidelines	42	72.4

Source: Garrod & Fennell (2004)

policy, as almost a universal, because of a significant degree of fragmentation amongst those responsible for tourism planning (see also McKercher, 1993). This has changed somewhat as a result of the onset of sustainable development, which has helped to clarify the role of governments and the private sector with regard to cultural and ecological integrity, including the expectation of accountability and responsibility (Fayos-Solá, 1996). The inertia behind this paradigmatic shift suggests that policy in the new millennium will be less about marketing, promotion, tax incentives and the support of the major sectors exclusively, and more about the natural environment, social impacts, and issues of rational and equitable access (Richter, 1991).

Non-voluntary

In general, the discussion on codes of ethics has included two general categories: regulatory or non-voluntary measures, and voluntary measures. Regulatory approaches (otherwise known as 'big stick' or 'command and control' approaches are more authoritative and designed to limit and restrict the activities of stakeholders operating in various sectors (Parker, 1999). Regulations are said to be essential for establishing the legal framework within which the private sector operates in tourism (Genot, 1995). Box 2.3, 'Knowing and respecting park regulations in Glacier National Park' is a good example of the regulation of tourist behaviour in a natural area. Readers will note the fines associated with certain transgressions of the rules.

The question that continues to be posed, but yet is exceedingly difficult to answer, is whether the industry should be left to regulate itself voluntarily, or whether it should be regulated by an external agent, such as government. Citing Forsyth (1993), Mason and Mowforth (1995) observe that, while tourism businesses acknowledge the important role that governments can play in taking responsibility for the tourism industry, the industry continues to be at odds with the implementation of regulatory devices which are perceived to be overly constraining to operations. Firms as a general rule usually resist governmental regulation as it is seen to restrict the freedom of action. Such regulation is thought to be unnecessary if companies and sectors can successfully demonstrate economic, social, and ecological management, through other means (e.g. codes of ethics, certification).

Two devices, licences and leases, have been discussed by Newsome *et al.* (2002) as important regulatory strategies in tourism. Licences are certificates or documents that give official permission to be involved in an activity. These are often necessary if service providers wish to undertake activities on crown land, for example. This allows the governmental agency to monitor the level of use and impact that results from these activities. Such is the case in Glacier Bay, Alaska, where cruise ships must obtain licences in order to view humpback whales. The licensing system serves not only to restrict the number of boats in the region (thus ensuring a higher-quality experience while disturbing the whales less), but also to assist cruise ships in planning their schedules (Gjerdalen & Williams, 2000). Either implicitly or explicitly the granting of licences comes with the expec-

Box 2.3 Knowing and respecting park regulations in Glacier National Park, Montana

The following is an excerpt from the 1999 Glacier National Park Backcountry Guide, Montana, USA. It provides a good illustration of park regulations and the penalties for not following them, as well as the organisation of permits and licenses. Park regulations are intended to protect natural and cultural resources and visitor experiences and to ensure visitor safety. It is your responsibility to know and respect these regulations. If you are unsure about the legality of a particular activity, please ask first. Stewardship of park lands depends as much on attitude and awareness as on rules and regulations. It is the policy of the National Park Service to apply the lowest level of law enforcement necessary to gain compliance. However, there are situations where offences may result in the issuance of a violation notice, which is punishable by a fine of up to $500 and/or six months in jail.

Backcountry use regulations

The following regulations and policies apply to all backcountry use (both day-use and overnight camping) in Glacier. They are essential to a safe and enjoyable trip:

- Pets, firearms, motorboats, snowmobiles and wheeled vehicles (including bicycles and canoe carts) are prohibited.
- All natural features are protected (fish, berries, or mushrooms may be caught or collected for personal consumption only).
- Hunting and trapping are prohibited.
- Wood fires are permitted in designated fire pits only.
- Pack out all refuse, including uneaten food and scraps.
- Stock use is restricted to designated trails and campgrounds.
- Grazing stock is prohibited.
- Feeding or disturbing wildlife is unsafe and illegal.
- Fishing does not require a license. Obtain the *Fishing Regulations* handout when you pick up your permit.
- Stay on maintained trails; shortcutting switchbacks is unsafe and illegal.
- Use pit toilets whenever possible; solid human waste must be deposited in a six to eight inch deep 'cathole' at least 200 feet from water sources.

Source: Glacier National Park (1999)

tation that service providers will act as good stewards in protecting the integrity of plants, animals or cultural heritage resources whilst undertaking their activities. Often, however, licensing becomes not a matter of conservation or user well being but a matter of satisfying institutional needs. This is suggested by McArthur (1998), who observed that licensing suffers from a lack of coordination across political units, little justification for any differences that exist in fees, and a lack of an incentives structure for the purpose of improving performance. By comparison, leases are issued to operators who have been given exclusive rights to areas for the purpose of service provision. This usually takes the form of a restaurant or lodge, or a recreational activity over an extended period of time.

Governments are also able to hold accountable those operators who maintain a permit to conduct tourism activities. Permits can be revoked if the offending party breaks any of a series of established regulations. This issue has come forward in Doubtful Sound, New Zealand, where a number of dolphin-watching operators with permits have been in violation of the government's Marine Mammal Protection Regulations. Lusseau (2004) reports that the benefit of holding a permit has been lost in this setting because non-permit holders can spend as much time with the animals as permit holders can, but without being legally bound to the requirements of the regulations. This has created a great deal of tension between the two groups and a culture of rule violation in both groups because of poor delineation within the system – a form of collective deviance based on the commons dilemma, i.e. rational individual benefit supersedes any form of sustainable control. The same holds true in Port Phillip Bay in Victoria, Australia, where swim-with-dolphins operators regularly fail to comply with all of the specified permit conditions (Scarpaci *et al.*, 2003).

With regard to the lack of coordination across political units illustrated above, Gjerdalen and Williams (2000, citing Beckmann, 1994) note that there are at least 36 federal and 20 provincial and territorial acts in Canada that deal with the protection of the marine environment. However, it is not at all clear which of these has the power to protect the whales from whale-watching activities. The problem is that there is no mechanism in place that allows for a cross over between marine protection and whale protection, and that has developed as a result of the complexity and growth of the whale-watching industry. Governments have simply not been able to keep pace with this growth (Garrod & Fennell, 2004).

Voluntary

The UNWTO (WTO, 2002) defines voluntary initiatives as social, ecological or economic measures that target a number of different groups or sectors (e.g. accommodation, food and beverage) where the initiator is not obliged by law to run the initiative, and where the target groups are not required to join. Examples include ecolabel and certification schemes, prizes, awards, environmental management systems, self-commitments, charters and declarations and codes of ethics. The Government of Canada (1998) provides a similar perspective by defining such mechanisms as: a set of non-legalised commitments that one or more organisations or individuals agrees to abide by, that are designed to influence, control or benchmark the actions of the target group, and are applied in a consistent manner across the board in reaching an outcome. In this regard, Stonehouse (1990, cited in Mason, 1997; see also Mason, 1994) notes that codes of conduct, codes of practice, and guidelines do not generally have legal status (see also Mason & Mowforth, 1996; Garrod & Fennell, 2004). The difference between non-voluntary and voluntary approaches is illustrated by contrasting the Boundary Waters Canoe Area Wilderness example (Box 2.4), with the example on Glacier National Park (Box 2.3).

Carter *et al.* (2004) argue that voluntary approaches may be more effective than the command-and-control mechanisms in achieving environmental goals because of their flexibility and ease of use. Regulations are viewed at times to be unnecessarily complicated by legislative and policy directives. The authors observe that environmental and conservation regulation, if it applies, is usually invoked in tourism at the developmental stages for the purposes of planning, impact assessment, waste control and zoning. Conversely, at the operational stage, where services are the main goods produced by providers, regulation of any form is rare. This means that legislative mechanisms typically apply at the early stages of tourism development, but that service industries like tourism are run more by self-regulatory approaches. The inculcation of ethically based mechanisms by which to guide the industry, like codes of ethics, accreditation, and so on, has thus evolved to fill the regulatory void, or where time is needed until more formal regulatory mechanisms can be put into place (WDCS, 2000, 2003). Carter *et al.* (2004) note that these mechanisms may only be effective on the basis of a foundational environmental ethic – enforcement by peer pressure and ethical obligation – that will influence the actions of service providers and tourists alike (see also Fennell, 2004).

The importance of the voluntary approach to management in tourism is discussed by Heckel *et al.* (2003), who found that whale-watching in Ensenada, Mexico has had to go through a period of evolution in order to recognise what constitutes a best-fit scenario socially, economically and ecologically. Over the span of about 15 years, interest in and the provision of services for viewing Eastern Pacific grey whales has grown tremendously. Heckel *et al.* define three major eras of management in efforts to control the impacts of this industry. The first era, deemed *'market-driven'*, was characterised by trip frequency dictated by demand. As no regulation existed at this early stage, a series of impacts emerged including competition leading to too many boats, the movement of the migration corridor further out into the ocean, fewer sightings, fewer persons watching whales and, later, financial losses. The response to this was to create *'regulation-driven whale watching'* through the enactment of an emergency whale-watching law in 1996 for the purpose of resuscitating the industry. Although this law led to some general improvements in the industry, including a permit system and guidelines for allowable manoeuvres, the effects on whale behaviour were still largely negative. This was because service providers offered different

Box 2.4 Accepting the wilderness challenge in the Boundary Waters Canoe Area Wilderness, Minnesota

The code of ethics developed by the Superior National Forest in regards to the Boundary Waters Canoe Area Wilderness can be contrasted with the regulations, above, pertaining to Glacier National Park. Here the focus is on 'suggestions' for being an ethical traveller, whereas in the former, regulations are stated and backed up by law.

Will you accept the wilderness challenge?

Wildernesses are managed to protect and maintain the environment in its natural state. As a wilderness visitor, your place within the wilderness is not as a conqueror or owner, but as a wise keeper of this land and water. The wilderness challenge is no longer 'Can you survive the wilderness?' The challenge now is *'can the wilderness survive you?'* Please do your part to preserve the BWCA Wilderness for the future by following these suggestions and reminders.

- Keep your group size small. Nine (9) people and four (4) watercraft are the maximum allowed in your party. You may not exceed this limit at any time or anywhere (on water, portages, campsites) in the BWCAW. Smaller groups increase your wilderness experience and decrease the impact.
- Travel and camp quietly. You will increase the chance of seeing wildlife and enhance the wilderness experience for yourself and others. Remember that noise carries a great distance across water.
- Make camp early enough in the day to ensure finding an available campsite. Sites off main travel routes and in back bays provide more privacy and solitude.
- Bring a small camp stove. They heat quicker and cleaner than a fire and come in handy during wet rainy weather.
- Leave your axe at home. By gathering small pieces of dead and down wood, which are easily broken by hand or cut with a small folding saw, you eliminate the need for an axe.
- Burn only dead wood found lying on the ground. Collect your firewood away from campsites where it's more abundant.
- Put all campfires DEAD OUT. Douse with water and stir ashes until they are cold to touch with a bare hand.
- Keep your drinking water clean. All soaps pollute water. Bathe and wash dishes at least 150 feet from lakes and streams.
- Pack a bag to carry out litter found on portages, landings and campsites. Pay attention to unburned foil, twist ties, and cigarette butts. Burning plastic is illegal.
- If you bring your dog, please respect other visitors' rights. Keep dogs under control at all times and prevent excessive barking. Bury faecal matter 150 feet from water sources.
- Leave tour campsite as you found it. Avoid removing rocks, flowers or moss. Refrain from cutting, peeling, or defacing live trees. Leave things in their natural state for others.
- Help preserve America's cultural heritage by leaving archaeological, historical, and rock painting sites undisturbed.

Box 2.4 – *continued*

- Fish entrails should be buried in the top 6 inches of soil well away from the campsite or place them on top of rocks at the water's edge at least 150 feet from portage or campsite to allow gulls to eat them. If they are not gone from the rocks before you break camp, they should be buried. State law prohibits putting the remains into the water.

Source: Superior National Forest (1998)

standards of conduct, resulting from reduced costs in securing market share, inappropriate manoeuvring of boats (insufficient compliance with law) to satisfy tourist expectations, too many vessels (some of which were unauthorised), lack of education among skippers who were unaware of the law and few resources available to enforce the law. In an effort to develop a solution to the problem, a local management process based on research, public participation and education – called the *'research- and management-driven whale-watching approach'* – was developed. In this third management era, skippers had to be trained as guides (including a mandatory environmental education programme in order to receive a license), there was a better system in place to educate people about the law, law enforcement was improved as a result of more resources (partly from a proper funding system), multi-stakeholder meetings were held on an on-going basis, and standards were developed based on the experiences of tour guides. Heckel *et al.* suggest that the multi-pronged approach provides fertile ground for a commitment to self-regulation, coupled with education of operators, the public and tourists, in ensuring compliance with measures developed for the activity.

The value of self-regulation in the marine tourism sector is further underscored by Watson *et al.* (1998: 255), who found that a range of measures, beyond permits, are required for effectively managing impacts to the Great Barrier Reef in Australia. These measures include:

(1) strategic policy and planning, which includes establishing a clear direction for managing marine tourism;
(2) direct management through well-defined, enforceable and effective management controls to protect the values of the marine park;
(3) self-regulation by the tourist industry, via the encouragement, assistance and promotion of environmental responsibility and professional presentation of the reef within the marine tourism industry; and
(4) active partnerships amongst members of the industry and other stakeholders, to be active partners in marine park management.

With reference to the third management strategy above, Watson and her colleagues (Watson *et al.*, 1998: 255) identify three main areas by which to promote and encourage environmental responsibility from the vantage point of tourism service provision, including:

(1) codes of conduct and best environmental practice;
(2) tourism industry training programmes; and
(3) accreditation.

An enhanced discussion of some of these measures is provided later in this chapter.

Codes by Whom and for Whom

Codes *by* whom?

Reporting on the UNEP (1995) study on codes of ethics in tourism, Genot (1995) illustrates that codes have been developed mainly by three groups: government, industry associations and NGOs. In a few cases codes have been developed by individuals, usually tourism scholars, in attempts to affect behaviour. Such codes have been targeted almost exclusively at the tourism industry, host communities and tourists themselves. We have taken the lead from these authors in providing a few examples of codes of ethics according to codes developed *by whom* and *for whom*, below and in Figure 2.1, which illustrates slight differences in the nature of the codes as they apply to industry, tourists and hosts, according to 'General behaviour' and 'Specific sectors, sites, individuals or activities'. Examples of codes developed by government, industry, NGOs and individuals are presented below.

Governmental codes

Governments have a history of involvement in the development of codes of ethics at all levels. The English Tourist Board is an example of a national entity that comes to mind by virtue of the number of references to this model in the literature (http://www.enjoyengland.com/; accessed 01.05).

Industry associations and other groups

The World Travel and Tourism Council (WTTC) is an example of an organisation that has developed a well-cited environmental code (http://www.wttc.org/frameset5.htm; accessed 01.05). At the regional level, the Pacific Asia Travel Association published a *Code for Environmental Responsible Tourism in the Pacific Asian Region* (http://www.pata.org/; accessed 01.05), which has also been widely cited. Included in this heading are a number of sector- and activity- specific codes for groups like hotels and accommodation. The International Hotels Environment Initiative has been innovative in generating positive change in the hotel sector (http://www.ihei.org/holding/index.htm; accessed 01.05). Amongst operators, the International Association of Antarctica Tour Operators' guidelines for operators and tourists (http://www.iaato.org/guidelines.html; accessed 01.05) is a good example of how operators can come together for common good (see also Splettstoesser, 1999).

NGO codes

Tourism Concern (http://www.tourismconcern.org.uk/; accessed 01.05) is one NGO that has been active in the development of codes of ethics for tourism. Other groups include the National Audubon Society, the World Wildlife Federation, and The International Ecotourism Society's Guidelines for Nature Tour Operators (http://www.pirt.org/TIES-Guidelines.htm; accessed 01.05).

Codes developed by individuals

See for example Boo's (1990) *Ecotourism: The Potentials and Pitfalls*, through the WWF. Stanley Plog has also developed a code of ethics for tourism (see Stark, 2002).

The importance of an examination of codes on the basis of author becomes important with reference to recent work by Parsons and Woods-Ballard (2003). These researchers found in the whale-watching industry of West Scotland that operators themselves were universal in their support of their own code of ethics over codes developed by government. In fact, none of the codes of ethics developed by government were used by any of the operators, and only 37% of operators knew of their existence. The reasons for ignoring the government codes ranged from resentment over being told how to act by government to the belief that the codes were not user-friendly. This tendency toward the 'bottom-up' type of control over the 'top-down' is a theme that needs to be further explored with respect not only to whale-watching but also to other forms of tourism. Parsons and Woods-Ballard also observed that codes of ethics should not be the only mechanism with which to protect cetaceans, but should be accompanied by sound research and legislation for better management of the industry.

Codes for whom

In general, codes of ethics have been targeted at three main groups: industry, tourists and hosts. The vast majority of these appear to be for tourists and outdoor recreationists, but there is an increasing number of professional codes of ethics designed specifically for the industry (A more elaborate comparison between different forms of codes of ethics is included in Table 2.2.)

Industry

Codes of ethics for the industry (e.g. accommodation providers, airlines) do not always come from within, but from other groups like government and NGOs. Such codes have the following characteristics: they usually

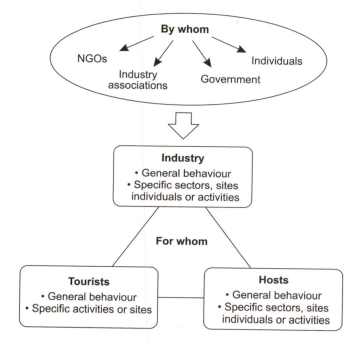

Figure 2.1 Codes of ethics: By whom and for whom

favour an ideal rather than a norm; they originate from coordinating bodies like the WTO or ASTA; codes usually promote self-regulation; codes produced by governments and NGOs tend to support regulation in the absence of statutory regulations; codes of ethics are seen as an important part of the regulation of the tourism industry; and codes developed by NGOs and citizens for industry refer to impacts, the role of host communities, and training and education (Mason & Mowforth, 1996).

Tourists

There are a great many codes of ethics in existence for specific tourist activities. Mason and Mowforth (1996) suggest that the majority of these types of codes: have been written by NGOs or citizens; the audience is both international and domestic tourists; the message is focused on ecology and socio-cultural factors; the code is short and usually confined to one sheet of paper; and the code is usually admonitory, with the list of 'DON'Ts' outnumbering the 'DOs'.

Hosts

Mason and Mowforth (1996) divide this category into codes for host governments and codes for host communities. They observe that: there are relatively few of these codes; they have been developed by citizens or

Table 2.2 Key elements of codes of conduct in tourism

Type of code	*Authorship*	*Audience*	*Message*
Visitor codes	Predominantly NGOs and concerned individuals, but also some government bodies such as Ministry of the Environment.	Domestic visitors and international visitors, especially overseas visitors to developing countries.	• Minimise environmental and socio-cultural damage to area visited. • Maximise economic benefit to host community. • Encourage more equality in relationships between visitors and hosts. • Promote more responsible and sustainable forms of tourism.
Industry codes	Predominantly coordinating bodies such as WTO and IATA also governments and to a lesser extent NGOs and concerned individuals; and exceptionally tourism companies, e.g. Chateau Whistler Hotel Group.	Tourism industry in general, and some codes for specific sectors such as the hotel industry.	• Appropriate training/ education for staff. • Honest marketing of product. • Develop awareness of environmental and socio-cultural impact of tourism. • Promote more responsible and sustainable forms of tourism. • Promote recycling.
Host codes	Predominantly NGOs and concerned individuals, some host communities in both developed and developing countries, and a small number of host governments.	Mainly host communities, especially in developing countries.	• Information and advice about visitors. • Minimise environmental and socio-cultural damage. • Minimise economic. benefits to host community. • Encourage more equality in relationship between host and visitors. • Advocate more democratic and participatory forms of tourism development

Source: Adapted from Mason & Mowforth (1996)

NGOs; governments have been slow to develop such codes for themselves; in both developing and developed countries host codes have been developed mostly by host communities for their own use; the message of these codes is geared towards the maximisation of benefits and the minimisation of costs; host codes are typically more democratic and participatory, encouraging more of a significant role in tourism development in the region.

Other Tools in the Search for Tourism Sustainability

Agenda 21, a programme of action adopted by 182 governments during the Earth Summit, was the first document of its kind to develop international consensus about the realisation of a sustainable future that is based on balancing human needs, collectively, with the physical and biological resources of the planet. In response to Agenda 21, the World Travel and Tourism Council in concert with the World Tourism Organisation and the Earth Council (WTTC, 1997), set forth an agenda of their own for the sustainable development of tourism. This report defined sustainable tourism development as that which

> meets the needs of present tourists and host regions while protecting and enhancing opportunity for the future. It is envisioned as leading to management of all resources in such a way that economic, social, and aesthetic needs can be fulfilled while maintaining cultural integrity, essential ecological processes, biological diversity, and life support systems. (WTO, as cited in WTTC, 1997: 6)

In Section 3 of the document, Responsibilities of Travel and Tourism Companies, a number of organisations and programmes are highlighted for the purpose of outlining the role of tourism companies in achieving the aims of Agenda 21. Voluntary programmes and initiatives form the core of approaches that companies can take in moving towards sustainability in their operations – a fact supported in the literature. For example, Mihalic (2000) argues that the effective management of tourism can take place along a continuum, including environmental management by: (1) environmental codes of conduct; (2) uncertified environmental practice and self-declared labels or brands; (3) green branding on the basis of prizes for environmental practice or certified environmental good practice; and (4) green branding on the basis of accreditation schemes (by internationally known ecolabels and ecoquality labels). Payne *et al.* (1999) have assembled these various tools into three main groups: scientific, managerial and principle-based. The scientific group includes indicators of ecosystem health, stress and resiliency, and baseline conditions that provide the means by which to scientifically measure change, and the acceptability of such change in the context of the setting. Managerial approaches focus on what the organisation should be doing to control the ecological impacts, through such measures as best practices, standards and environmental management systems. Principle-based approaches, which address the ecological and social impacts of tourism through a code of ethics, are premised on the need for actors to follow a set of precepts in generating appropriate behaviours. Payne *et al.* conclude by suggesting that, although distinct in theory, these three approaches should overlap in practice with the benefit of enhancing sustainability.

What is perhaps most significant about these approaches, apart from what they attempt to do, is their growth and volume over a relatively short period of time. While Payne *et al.* view this as a positive step in tourism's attempt to be more sustainable, their onset has incorporated a complex set of new terms that have complicated tourism's theoretical and applied landscape. With regard to eco-certification schemes alone, Yunis (2002, as cited in Buckley, 2002a) has identified more than 100 of these, involving some 7000 member companies. This means that, in terms of the evolution of sustainability in tourism, these schemes cannot be ignored because, like codes of ethics, they seek to improve the performance of a target group. We can say that the connection between codes of ethics and certification and environmental management is based primarily on intent (i.e. sustainability). This is supported by Bendell and Harris (2004), who suggest that the standards forming the basis of certification have in fact evolved from codes of ethics through the incorporation of measuring and monitoring methods. This corroborates not only what Payne *et al.* (1999) say above with reference to the overlap of these various measures, but also corroborates Clarke (2002), who links codes of ethics with ecolabels, awards, environmental management systems, and other initiatives in efforts to implement sustainable tourism.

Of these various measures, best practice, benchmarking, auditing, certification and ecolabels, will be highlighted below, albeit briefly, in an effort to examine the emergence of managerial efforts to generate sustainable practices in tourism. Issaverdis (2001) illustrates that even though a tourism service provider may take part in benchmarking, accreditation and best practice, the element of auditing may be missing. However, the ideal situation is if service providers subscribe to all three elements – i.e. the firm has established operational benchmarks, is accredited, is performing at the level of best practice and, finally, has gone one step further in conducting regular audits, both internal (by someone inside the firm) and external (by someone outside the firm) audits. Each of the foregoing is discussed in more detail below.

Best practice in tourism

Best practice includes, 'those practices that are considered the most effective and efficient at the time. Best practice is a management approach to operations and customer service, which demands the highest standard of performance at all times' (Issaverdis, 2001: 587). It has also been defined as a mechanism by which to designate highest quality, excellence or superior practices in a particular field by a tourism operator (Honey & Rome, 2001; see also Hawkes & Williams, 1993). Best practice is widely used in many award and certification programmes, as well as in academic studies, to designate best in a particular class or a leader in the field. The authors observe that 'best' is a contextual term, with often no set standard for use in measurement of what qualifies as best or not. Issaverdis (2001) suggests that there are a few key principles that are linked to companies that continually strive to achieve best practice. These include commitment to change and continuous improvement, retaining a highly-skilled base of employees, employing a team-based management style, adopting innovative technologies, focusing on customer needs, developing superior communication networks, using performance measurement systems, and benchmarking.

In 2001, the UK-based Tearfund published a report on the responsible business practices of 65 service providers in the United Kingdom. The thrust of this publication was to examine industry best practice in four main areas: benefits to the local community, charitable giving, partnerships and responsible tourism practices, all of which were scrutinised on the basis of findings, commentary and recommendations. Although too detailed to discuss here at length, the general conclusions drawn from the study (Tearfund, 2001) were summarised as follows:

(1) the tourism industry lags behind other industries in terms of fulfilling social and economic obligations in regards to local communities;
(2) tour operators need to be more vigilant in providing tourists with appropriate information (e.g. codes of ethics) in regards to acceptable behaviour at destinations;
(3) operators need to do more to stimulate local partnerships, particularly in reference to helping local entrepreneurs; and
(4) there is a challenge to establish priorities over a longer period of time.

Too often success is defined on the basis of quarterly earnings and 2- or 3-year plans. What is perhaps most impressive about the terminology used in describing this last point is the observation that companies will need to be *bold* and inspired in accomplishing this end.

An organisation that appears to have pushed the envelope on best practice is the Haliburton Forest and Wild Life Reserve Ltd, located in the Haliburton Highlands of central Ontario, Canada (http://www.haliburton forest.com/bacl.htm; accessed 15.03.06). This is the largest privately-owned property in Canada comprising over 60,000 acres of rolling hardwood forests, pristine lakes, meandering rivers and extensive wetlands. It is also Canada's first certified sustainable forest, meeting the stringent standards of the Forest Stewardship Council, an NGO supported by such organisations as the WWF and the Sierra Club. Until the late 1950s, the area had been logged so extensively that it was deemed worthless to the Canadian government. With few other ways to manage the land (which is located on the Canadian Shield and therefore has poor agricultural value) the government chose to sell it, but had trouble doing so. In 1962, Baron von Fuerstenberg, a German forester who had immigrated to Canada, purchased the land for the purpose of restoring it to its original productive state. In order to do this, he employed a 100-year plan to bring the forest back to its original health through the practice of wise forestry management – selective cutting not of the healthiest trees, but of the least healthy trees in order to restore the genetic health of the ecosystem. In order to realise von Fuerstenberg's sustainable plan, recently passed down to his son, a number of adventure and ecotourism activities have been used to provide the financial means to supplement the forestry operation. These activities include a Wolf Centre (at present this has 10 timber wolves on 15 acres, with an observatory), a Walk in the Clouds forest canopy tour, groomed snowmobile trails, mountain biking, dog-sledding, hiking, astronomy, wildlife observation, semi-wilderness camping and accommodation, and a six-passenger submarine that takes tourists down into one of the region's lakes. There are also outdoor education seminars and workshops (e.g. for school groups) and the centre also offers executive and corporate training programmes in a wilderness retreat setting.

Benchmarking

Honey and Rome (2001: 5) define benchmarking as 'the process of comparing performance and processes within an industry to assess relative position against either a set industry standard or against those who are "best in the class"'. The benchmark becomes the point of reference from which to evaluate the operational practices of one company against another. National or international standards or sector-specific indicators may be used to develop the benchmark for the purpose of gauging sub-par performance, par performance or, as noted above, performance that is deemed well above the norm. Issaverdis (2001) contends that there is a critical difference between benchmarking and best practice, with benchmarking viewed as more of a point of reference for systematic comparison (with others), while best practice represents those entities that are most effective or efficient in time and space, as compared with others in the same class. In this regard, Pigram (2000) suggests that organisational efficiency with reference to benchmarking would include identifying industry leaders and comparing products, services and practices, and then implementing procedures to both upgrade performance and to match or surpass competitors.

Auditing

Auditing is 'the process a business undergoes to identify and confirm benchmarks, to provide accreditation with reliability and validity, and measure and verify best practice' (Issaverdis, 2001: 589). It entails a process of measuring and the development of effective guidelines for the purpose of gauging the level of adherence to these guidelines. These guidelines are usually designed to evaluate the operational strategies, broadly defined, of the service provider. Goodall (1995) observes that audits may provide the following benefits in the context of the environment:

- more efficient use of resources will result in cost savings;
- environmental problems may be identified before they turn into liabilities;
- positive environmental practice benchmarks may be more easily established;
- an organisation's corporate image may be improved;
- marketing advantages may be realised;
- investors, regulators, customers and the community will have heightened confidence in the quality of the product; and
- the company will have the latitude to hire better employees who are more intrinsically motivated.

Certification/accreditation and ecolabels

Certification and accreditation, treated synonymously here, are part of a continuum, as noted above, that is designed to improve standards, professionalism and overall quality (Harris & Jago, 2001). They include 'programmes that provide a means of establishing the extent to which a business offering tourism experiences meets industry nominated standards' (Issaverdis, 2001: 583). Honey (2001, see also 2002) notes that all certification programmes currently in existence share five elements:

(1) participation by service providers is strictly voluntary;
(2) all programmes award a logo that is used by service providers for competitive advantage;
(3) participants must comply with or improve upon standards or regulations;
(4) the logo is awarded on the basis of an audit or assessment; and
(5) most programmes charge a fee to those seeking certification.

What is driving the new wave of certification in tourism is the expectation on the part of consumers that their products should be not only safe but of the highest standards. Perhaps more succinctly it means that such programmes are developed for the purpose of reducing purchase risk, by letting consumers know that the service provider has achieved certain levels of skill, competence and knowledge. The earliest of these schemes was Blue Flag in 1985, followed by Green Globe in 1998 (Font, 2002). The following two examples provide a snapshot of the nature of certification in tourism.

The Certification for Sustainable Tourism (CST), Costa Rica

This is a programme that categorises and certifies each tourism company according to the manner in which it complies with a model of sustainability. Evaluation is based on 153 yes/no performance-based questions according to:

(1) physical–biological parameters, including interactions between the company and natural habitat;
(2) infrastructure and services, which entails management policies and operational systems of the company;
(3) how much the company allows and invites the client to be an active contributor to the company's policies on sustainability; and
(4) socio-economic environment, which includes an evaluation of the interaction of the company with the local communities and populations which it encounters (www.turismo-sostenible.co.cr/EN/sobreCST/about-cst.shtml; accessed 15.11.05).

Lapas Rios, a 1000-acre private ecotourism reserve in Costa Rica, is one of the best examples of Costa' Rica's CST programme. Birding, night hikes and boat trips to a botanical garden are some of the most popular activities of one of Costa Rica's greenest hotels (Honey, 2003).

The SmartVoyager programme

Established by the NGO Rainforest Alliance for tourism boat operators in the Galapagos Islands, Ecuador, this programme awards a green seal of approval to those operators who meet strict standards for protecting wild-life, workers and local communities. While the programme was designed initially for large vessels, it has more recently been adapted for smaller ones. Certification standards are grouped into 11 categories, including company policy, conservation of natural ecosystems, reduction of negative environmental impacts, lowering the risk of introduction and dispersal of exotic species, just and proper treatment of workers, employee training, community relations and local welfare, strict control of use, supply, and storage of materials, integrated waste management, commitment on the part of the tourists and planning and monitoring (www.rainforest-alliance.org/programs/tourism/smartvoyager; accessed 15.11.05).

The platforms developed by organisations such as Pro-Poor Tourism and Tourism Concern along the lines of justice, equity, rights, child labour, discrimination and health and safety appear to be on the cutting edge of this new wave of ethical thought and action. This is a welcome change, according to Font and Harris (2004), who conclude that most certification schemes (and the content found within them) deal more with traditional aspects of tourism issues, such as environmental impacts and cost-saving devices. Based on an interview-style methodology framed by the Pro-Poor Tourism agenda, these authors examined the social mandates of five certification schemes operating in the less well-developed countries. Questions included, for example, 'Do you encourage support of local enterprises?', 'Can you address issues of poor working conditions?', and 'Do criteria encourage respect of customary/legal rights of access by locals to natural resources?' Font and Harris (2004) concluded by suggesting that there are severe limitations with regard to the measurement and application of these social standards on many levels. Foremost is the difficulty in measuring largely subjective issues according to basic standards (i.e. the issues are a great deal more complex than might be surmised through standards questions that demand only 'yes' or 'no' responses). The standards in use, therefore, were found to be ambiguous, the assessment methodologies used by certifying bodies were largely inconsistent, there is huge variability regarding what is and is not sustainable, and those companies working most diligently on being socially conscious are those most challenged to expand. This led Font and Harris (2004) to suggest that considerable work is needed in order to determine what best practice is as a benchmark for sustainable certification, broadly defined (see also Bendell & Font, 2004, with reference to best practice for setting, implementing, monitoring and the certification of sustainable tourism standards).

An important aspect of certification programmes is the label (e.g. ecolabel), which is defined as 'methods to standardise the promotion of environmental claims by following compliance to set criteria, generally based on third-party, impartial verification, usually by governments or non-profit organisations' (Font, 2001: 3). To be meaningful, an ecolabel needs to be tied to an ecolabel scheme and administered by a reputable organisation, without which it may be rightfully judged to be meaningless beyond its utility as a marketing hook (Buckley, 2001). The value of the eco-label to consumers is judged on the basis of: (1) how much consumers care about the environment in the context of their chosen activity (e.g. tourism); and (2) how much difference they perceive in programme offerings that are ecolabeled versus those that are not (Buckley, 2001). Apart from Blue Flag, one of the most widely acclaimed eco-labels is the Australian Nature and Ecotourism Accreditation Programme (NEAP2), which signifies quality, especially in regards to the advanced ecotourism accreditation standard which many Australian ecotourism operators have attained.

As a postscript to this section, a new international certification scheme entitled the, International Ecotourism Standard (IES), was unveiled at the 2002 Ecotourism Summit in Quebec City. The IES is jointly owned by the Nature and Ecotourism Accreditation Program of Australia and the CRC for Sustainable Tourism also of Australia, and is exclusively licensed to Green Globe 21 for its use internationally (Crabtree *et al.*, 2002). The new standard is based on the international standards for ecotourism developed at the Mohonk Conference, New York (Honey & Rome, 2001), the

Australian NEAP, and the standards that have been used by Green Globe 21. The resultant certification standard is said to, 'provide a blueprint for ecotourism development, a benchmark and incentive to promote best practice and a means of identifying genuine ecotourism' (Crabtree *et al.*, 2002: 1). In order for the system to work, Green Globe 21 had to respond to a number of criticisms that their sustainable tourism indicators were more process-oriented than performance-oriented. In general, the World Wildlife Fund (WWF, 2000) criticised tourism certification programmes around the world, with a particular focus on Green Globe 21 – cited as the world's most frequently used programme. In their report, the WWF identified a series of drawbacks to the system, including the fact that Green Globe allowed its logo to be used even though full certification had not been achieved. This meant that a company could be perceived as certified, even though their organisational practices might be found to be damaging to the natural environment. The WWF report acknowledges that good certification programmes are those that require service providers to meet or exceed benchmark standards prior to certification and any use of an ecolabel. The other main criticism against Green Globe 21 surrounded the for-profit nature of their operations (Font, 2002).

The IES system is premised on quantified on-site performance standards (known as 'Earth Check') that are later compared with baseline standards. This benchmarking component is essential to the system, as service providers will be certified only if they can demonstrate operations that exceed the benchmark indicators. The verification of these measures takes place through an on-site third party audit. And while there are perceived complications with establishing a benchmarking system that is universal, the authors have attempted to overcome this difficulty by establishing benchmarking indicators that are country specific, at baseline and best practice levels. As noted by the authors, 'baseline and best practice levels for these indicators are analysed according to that countries [*sic*] environmental performance data, or if this is not available, a country with similar technology and infrastructure' (Crabtree *et al.*, 2002: 7). All benchmarking indicators that have either met or exceeded the best practice level will be subsequently identified through awards or other means. This has prompted the IES to develop two levels of criteria for certifying an ecotourism product: 'Ecotourism' and 'Advanced Ecotourism'. This means that the 'Advanced Ecotourism' certification will be given to products that meet or exceed a specified percentage of best practice criteria as developed by the standard. In addition, the new system is subject to periodic review given changing conditions, there are built-in incentives to continually improve, logo use will be strongly controlled, and certification can be withdrawn as a result of non-compliance.

This example serves to cast further light on the many different terms identified above. IES is a certification scheme; it has an ecolabel; benchmarking is an integral aspect of the system (in the way baseline data has been amassed); and it does have a provision for best practice built into it. But, although the extensiveness of the system (based on current knowledge) is not in doubt, there is something very unsettling about the whole endeavour. Perhaps it is the marriage of a global approach with ownership/exclusivity that is most troubling. Presumably the Ecotourism Association of Australia and the CRC for Sustainable Tourism both stand to make a great deal of money from this venture, not to mention the money that Green Globe 21 makes as well – by 2001, 1000 companies in more than 100 countries had become members of Green Globe 21 (Green Globe 21, 2001). Added to this is the notion that perhaps there is something wrong about capitalising on intellectual assets. That is, certification schemes have benefited from the work of countless other people and other systems that have gone before.

Buckley (2002a, citing Gunningham *et al.*, 1998) writes that tourists are right to be suspicious of ecolabels and other related forms of self-regulation that come at a price, because these are operated by private firms or industry associations. In such cases consumers cannot be confident that what they are purchasing does not come with a focus on profit over conservation. Missing is oversight from governmental agencies who regulate standards on innumerable products and globally respected NGOs whose endorsement means a great deal more to consumers than an industry label does. There should also be penalties to operators for non-compliance (see Chapter 3), and this information should be shared with the public at large and with companies who are thinking about joining the ecolabel scheme in question (Buckley, 2002b). Consumers might also be suspicious of accreditation and ecolabels schemes on the basis of their standards, particularly if there is a lack of solid data on the actual performance of these companies in relation to the standards of the accrediting body. Does this inspire confidence? Not likely, but it does allude to the oft-quoted adage, 'Buyer beware'. Buckley (2002a) sums up his discussion on certification and ecolabels by asking whether or not we ought to care about this recent phenomenon. He observes that all the time and effort we have placed into these in the last decade may have been misplaced. In the end he feels that they may be far less effective than simple government actions like codes of ethics or permits. As with any political beast, the more layers of bureaucracy built into a system, the more mouths there are to feed. (See Sasidharan *et al.* (2002) and Jamal *et al.* (2006) for well-balanced criticisms of ecolabels and certification.)

Conclusion

This broadly-based chapter has sought to accomplish two main ends.

The first was to provide a brief overview of the tourism ethics literature, including an historical overview of codes of ethics. This was coupled with a discussion of voluntary and non-voluntary approaches to tourism management. Non-voluntary measures were deemed more essential in the development or early stages of tourism, whilst voluntary measures were viewed as more essential in the day-to-day operations of the industry. A number of examples of codes from the perspective of who they were developed by and for were included to illustrate the spectrum of involvement in tourism from the perspective of government, NGOs, tourism associations, communities, and other stakeholder groups. The second aim of the chapter was to frame codes of ethics in the broader sustainability concept by drawing a link between codes and these other initiatives (e.g. certification). Theorists have suggested that these more advanced initiatives have emerged from codes and, further, that all these various tools exist as part of a range of possibilities for generating sustainable tourism ends. The chapter concluded with observations by Buckley, who feels that the time and effort put into certification schemes and ecolabels might be misplaced. As such, these tools may be less effective than traditional mechanisms like codes and other regulatory devices, such as permits. These comments provide fertile grounds for further investigation of these various measures in time, space and circumstance.

Chapter 3

Code Development and Compliance

Introduction

Implicit in a code is the belief or hope that the outcome of adhering to the code is ethical behaviour. However, the dynamics are much more complex than one might initially suppose. In this chapter we explore generic examples of the code development process, followed by specific examples in a tourism context. Examples of a tourism nature include British Columbia, the Arctic and Scotland. Questions related to the formation of codes of ethics and how they should be communicated are also examined. The second major aspect of the chapter, compliance, is included with a focus on implementation, monitoring and the enforcement of codes. As perhaps the least documented aspect of codes of ethics, based on what appears to be absent from the literature, recommendations are made to provide more insight into this important component. We also summarise some of the main pros and cons of codes of ethics. Although the 'cons' section of this analysis is more robust, the two dovetail in the sense that both contribute to an overall sense of what a successful code of ethics ought to look like.

Code Development in General

A Government of Canada (1998) report on the code development process suggests that, because codes often emerge as a result of pressures from consumers, competitors and/or fear of regulation, they must be carefully conceived and developed. Doing otherwise simply undermines the importance of these pressures, with the end result that extensive time and effort has been wasted with little forward progress demonstrated. The report further acknowledges that the hallmark of a well-developed code of ethics is the inclusion of the public in the process, the generation of public confidence as a result of the code, and the successful attention to concerns in any number of different forms, including quality, price, choice, privacy, environment, labour standards, human rights, health and safety, advertising,and issues of morality (Government of Canada, 1998).

Taken from the aforementioned report, the code development process depicted in Figure 3.1 illustrates 8 different stages and associated tips

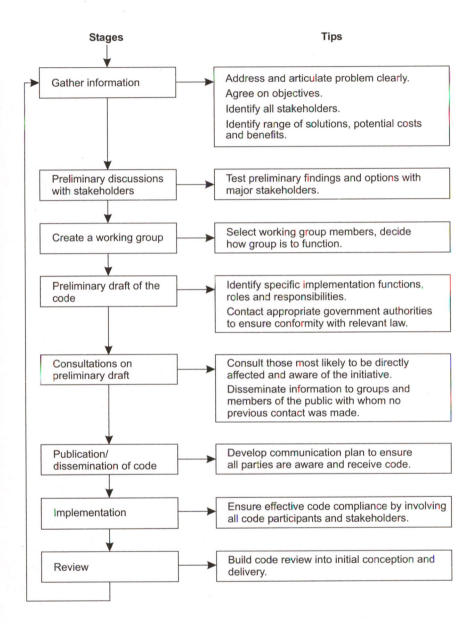

Figure 3.1 Code development process

Source: Adapted from Government of Canada (1998)

which will help ensure that the code is designed to accomplish its intended goal. It is important to point out that, as with strategic processes in general, there is a feedback loop that allows the 'system' to learn. That is, after a process of review, the code of ethics should be adapted to meet any of the changing needs or circumstances of the activities in question. One of the key advantages of this process is the inclusion, at several stages, of the stakeholders who will be involved or affected by the code of ethics. It also highlights the importance of compliance in the implementation stage, and the review process, as noted above.

The Canadian Government report goes on to identify a number of key roles that governments should be willing to adopt in balancing the many different stakeholder groups and interests for the good of an industry or sector (Box 3.1). Included are contributions along the lines of catalyst, facilitator, endorser, and/or provider of regulatory support. With reference to the facilitator role, governments could be instrumental in providing physical space, special documents or even monetary resources for the purpose of generating enthusiasm within a group for the active pursuit of a code of ethics.

If government has been able to contribute in a facilitating or enabling fashion, there is still the task of sitting down and generating the actual code document. A series of questions will need to be generated in respect of current knowledge, background and history, current and future needs, and so on, in assembling the right people and knowledge base to proceed with the code. Appendix 1 describes how the municipal government of San Martin de los Andes, a Patagonian tourist resort, set about developing its own environmental code of conduct.

Although not established on the basis of a conceptual framework, Saltzman (2004) has written 12 useful tips for the development of a code of ethics in business (Box 3.2). He explains that the most effective way to discover the ethics that are important for one's company is to write them down (i.e. to formalise or codify them). In doing so, the company becomes empowered with the opportunity to make sound ethical decisions. Essential components of this process include, for example, making good choices around who will draft the code, looking both inside and outside one's industry for leadership, looking at the positives and negatives of conduct in the past, allowing everyone to know what the rules are and how they ought to be followed, and the establishming a clear mechanism for reporting problems. Many of these features will be discussed in the following practical examples of codes developed in tourism.

Box 3.1 The role of government in code initiation and development

Government departments and agencies can contribute to the initiation, development and implementation of voluntary codes in many ways. However, government's role must be defined at the beginning to prevent confusion on the part of the public about the code's status, frustration on the part of the code developers and government liability in non-compliance situations.

Catalyst. Government representatives can encourage parties to explore voluntary approaches even if laws or regulations are not imminent. Government research, analysis and consultations can reveal concerns that stimulate action.

Facilitator. Governments can provide meeting rooms, teleconference facilities, information (for example, reports and case studies), advice – and, in some cases, financial assistance – in the early stages of code development.

Endorser. In some circumstances government departments or agencies can explicitly endorse a particular code or association that satisfies the provisions of a code. However, it is important that clear legal authority for such endorsements exists.

Provider of framework rules and regulatory support. Although voluntary codes may not be required by legislation, the existence of such codes may help to achieve regulatory objectives and could have regulatory implications. For example, in a regulatory enforcement action a company could point to its adherence to a voluntary code to help establish 'due diligence'. Conversely, failure to adhere to a voluntary code may assist prosecutors. In some circumstances, a regulatory authority could insist on adherence to voluntary codes as a condition of issuing a licence, and enforcement and procurement policies can encourage voluntary code compliance. Consistent, rigorous law enforcement is an essential backdrop to the effective development and use of voluntary codes.

Government officials must assess their involvement in relation to the broader public interest. They must also be scrupulously open, fair, and consistent in their dealings with all parties. Governments must not condone any activity that would lessen competition or otherwise contravene the Competition Act or other statute. Governments must also ensure that voluntary codes do not act as barriers to trade. Given that it could cost a department considerable money to help develop and monitor a voluntary code, it may want to conduct at least a notional cost-benefit analysis of the initiative along the lines of the federal Regulatory Impact Assessment Statement.

As the code is developed, governments must remain flexible and willing to shift approaches if necessary. If evidence surfaces that a voluntary initiative is not working as intended, or that the public interest is at risk, governments should be prepared to act, taking legislative or enforcement actions

Source: Government of Canada (1998: 6)

Box 3.2 Saltzman's tips for the development of codes of ethics in business

(1) *Choose your drafter carefully.* This can be done through a special committee or through individuals who have experience or training in this area.

(2) *Look to your industry.* The industry itself may have a code of ethics, which may be easily incorporated into the firm. There may also be specific businesses within your sector (e.g. ecotourism) which are more appropriate and can be easily integrated.

(3) *Look outside our industry.* It is important to study what is taking place outside one's industry for the purpose of diversifying thought and finding superior examples.

(4) *Get inspired by others.* In line with the previous tip, allow yourself to be inspired by the concepts and ideas from other companies.

(5) *Put first things first.* It is important to start with a general statement that outlines your company's mission, values and ideals. This helps put into perspective the broad mandate of your firm and the values of all who work there. For example, Tylenol's 'Our Credo' is as follows:

> We believe our first responsibility is to the doctors, nurses, and patients, to mothers and fathers and all others who use our products and services.

(6) *Look to your past.* Draw on cases and situations that helped to stimulate and challenge your progression. These events are important in forming a shared memory of the good times and the bad. Integrate the lessons learned from these into your code of ethics.

(7) *Create a first draft.* Although this is a big step it is likely that you will need multiple drafts of the document after sufficient time to filter the information. This will help ensure the final draft is clear, concise and meaningful.

(8) *Keep it simple.* Understand what it is that you are responsible for and work towards ensuring that this takes place. The document does not have to be long.

(9) *Make sure everyone knows 'These are the rules'.* This means distributing the code to all employees and posting it in convenient places so that both employees, people that you do business with and clients are aware of it.

(10) *Make sure everyone knows 'Here's how you FOLLOW the rules'.* Make it easy for employees to ask if they are doing the right thing or not. It makes sense to collect these ethical enquiries and communicate these to the company for their scrutiny and awareness. Ask employees to periodically assess how well the company is doing in regards to the code of ethics.

(11) *Establish a mechanism for reporting problems.* Establish a 'cool line' where employees can report any problems anonymously. Ensure that, if employees go the distance to report a wrong doing, they are assured that the company will follow through with the report. Also tell them that there is never a penalty for reporting such incidents. Also make sure that the caller is not identified, through identification or other means, and that all calls are not recorded and are permanently deleted after being received.

(12) *Look to your present (and your future).* Avoid changes that would appear to lower the ethical bar. Enron, for example, voted twice to place profit ahead of ethics in their code of ethics. Look to see how present and future events will affect your company and try to stay clear of the negative repercussions that will compromise the company's ethical integrity.

Source: Saltzman (2004)

The Language of Codes

In this section we provide a summary of the literature with regard to some fundamental aspects of code form, who should develop it and how it should be communicated. As such, it provides somewhat more sophistication with regard to the language of codes beyond what is introduced above. For this we rely on research from a broad spectrum of different fields, ranging from medicine to business.

The form of the code of ethics refers to its linguistic and grammatical style. Initial research by Farrell and Farrell (1998) explored the impact that the actual writing style of the code had on its adherence by the reader. Hadjistavropoulos, *et al.* (2002: 41) pursued this line of code analysis in the health fields of nursing and medicine, and assessed codes in terms of the following seven subcategories of syntax and lexicosemantics:

(1) *Passive constructions* – depersonalises the action (verb structure) to be carried out by not indicating who the agent of the action is or the recipient of the action (e.g. 'appropriate care is provided until alternative care arrangements are in place';

(2) *Relational process* – the use of verbs that imply certainty, such as 'is' and 'are' (e.g. 'self-regulation of the profession is a privilege';

(3) *Mode* (indicative and imperative) – the indicative mode implies fact (e.g. 'Nurses foster well-being'; whereas the imperative mode implies authority (e.g. 'use health care resources prudently';

(4) *Nominalisation* – occurs when nouns or noun phrases are constructed in which no agent is identified (e.g. 'development, implementation, and ongoing review of policies';

(5) *Modality* – this refers to the nuance of the verb used (e.g. should or will or may);

(6) *Lexical choice* – the use of terminology (e.g. member vs. subordinate)

(7) *Lexical avoidance* – this technique replaces words that are not palatable or politically correct (e.g. collateral damage vs. innocent bystander)

The conclusion reached, in terms of linguistic and grammatical structures, was that statements that depersonalised the reader (i.e. passive constructions and nominalisation), used the imperative mode, selected the authoritarian modality 'should', and made use of lexical avoidance were not as effective in transmitting the message to the reader as those that were personalised and offered the reader some degree of flexibility in terms of modality.

Put another way, codes should be written so that the reader will identify with the intent and goal of the statement. Impersonal messages distance the reader from the writer. Codes *should* be written (oddly enough) without the use of the word, *should*. This implies an authoritarian nature that may turn away the competent reader who could interpret the use of *should* or *will* as overly paternalistic. Finally, the choice of words is critical. Wal-Mart employees are called *associates* rather than *workers*; psychologists care for *clients* as opposed to *patients*; universities have *professors* and high schools have *teachers*. Each of these semantic distinctions is important and each demonstrates a degree of respect that the particular institution has for its *stakeholder*.

Generally, codes are the product of senior administration. This is true despite the truism that codes (and other philosophical statements describing the organisation) that are developed with the input from all corners of the organisation are more apt to instil a sense of commitment and camaraderie than dicta from above. Having said this though, it is senior administration who provide the organisation with leadership – moral and technical (see Burns, 1978) – and thus it perhaps ought to fall on their shoulders to develop the philosophical vision for its membership. This of course raises the age-old debate over who in fact is a leader and what are the responsibilities of this individual (Hodgkinson, 1996; Lang & Malloy, 2006).

That the code of ethics should be communicated at all is a major step forward for many organisations, which are often prepared to develop the document and then shelve it safely away in a manual. In these organisations, individual may be aware of the code, but they are often unable to recall its contents (Adams *et al.*, 2001). However, for those organisations that wish to make the code an active document, a variety of methods and mediums can be employed. First, the document needs to be written in a clear, concise and relevant fashion. If the message is sent, yet unclear, it will fail to make an impact on behaviour. Once this most basic and important task is accomplished, then it needs to be distributed. Possible locations include the following:

- policy and procedure manuals;
- web sites;
- employee handbook;
- newsletters;
- financial statements;
- employee orientation manual;
- telephone/email directories;
- brochures;
- training/educational manuals, videos, cds;
- identification cards;
- business cards.

The essential point to be made here is that the code needs to be part of all organisational activity. It needs to be part of the organisational culture (*the way we do things around here*) rather than a tool that is dug up each time a potentially unethical issue rears its ugly head. As Aristotle argued (1992), ethics must be lived as opposed to periodically imposed. Having a code does not make an organisation ethical, but living by and through the code does make it an ethical organisation.

The ability to affect decision-making is directly related to the value that members place on the code. For example, if the code is weakly valued, chances are that it will not be internalised nor put into action. On the other hand, if the values the organisation espouses are also core values of the individual, then it will become the conceptual basis of individual behaviour. The importance of values as cornerstones of good codes is observed by Coughlan (2001), who provides a useful synthesis of the work of three theorists, Raiborn and Payne (1990), Tucker *et al.* (1999), and Wiley (2000); all of whom isolate main values that form the essence of codes. Values isolated by Raiborn and Payne (1990) included justice (e.g. conscientiousness), competence (e.g. reliability), utility (e.g. efficacy) and integrity (e.g. honesty). These differ from those identified by Tucker *et al.*, which included integrity (e.g. trust), equality, economic efficiency, equivalence (e.g. one equal to another), equal distribution of benefits, support for the group and environmental prudence (e.g. political participation and community impacts). These in turn were inconsistent with those suggested by Wiley (integrity, proficiency, legality, loyalty and confidentiality).

Preferring Raiborn and Payne's (1990) list of values, Coughlan (2001) analysed four professional codes of ethics in the hospitality industry for the purpose of detecting the level of adherence to such values. In general, he found all four values (justice, competence, utility, and integrity) in the American Society of Association Executives Standards of Conduct and in the Meeting Professionals International Principles of Professionalism. Less representative were the Professional Convention Management Association Principles of Professional and Ethical Conduct and the Hospitality Sales and Marketing Association International Code of Ethics, both of which lacked at least one of the necessary values identified by Raiborn and Payne. The study indicates that many of the core values that organisations should project in their dealings with the public, and amongst themselves, ought to be communicated and upheld through effective codes of ethics (see Stefanovic, 1997 for a good overview of the pros and cons of codes of ethics).

Based upon the foregoing, and as a conclusion to this section, the here is our recommendation for the development of **successful** codes. A code should:

(1) reflect the actual organisational philosophy
(2) be written clearly and concisely in order for it to be accessible by all members;
(3) be written in order for the reader to feel that he or she is part of the process rather than the recipient of a directive;

(4)   be a document that will lead to a behavioural change or to the rein-forcement of previously held values;

(5)   clearly relate to actual decision-making behaviour (i.e. it should be part of the decision-making process in the organisation);

(6)   clarify the ethically ambiguous;

(7)   be widely and constantly communicated;

(8)   reflect the behaviour and values of the leadership;

(9)   be enforceable;

(10) inspire, educate, and regulate.

Criticisms

One of the primary criticisms of codes of ethics is that they are essentially public relations platitudes. They are dicta from senior management with little input from the membership at large. They are too vague to be practical or too specific to be of use in the myriad dilemmas that confront the individual. They are not enforceable. They are paternalistic. They are too negative, too idealistic, and too cryptic. They portray the obvious in an environment in which resolving the ambiguous is the true requirement of a guiding document – one does not need a map when the path is clear, only when it is a maze to be negotiated. Unless a code has an obvious role to play in the actual functioning of the organisation, it is more often than not regarded with some suspicion. Another drawback is that codes are often left in the hands of people who may or may not be able to interpret them. In the case of the latter, actions that are based on inability or incompetence are not really unethical; those who carry them out may be ignorant, but we can't call them unethical if they do not have the intellectual or practical tools to make informed decisions. It is perhaps their boss who is unethical for not properly training the firm's personnel.

The problems identified above can be seen in the following few cases. Buchholz (2004) writes that many codes of ethics consist merely of a handful of proscriptions. He cites the National Education Association's *Code of Ethics of the Education Profession*, which identifies the following statement, among others, 'Shall not unreasonably restrain the student from independent action in the pursuit of learning'. The ambiguity behind this and other similar proscriptions leaves much to the imagination of the agent. The intent of these, it is claimed, is not to guide, specifically, but rather to set a specific tone to the profession. It is then up to the discretion of the professional to interpret the statement and act accordingly in the best interests of all students. But the danger of this is that such phrasings become encoded, in Buchholz's (2000) terms, where meaning is caught in semantic entanglements which ultimately render the code meaningless (see above). Semantics can be exacerbated if outside influences (e.g. NGOs) responsible for code development are out of touch with the demands of the group they are advocating for. In the case of NGOs, Sethi (2000) suggests that they are rarely themselves among the marginalised groups covered by the proposed codes; their code proposals are usually framed in absolute terms rather in terms that are most meaningful to the group in question; and they often target groups that are most susceptible to pressure in working towards reforms.

Although there appears to be no available research gauging the importance/effectiveness of codes from the perspective of scholars and practitioners, there appears to be general acceptance of their utility. Having said this, codes are not without their critics. Ashcroft (1993), for example, has found the development of principles for sustainable tourism to contain too many unanswered questions; while Wheeller has commented at length on the limitations, stating that there is simply:

> A never-ending series of laughable codes of ethics: codes of ethics for travelers; codes of ethics for tourists, for government, and for tourism businesses. Codes for all – or, more likely, codeine for all..But who really believes these codes are effective? I am pretty wary of platitudinous phrases like 'we are monitoring progress'. Has there been any progress – indeed, has there been any monitoring? Perhaps I am missing it and the answer itself is actually in code. (Wheeller, 1994: 651)

In a similar vein, Weeden, although a proponent of ethical tourism, writes that:

> codes of conduct and codes of ethics have been dismissed as mere PR 'puff', and a tourism code of ethics is fraught with difficulties in such a complex and fragmented industry that covers a wide diversity of cultural and business practices. (Weeden, 2001: 144)

A number of issues arise in considering the importance of codes of ethics for tourism. Valentine (1992) argues that codes of ethics need to be tailored to the needs and expectations of different groups in the same setting. Operators and tourists have different motives, but both groups should at least be talking the same language with regards to the protection of the socio-cultural and ecological integrity of the region. Weeden (2005) suggests that concern over codes of ethics have been expressed by operators who feel that there are just too many different codes of ethics in existence which confuse tourists by means of information overload. Coupled with this is concern by tourists in regards to what Weeden (2005) has referred to as 'ethical wash', where industry codes are not supported by operators themselves.

Varandani (1999) argues for an expanded role for codes of ethics in tourism, beyond the typical reliance on aspects such as pollution and design controls. If sustainable tourism is to be realised it will come on the back of other facets such as education, outreach, community development, the reinvestment of profits back into the environment, wildlife protection, social impacts and heritage conservation, infrastructure development and alternative sources of energy. Perhaps most important in this message is that the demonstration of compliance to requirements that are not congruent with sustainable tourism is misleading to all stakeholder groups in the tourism industry. In a similar context, Genot (1995) identifies six main issues at the core of codes of ethics for tourism, which she says can be generalised across the board in reference to the environmental aspects of tourism, including:

(1) the expression of overall environmental commitment;
(2) recognising the importance of taking responsibility;
(3) the integration of tourism planning and development with other land-use policies;
(4) the importance of environmental management practices (e.g. audits);
(5) co-operation between different decision-making groups; and
(6) making the public aware at all levels.

With reference to the last two of the foregoing list, Genot (1995) writes that the lack of co-operation and coordination between tourism stakeholders was the major obstacle to environmentally sound tourism management.

With regard to the whale-watching sector, Garrod and Fennell (2004) note that few attempts have been made to combine the efforts of government, industry and other stakeholders in the development of codes of ethics. The unwillingness of governments to facilitate a collaborative approach in this regard is one of the most significant challenges to an ethical tourism industry, as it is for many of the other resource industries (Pinkerton & Weinstein, 1995). Doing so (i.e. working with others) necessitates an opening of the door and an inclusiveness that is a rather labour-intensive process, not to say expensive in terms of time and other resources – as noted earlier in this book.

In practice, the code of ethics is also constrained by factors such as ownership (i.e. who develops the code and who abides by it) (see Garrod & Fennell, 2004; Hughes, 2001; Gjerdalen & Williams, 2000; Gjerdalen & Symko, 1999). Garrod *et al.* (2001) found that codes tend to be more consistently followed if developed by those who are most affected by them. A parallel to this can be seen in the recreation literature through 'positive affect', which is one of a few key leisure-defining concepts where, 'A more rewarding experience results when individuals have some control or influence within the leisure process' (Edginton *et al.*, 1995: 34). While this does not mean that recreationists should be involved in programming or policy development, it does mean that, if we are more inclusive in the decision-making process, people often have a more enhanced overall experience. Empowering participants (e.g. service providers) with the ability to take an active role in preserving a resource allows for the expression of co-operation at a level that might never have existed before. This is better, it is argued, for all parties involved.

Another noteworthy constraint to the development of an effective code of ethics is said to rest on the science on which it is based. Garrod and Fennell (2004) found that there is a wide array of approach distances used to limit proximity to cetaceans (e.g. ranges from 10–49 metres to 500 metres). With so much ambiguity in distance – compounded by species-dependant characteristics – there appears to be no clear understanding of appropriate animal–boat distances. In the absence of precise data, the authors argue that the industry must exercise precaution in an effort to do as little harm as possible (Fennell & Ebert, 2004). They further suggest that the most effective way to get past this dearth of critical scientific knowledge is by way of more intensive interdisciplinary research (including biologists, environmental scientists and animal behaviourists). In this the advantages would surely outweigh the disadvantages in helping to move closer to more sustainable practices (see Berrow, 2003).

Tied to discourses on effective community empowerment, Stark (2002) notes that development and policy making are often decidedly unidirectional, with administrators and technocrats involved in decision-making to the exclusion of those people who stand to lose the most from a tourism enterprise (see also D'Sa, 1999). In citing the work of Peterson (1997), Stark illustrates that 'technological discourses' used by scientific experts and governmental officials tend to overwhelm the 'creative discourses' of aboriginal and local people. What this means is that policy documents and scientific evidence are seen to more credible than the cultural traditions and land–environment nexus that has been created over countless generations (see Chapter 1 and the discussion on calculative and meditative thinking). The corollary of this is an insurmountable impasse that prevents discussions from reaching meta-discourses in providing clear and even-sided communications to the benefit of all. In stressing the need for a deeper philosophical foundation in the development of codes of ethics, Stark uses one of Plog's maxim's to explain what is needed:

> Plog's maxim 1: 'Protect what is natural and beautiful for the benefit of "natives" and tourists'. (Stark, 2002: 107)

Stark argues that the strong anthropocentric nature of this guideline is not difficult to see. Protection is important only in so far as it provides benefits to local people and tourists themselves. That is, there is no intrinsic rationale for the protection of natural capital for its own sake. According to Stark, Plog does not penetrate any deeper beyond the anthropocentric in any of his other maxims. This, she says, is attributed to the fact that Plog was writing for the purpose of protecting the virtues of tourism industry development over other interests.

The importance of an intrinsic rationale should not be easily dismissed. Citing Grundy (1987), Tribe (2002) writes that we ought to be able to distinguish between that which is 'good' and that which is 'correct', both of which can be differentiated by consideration of moral consciousness. Being correct merely suggests that one is able to follow a set of rules with little sense of the intrinsic nature of 'good'. It is an oft-quoted contention in ethics that actions are deemed additionally moral if the agent has performed it on the basis of intrinsic motivations rather than extrinsic ones. The example that Tribe uses is a code of ethics. We can follow the code to the letter of the law and, in doing so, be correct. But what is even more meaningful is the development of an orientation to what is good, intrinsically, which allows simple statements to have both cognitive and affective resonance.

Code Development in Practice: Tourism Examples

In 1993, ten local whale-watching operators in Johnstone Straight – the northwest coast of British Columbia – worked together with the goal of creating a code of ethics to guide the future of their industry. They did this first by recognising a number of key values (e.g. professionalism, safety, communication) considered essential for the long-term viability of the industry. They also recognised that any code-development process had to include all stakeholders with a vested interest in the resource base and industry – groups that could pinpoint the many unique social and ecological issues that were most pressing to the industry and the whales. Important in this process was the promotion of open face-to-face meetings with all involved, with decision-making based on consensus to ensure that as many perspectives as possible were factored into the code of conduct. This inclusiveness was a motivating factor to engender a culture of responsible stewardship, but it also had the added benefit of building trust and co-operation amongst the various groups involved.

A similar story emerges from the work of Johnston and Twynam (1999, 2001), who summarised the code development process initiated by the Arctic branch of the WWF during the mid-1990s. Central to this process was a conference held in Longyearbyen, Norway, in 1996 for the purpose of gathering information on the scope and design of the code of ethics for tourism activities. Participants included tour operators, government, researchers, residents, indigenous peoples and NGOs, all of whom contributed to a memorandum of understanding along with key principles for Arctic tourism. Principles included the ideas that: (1) tourism and conservation should be compatible, and (2) tourism should recognise and respect local culture. The resultant code of ethics articulated these broad principles through a number of rules of behaviour, (i.e. the actions that should or should not take place within the context of the principles). Following from the first of the two principles identified above, the code stated that operators should: support conservation, plan tourism activities so that they do not conflict with conservation efforts, ensure that clients understand the laws and regulations as they apply to import and export of products made from wildlife, develop an environmental management plan for daily operations, and do post-trip evaluations to confirm that activities were conducted in an environmentally sound manner (WWF, 1997, cited in Johnston & Twynam, 2001). In this way, each of the guidelines in the code of ethics was directly linked to a broader principle. A subsequent workshop in Longyearbyen the following year focused on how best to implement the code of ethics (discussed at greater length in the section on implementation, below).

The importance of incorporating all user interests is reflected in a study by Stefanovic (1997), who set out to develop a code of ethics for Short Hills Provincial Park, located on the Niagara Escarpment at St Catharines, Ontario, Canada. This case demonstrates the importance of reconciling ecocentric and anthropocentric needs, given the special biophysical attributes of the park and the number of different users with interests in the area (horseback riding, mountain biking, hiking and fishing). Through a review of literature, the author found that studies have confirmed the importance of positive reinforcement, prompts (like garbage bins), cues, information dissemination and better education in minimising friction between user groups, beyond more stringent methods such as enforcement officers. There was also the realisation that park user groups have become accustomed to a degree of freedom in using common pool resources (such as parks) that is not afforded in more politically and socially restrictive settings.

A phenomenological approach was used in Stefanovic's study to mediate between subjectivist (values) and objectivist (facts) extremes, and to discover the inherent value of the resource and the sense of place of the park as a whole. The methodology employed in this study included a survey to all user groups, in-depth interviews with user groups, community meetings, and a bottom-up method of developing the code based on user group feedback. Stefanovic (1997) discussed the ontological basis of values and facts with the realisation that: (1) facts are rarely ever value free, and (2) values cannot afford to be unmarried to facts. The assignment of significance to the park was thus a function not only of the accumulation of scientific facts (e.g. trees and trails) but also the values and moral considerability of the park and its various user groups in their own right. This was further described as 'the ontological relations between humans and the environments within which they find themselves' (Stefanovic,

1997: 251), and translated into the ability to move away from assigning ontological priority to humans (which would have been consistent with the anthropocentric world view) over the natural world (see Chapter 4). This is often reflected in the instrumental assumption that parks and protected areas are constructed primarily for human use. Based on the philosophical and methodological approach used by Stefanovic, a code of ethics was presented to the community at a workshop, where small groups of 4–5 participants had the opportunity to work on the draft and modifications were incorporated into a later final document.

Recently, Scottish Natural Heritage, with the aid of a consulting firm, launched an innovative process for the development of a marine wildlife-watching code for Scotland (Scottish Natural Heritage, 2005). This organisation undertook the initiative in response to the Nature Conservation Act of 2004, specifying that Scottish Natural Heritage must develop and issue a marine-watching code that sets out recommendations, advice and information relating to commercial and leisure activities involving the watching of marine wildlife (Scottish Natural Heritage, 2005). Not only should the code strive to protect marine wildlife such as whales, dolphins, sharks, seals, otters, turtles, seabirds and shore birds, but it will also seek to care for the various habitats in which they live, breed and feed. What is innovative about the scheme is the use of the Internet to tap into many affected parties in association with a more traditional attempt to incorporate community sentiment. Interested parties (e.g. operators and recreationists) were encouraged to explore a series of links that display older codes of ethics in an effort to educate these parties before submitting their own version of the new code. A number of advertised workshops were planned for the spring of 2005, including objectives and meeting agendas specified on the website. Once comments were obtained and the workshops had taken place, a draft code was posted on the website for comment and further consultation, with the intention of finalising the document at a later date.

Given the nature of tourism, where there is a complex interaction between human groups and ecology, special care needs to be extended in an effort to balance use and conservation. The preceding example demonstrates the important role that non-governmental organisations can play in the development of codes of ethics in striking this balance. While the Government of Canada (1998) document mentioned earlier in this chapter provided good advice on how governments may aid the code-development process, the same document summarises some of the most fundamental questions and challenges guiding NGO participation in the development of codes of ethics (Box 3.3). Some of these have been discussed by Fleckenstein and Huebsch (1999), who are argue that creating a code of ethics for many different types of tourism organisations (e.g. NGOs, governments and industry) is challenging because of the self-interest of these organisations in the face of 'competing' forces from others (see Fennell and Plummer, in press, who discuss co-operation in adaptive co-management situations).

The preceding discussion demonstrates the importance of values from both individual and organisational perspectives. In consideration of the wider context, Frankl (1989) contends that organisations and professions on the whole have been granted power and privilege by society, which comes packaged with the expectation of a contribution to the broader social well-being through a shared appreciation of overlapping values. Just as the profession is bound by a set of values (e.g. ecological integrity and safety) these must emerge as a function of common purpose. If the profession acts outside this nexus, there is a chance that the scope of moral evaluation (the societal norms that govern behaviour) will become both narrowed and flattened, leading to the disintegration of trust between the community and the firm/profession. This suggests that the profession and society in general must be intricately intertwined in a relationship that is bound by reciprocity and symbiosis (more on the importance of reciprocity in Chapter 4). The following two examples attempt to project differing perspectives on

Box 3.3 Key questions to guide NGO participation in code development

Are all of the major players – including customers, key suppliers and NGOs – at the table? Is there meaningful participation by government at all stages? Is a strong industry association in place to manage code development and implementation?

Does the industry have a good record of similar initiatives in the past? Are the industry leaders demonstrating strong commitment? Have the background conditions and motivations been clearly identified?

Are the proponents inviting meaningful third-party representation and involvement by consumer groups, other NGOs and standard-setting bodies, and are they prepared to pay for this involvement?

Are the processes for developing and implementing the code open and transparent? Is there a clear articulation and understanding of the rights and responsibilities of all stakeholders?

Is there clear evidence that the code will promote the public interest in areas such as health, safety, and the environment, and address consumer concerns?

Does the code include effective complaints-handling and redress mechanisms accessible to everyone, effective programs to inform consumers and the public, and an evaluation framework to track progress and provide credible evidence of success and failure? Will a reputable third party regularly monitor the code?

Does the code have the capacity to mature through time and respond to new learning and developments?

Source: Government of Canada (1998: 18)

how values play heavily in the development of codes of ethics at a broader level. One is said to be a value-driven approach, while the other is felt to reflect more of a market-driven perspective. The ends that each achieve for society may be different, emphasising the importance of establishing good processes that are built on inclusive core values.

A value-driven process

Ritchie (1999: 273) writes that the concept of visioning, 'a statement that provides an inspirational portrait of a desired future for the destination', has received scant attention in the tourism literature. His account of the visioning process that took place in the Banff-Bow valley (the valley includes Canada's famous Banff National Park) is indicative of the overall importance of this process in achieving balanced, sustainable improvement in communities. Visioning was described by Ritchie as both time consuming and labour intensive. But although costly in this way, it forces tourism planners to look well into the future in devising their policies and plans – a mindset that is not universally shared. What is achieved in this process is a future desired state for the destination, a benchmark from which to direct efforts, and a reflection of the values of the stakeholders for whom it was developed. This last outcome should not be treated lightly, as the values of tourists, ecologists, economists and planners, among others, have not been congruent. The Banff-Bow Valley visioning process accommodated 14 different stakeholder groups at the table, including representatives from cultural heritage, natural environment, local environment, municipal government, federal government, aboriginal people (Siksika, First Nations, Wesley), park users, Banff-Bow Valley task Force, infrastructure-transportation, social/health/education, commercial outdoor recreation, commercial visitor services, and tourism marketing. Each group was able to elect a Chair, who reported to a working committee, who, in turn, reported to a constituency representing three different scales of involvement. The participants agreed upon a conceptual framework to guide the proceedings (see Figure 3.2), based on the following five components

(1) *Preamble*. A general introduction which acted both as a preamble to the vision process and a means by which to contextualised the purpose, structure, and content of the vision.

(2) *Core vision*. As the heart of the visioning process, the core vision consolidated the key dimensions of the desired future for the destination, as follows:

> 'The Bow Valley in Banff National Park reveals the majesty and wildness of the Rocky Mountains. It is symbol of Canada, a place of great beauty, where nature is able to flourish and evolve. People from around the world participate in the life of the valley, finding

inspiration, enjoyment, livelihoods and understanding. Through their wisdom and foresight in protecting this small part of the planet, Canadians demonstrate leadership in forging healthy relationships between people and nature. The Banff-Bow Valley is, above all else, a place of wonder, where the richness of life is respected and celebrated. (Ritchie, 1999: 277)

(3) *Elements of the vision.* After accepting the core vision, several supporting themes were identified for the purpose of developing key messages in detail. These themes included (a) ecology, (b) visitor experience, (c) awareness/education, (d) economy and (e) community.

(4) *Values on which the vision is based.* These are stated in full in Box 3.4.

(5) *Principles guiding implementation of the vision.* The vision strategy is being realised through a series of guiding principles that have evolved from the process. Five of the 22 principles are outlined in Box 3.5.

The Banff-Bow Valley planning process, and the resulting principles, have led to the modification of the Banff National Park Management Plan, the implementation of a heritage tourism strategy, and the decision by the federal government to cap future development and return 17% of Banff townsite into parkland. Ritchie notes in concluding his overview of the process, that the heart of the vision is not to be found in the words of the document, but rather in the spirit of co-operation and collaboration that

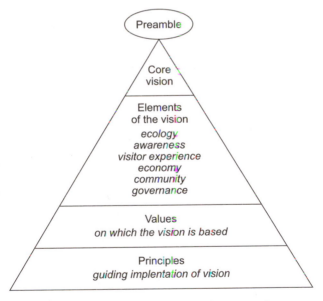

Figure 3.2 Destination vision: A conceptual framework

Source: Adapted from Ritchie (1999)

Box 3.4 The values on which the vision for Banff-Bow Valley is based

The value of ...
- exercising restraint and self-discipline today, for the sake of future generations;
- nature in and of itself;
- nature to human experience;
- national parks as protected areas;
- Banff National Park for all the people of the world as a World Heritage Site;
- Banff-Bow Valley for its ecological role in the context of the park and the larger ecosystem;
- Banff-Bow Valley, including the transportation corridor, to national, regional and local economy;
- safe, healthy and hospitable communities;
- culture and history;
- open, participatory decision making;
- equal opportunity for wilderness and park experience;
- predictable, consistent and fair regulation;
- competent, accountable management;
- National parks for Canadians' sense of identity;
- wilderness preservation to Canada's image around the world;
- respect for others;
- freedom of access;
- education, enjoyment and other park-related benefits of the Bow Valley to visitors.

Source: BBVS (1996) as reported in Ritchie (1999: 279)

Box 3.5 Principles guiding implementation of the vision

The following principles guide all actions by government, business, communities, and the public:
- Regulation and decision-making are responsive, open, participatory, consistent, and equitable.
- There is individual and shared responsibility to provide for protection and preservation of heritage resources, including buildings, within the park.
- Proactive, adaptive, and precautionary management take into account cumulative effects and limits to growth in recognition of the finite nature of the Valley.
- Stewardship, based on sound science, is practised through environmentally sensitive management, mitigation, and restoration.
- The geographic area of the Town of Banff will not change, although the boundaries may be adjusted to achieve the goals of ecological integrity.

Source: BBVS (1996) as cited in Ritchie (1999)

took place throughout the rather long course of the proceedings. It is indeed significant to note the words of Senge in this regard, who said that 'Few, if any forces in human affairs are as powerful as a shared vision' (Senge, 1990 in Ritchie, 1999: 276).

This example is an important one for our purposes here as it shows yet another methodology that may be used for the purpose of developing meaningful values and principles that might cross over into other settings and circumstances (refer back to Chapter 1). In commenting on the challenges inherent in the new tourism, Ryan (2002) observes that communities need to construct vision statements before they entertain proposals for new tourism developments. The implications of this are obvious, and they have everything to do with balancing profit with socio-ecological concerns. Tourism thus comes at a cost, as noted above and by Ryan, requiring new types of management as well as innovative efforts to monitor the return, broadly defined, from our labours. This example further illustrates the importance of core values that are shared not only by one individual or one organisation, but across many diverse groups that form the impetus for positive action.

A market value-driven process

The community of 'X', also in Canada, developed a comprehensive tourism development strategy during the mid-1990s, on the basis of a community vision and tourism vision, and also developed a number of tourism objectives based on a number of core values. These statements are illustrated below.

Community vision

- 'X' will be a leader in achieving a sustainable community by balancing environmental, social and economic values within a local, regional and global context.
- Building on its rich heritage and natural beauty, this historic mountain community will pursue quality and excellence. 'X' will be seen as vibrant, healthy, clean, hospitable, resilient and forward thinking. It will be committed to exercising its rights with respect to decisions affecting the region.
- Community priorities include: opportunities for youth; economic growth an stability; environmental citizenship; personal safety and security; a responsible and caring social support system; a first-class education system; local access to life-long learning, spiritual and cultural values; and diverse forms of recreation.
- All residents and visitors shall have access to the opportunities afforded by this community.

Tourism vision

- To use the region's natural and heritage resources to foster the development of tourism in 'X' as a viable sector in the economy in a manner that complements the scale, quality and unique features of the community, balances the interests of tourism with the interests of other industries, and balances the needs of visitors with the needs of residents.

Tourism objectives

- To position 'X' as a four-season tourism and outdoor adventure destination and to establish a recognisable image of the community among travellers.
- To encourage development and marketing initiatives that build on existing tourism strengths and are compatible with this destination focus.
- To ensure that tourism development is a well-managed process, in keeping with the character and servicing of the community.
- To foster the creation of jobs and the generation of investment income so as to enhance the viability and sustainability of 'X's' economy.
- To promote co-operation and goodwill among tourism industry operators, business and development agencies, and local government representatives in order to facilitate the realisation of these objectives and the achievement of 'X's' tourism vision.

This example demonstrates that tourism by nature is somehow incongruent with many of the more altruistic values that seem to be important in defining community. What are often cherished as core values in describing the community, therefore, do not always lie within the realm of progressive community economic development. This legacy is perpetuated by community 'X', above, where the tourism vision and objectives are primarily devoted to the maximisation of profit. Unfortunately, this goes in contrast to the community vision, where economic development is one of many values that are described. Other values in the community vision include sustainability, the pursuit of quality, hospitality, cleanliness, rights in terms of decision-making, and accessibility. Unhappily, however, the tourism vision refers only to using the region's resources for further developing tourism in the region. The focus on economic development is even more pronounced in the tourism objectives section, where extending the destination to a four-season resort, marketing, management in the context of growth, jobs and investment, and co-operation and goodwill are encouraged for overall economic success.

The difficulties inherent in failing to have a common vision between public and private sectors, and national, regional, and local levels, is evident in the work of Ladkin and Martinez Bertramini (2002). These authors found in the case of Cusco in Peru that, although there was cohesion around a tourism vision at the national level (to be 'competitive' and 'sustainable'), this message had not filtered down to the regional level, where tourism is viewed as an economic engine for the region to the exclusion of other values. Martin (1998) reminds us that 'being ethical' is not just an either/or choice, but rather a choice of degree, where the ethical behaviour of an entity, like an organisation or a community, can be judged on the basis of an ascending scale. How far the entity goes towards being ethical is a function of values – demonstrated through the aforementioned case studies. In answering the question, 'Why should a company act ethically?' Martin contends that it reflects upon how the organisation sees itself (a point we discussed previously). If we see tourism only through commercial eyes, then visitors may be reduced to units of measurement (measured in dollars, Euros, and so on), regardless of the public image that has been created to suggest otherwise.

Compliance

Kolk and Tulder (2002) write that compliance is a broad term that encompasses implementation, monitoring, reporting, auditing, verification and enforceability, all of which serve to increase the likelihood of stakeholders following a code. We will deal briefly with each of these aspects in turn, in an attempt to illustrate the extent to which tourism groups can go to ensure their codes of ethics have the broadest possible impact. Having said this, one of the key findings of this chapter is that very little currently exists in the tourism literature on compliance, especially with respect to codes of ethics. This is almost as true today as it was a decade ago when Mason and Mowforth (1995) observed that one of the most important issues facing codes of ethics is the lack of monitoring and evaluation in gauging code effectiveness. To this end, they uncovered virtually no examples of compliance factors in their search of the literature.

Implementation

Although often neglected in the provision of tourism services, effective implementation strategies have the potential to save money and secure intended programmatic outcomes (Fennell, 2002). This is substantiated by Genot (1995) in the context of tourism codes of ethics, who explains that if a code has any value it must be widely promoted and put into practice (i.e. implemented). In this regard, the UNEP (1995: 45) document on environmental codes of conduct states that 'the implementation process is best begun by appointing a working group or task force to plan and carry out implementation of the code'. The implementation of the Tourism Industry

Association of Canada code of ethics, for example, took place through collaboration with a number of different groups who were representative of the National Round Table on Environment and the Economy. Seven strategies were broadly considered in the UNEP document for the purpose of code implementation, including:

- *Dissemination and publicity campaigns.* Letting people know the existence of the code of ethics is stated to be the first and most important step in implementation. This may be accomplished through press, radio, television, display, videos, brochures, books and lectures.
- *Publications.* The production of newsletters and occasional reports is an excellent way of getting the point across to any number of target groups. An example includes The International Conference on Monuments and Sites (ICOMOS), which has produced a publication, entitled *Management of Tourism in World Heritage Sites.*
- *Seminars and conferences.* These can be used to educate the general population on such things as environmental stewardship and sustainable tourism. In the process, sponsoring organisations, whether governmental or NGO, build support not only for the issue at hand but also for themselves.
- *Pilot projects.* Seen as one of the first steps in the implementation process, these are designed to demonstrate and test the value of different development strategies. For example, after the successful launch of the publication *Green Light* (http://www.countryside. gov.uk/Publications/articles/Publication_tcm2-4188.asp; accessed 04.12.06), the English Tourist Board, the Countryside Commission and the Rural Development Board initiated a national demonstration project which resulted in the development of an environmental kit for small and medium-sized tourism businesses.
- *Awards.* Notoriety through award schemes is stated to be an effective means by which to implement codes of ethics or other standards. Examples include Blue Flag (European beaches) and Green Globe (sustainable tourism businesses), both of which recognise best practice in the tourism industry (see Chapter 2).
- *Education and training.* Performance can be enhanced through any number of different education and training programmes. A recent example of the importance of training and education in tourism is the WTTCs World Travel and Tourism Human Resource Centre, centred in Vancouver, B.C. This organisation has developed a number of packages designed to educate those working in the field, reported in the WTTHRC's publication, entitled *Steps to Success* (WRRTC, 1998).
- *Technical assistance.* This comes in the form of expert missions at the request of international organisations or in the form of research

networks or task forces designed to make recommendations on how destinations, programmes, planning, and services can be improved. Technical assistance may also come in the form of databases or academic resource centres to help disseminate information on improving performance through codes of ethics.

A good example of the use of pilot projects in measuring the relevance and applicability of codes can be seen in the earlier example of the WWF Arctic code of ethics (Johnston & Twynam, 2001). An interim code development committee was responsible for: promoting the goals of the initiative; establishing a membership organisation; disseminating guidelines; developing a website, database and a logo; encouraging communication from all interested/involved parties; and organising a monitoring programme (among other duties). In 1998, a meeting was convened to examine pilot project development and to revise and engage in consultation. A subsequent meeting in March, 1999 (Husum, Germany), provided an opportunity to learn about some of the unique benefits and challenges in implementing the codes of ethics as a result of the on-going pilot projects. The authors identified a number of specific recommendations that were discussed in meetings and written in reports, as follows (see also Johnston & Twynam, 1999):

- results of the pilot projects showed a high level of interest in conservation efforts;
- the need to change the order of the principles and code items so conservation and requests for money do not come first;
- the necessity of changing materials to reflect the views and needs of local and indigenous peoples;
- reduce the content of the code so that it may be easily read;
- provide information on education and training for local and indigenous peoples;
- provide information to assist operators in identifying what qualifies as conservation issues.

At the time of publication, Johnston and Tywnam (1999) stated that there was some disagreement as to how the membership organisation was to evolve, as well as the methods for evaluation. Suggestions for the latter included an award for operators who demonstrated best practice in Arctic tourism, operator self-assessments, client assessment and a panel review. While details surrounding the lack of agreement were not well understood, it appears that there was ample room for further discussion on the merits of operator evaluation. For example, Johnston and Tywnam note that in the baseline data for the Nunavet case study, all 52 operators (100%) said they followed local laws. However, there is substantive evidence to support the notion that in Pond Inlet (Canadian High Arctic) hunters do not follow local laws (Buckley, 2005). Discrepancies in research and practice are not just central to this region, but these contrasting results point to the need for more rigour, knowledge, communication and education in efforts to protect ecological and cultural resources.

The authors concluded by noting that the development and implementation of principles and codes of ethics must be inclusive of a broad spectrum of interests if they are to be successful. Achievement is therefore strongly tied to ownership. Coupled with this is the need to have effective implementation strategies because, as noted by Johnston and Tywnam, the most effective codes are of little use if not accompanied by a plan to support not only the procedural aspects of implementation, but also those who must make it happen (e.g. through education and other forms of assistance), as noted above. Evaluation was also seen as an integral part, which must be considered early on in the planning process. Failing to do so undermines the ability to adequately monitor the project through measurable outcomes.

Monitoring

It is not enough for the tourism industry to state its responsibility. It must also demonstrate it. This means the development of a monitoring framework (Genot, 1995), which is the collection of information on the effectiveness of codes of ethics, and the assessment of whether the information is accurate, complete, relevant, and reliable (Kolk & Tulder, 2002). The UNEP (1995) report (citing the ICC Business Charter for Sustainable Development), notes that the chief benefits of monitoring are: (1) the improvement of policy and performance; (2) the promotion of openness; and (3) the assessment of progress. Other benefits are said to lie in the opportunity to inform customers of environmental policies and efforts; improvement of the corporate image; the ability to assess customer awareness and attitudes to codes of ethics; the measurement of response and acceptance of the code of ethics; the measurement of how extensive the code has been implemented; and the identification of gaps or weaknesses in implementation (UNEP, 1995).

A recent example of monitoring in tourism from Berrow (2003), suggests that despite the global economic importance of whale watching, there have been relatively few efforts to monitor its consequences. More typically, researchers have undertaken short-term studies that have been designed to investigate the behavioural responses of whales and other cetaceans to the presence of whale-watching boats. For example, Lusseau (2003) examined the short-term reactions of bottlenose dolphins to tour boat traffic. The study found that males started to avoid boats as soon as they were present; while females switched to a vertical avoidance strategy only when interactions became intrusive. These different avoidance strategies between sexes were attributed to the fact that males were better able to match the cost of vertical avoidance of boats because of their greater energy stores. It appears also that visitor satisfaction has been monitored sparingly, although there is evidence of increased activity in this area as new publications continue to document human–cetacean interactions in this fast-developing industry.

With reference to the Johnstone Straight Code of Conduct discussed above, compliance was much more easily achieved amongst operators because of the planning foundations built into the process. Interviews by the authors some three years after the implementation of the code confirmed that moral obligations linked to personal guilt and shame were key factors motivating operators to comply. Non-compliance was thus seen to be a betrayal of the community of operators and a deviation of their commitment to stewardship. Socially, reasons for compliance with the code of conduct included a reliance on the whale-sighting network (as each oper- ator's livelihood depends on co-operation with others), a dependence on others for safety, business referral and camaraderie. Operators also felt that it was important to maintain a sense of belonging to the community and to avoid peer-inflicted repercussions. Although the code of conduct has largely been successful in the community of operators in Johnstone Straight, there is a belief on the part of the operators that the code must be dynamic (i.e. ongoing evaluation and monitoring of the code is essential to being socially and ecologically proactive for the purpose of protecting the resource and the experience of participants).

As noted earlier, compliance is articulated in the broadest sense in this chapter, and includes monitoring, implementation, reporting, auditing, verification and enforceability. However, the more specific reference to compliance in tourism is observed in a detailed set of factors identified by Gjerdalen and Williams (2000), below. Following from Gramann and Vander Stoep (1987), Gjerdalen and Williams identify the many reasons why stakeholders *may* (compliance) or *may not* (non-compliance) subscribe to a code of ethics.

Compliance

- *Moral obligation.* This factor touches on the desire to do the right thing depending on circumstance. When we are made aware of the conse- quences of our actions we may exercise this desire.
- *Need to belong.* Being part of a tour group often comes packaged with the desire to comply with certain normative standards that quickly emerge through interaction or education. Complying with these stan- dards allows for a sense of belonging and security.
- *The threat of punishment.* Compliance will emerge if the threat of an external body is too heavy. For example, service providers will

comply with standards if they feel they will lose market share or be penalised by the external body.

- *The threat of shame and embarrassment.* While shame is a self- imposed punishment, embarrassment is a socially-derived sanction. Both may strengthen the willingness to comply with normative standards.
- *The extent of social bonding.* Service providers who have a strong social bond to the group (other service providers) will be less likely to deviate away from the accepted norms for fear of being ostracised from the group.

Non-compliance

- *Limited awareness of accepted norms.* If the individual or group is unaware of the proper procedures they will be unable to follow them. Actions may be completely innocent because of a lack of knowledge.
- *Inappropriate environmental behaviour.* The inappropriate behaviour of one individual or group may be assumed to be acceptable to others (e.g. going off the trail to take photographs). .
- *Limited awareness of negative consequences.* Some service providers may be unaware of the significance of the violation under scrutiny. Without this knowledge, the code violation is seen as frivolous.
- *Perceived irrelevant and unrealistic guidelines.* Non-compliance is rationalised by the fact that the code is not founded on an under-standing of the needs of service providers or participants. The feeling is that it may be based on erroneous assumptions or information.
- *Deliberate violations based on financial gain, ideological protest, revenge, malice or fun.* This may include, for example, local people not following a code of ethics because they have not been asked to do so. Those operating motor boats off the coast of British Columbia and Washington State have been observed cruising alongside orcas, which is in clear violation of the operators' code of ethics (see Fennell, 2003).

One of the chief constraints to monitoring in tourism is the lack of available funds to initiate such programmes. Theorists argue that research funding can come through membership fees or trip levies, with the belief that the willingness to pay for such levies is much greater if the operator can demonstrate that the money gathered does in fact go to research and monitoring (Orams, 2000). The argument carried forward from this is that we might all stand to gain in our efforts to become more sustainable if we were able to channel funds into monitoring for the purpose of making tourists and tourism service providers more responsible and accountable. While this makes sense in theory, the recognisable problem with this is the difficulty in sacrificing immediate financial gains in order to secure long-term well-being (see the example of Haliburton Sustainable Forest in Chapter 2).

Not surprisingly, the scarcity of monitoring is not solely a tourism problem. In their research on codes of ethics of international companies, Kolk and Tulder (2002) found that not one of four categories of organisations (social interest groups, business support groups, international organisations and firms) had more than 50% of their codes of conduct that could be classified as having a 'clear' monitoring system in place (based on a four point scale of 'none', 'vague', 'vague/clear' or 'clear'). Kolk and Tulder also reported on the type of party that was responsible for monitoring of the code of conduct, if any, along with a number of assessment options, including:

- *none* – no monitoring party at all;
- *first party* – the firms themselves;
- *second party* – business support groups such as trade and industry associations;
- *third party* – external professionals paid by the firm which is observed;
- *fourth party* – combinations of different actors (e.g. business support groups and social interest groups);
- *fifth party* – social interest groups only, without involvement of the firm;
- *sixth party* – legal authorities.

Kolk and Tulder (2002) found that 45.5% of the four groups had no monitoring party; 27.8% had first party monitoring; 3.3% had second party; 2.5% had third party; 10.0% had fourth party; there was no fifth party monitoring; and 9.1% had sixth party monitoring. Of this last category, only international organisations were subjected to legal authority monitoring. The authors also discussed the tendency for groups to form coalitions for the purpose of developing more substantive codes. For example, transnational corporations have had significant impacts on the codes developed by international organisations and social interest groups. What has followed is the development of new monitoring agencies to measure the level of compliance with codes of ethics. For example, The Social Accountability 8000 standard, a third-party monitoring system developed by the Council on Economic Priorities (CEP) is thought to hold much potential for the regulation of various labour practices. Some of the world's largest certification bodies have already subscribed to the Social Accountability 8000, for which accreditation began in 1998. (See Rivera, 2004, for a description of Costa Rica's Certification of Sustainable Tourism as an example of a third-party performance-based initiative in tourism; see also Chapter 2.)

Reporting and auditing

Reporting can be viewed in two very different contexts. The first of these is referred to as wrongdoing and includes the reporting or whistle-blowing that often follows from unethical acts in the organisation. Wrongdoing is defined as 'behaviour which is morally wrong as well as behaviour which is illegal, unethical, wasteful, inefficient, neglectful, an abuse of power, or violates organisational rules or professional standards' (McLain & Keenan, 1999: 256).

The importance of engendering an environment or culture where people can feel free to identify and report wrongdoing is discussed by Swenson (2000). In illustrating the ethical policies of the management consulting firm KPMG, Swenson says that: (1) good people should feel free to step forward and communicate concerns; (2) policy and practice should not be geared towards shooting the messenger, but rather towards fixing the problem; and (3) bad news is sought so that small problems don't fester into big ones (see also Messmer, 2003).

The second context of reporting that has relevance to codes, and which occurs at a broader level, is the new trend amongst multinational enterprises surrounding the description of environmental and social impacts of operations through a 'sustainability report' (Mamic, 2004). The UN Global Reporting Initiative (GRI), a framework designed to create a lingua franca for the voluntary reporting of economic, social and ecological impacts, has met with mixed emotions. Mamic found that the initiative has been criticised for its inconsistencies in criteria for reporting and for its mandatory application, which voids its 'voluntary' status. Questions have also been raised about the level of disclosure of certain practices that organisations may or may not detail. The logical next question would be to ascertain whether or not tourism organisations would be willing to devise such a system. This might be an alternative or an additive to some of the global certification systems that have recently emerged, as discussed in Chapter 2.

Auditing is a process that allows for the assessment of performance against goals or other stated criteria. In the context of environmental management systems (EMS), Tribe *et al.* (2000) view the auditing system as an evaluation of whether an EMS is effective, whether it performs against various targets set out in policy and whether environmental impacts are being recognised. Theorists such as McDonald (1999), argue for the inclusion of an ethics audit within the organisation over and above the annual fiscal audit (or the EMS), as a commitment that serves to bring the organisation's core values back into focus along with conveying the importance of sharing these values.

In business, Mamic (2004) suggests that a growing trend is the development of external verification services, including global auditing firms, consultants and NGOs. Key issues surrounding the audit include the independence of the entity undertaking the audit, as well as whether the audit is done internally or externally. With regard to third-party auditing, such as what would be conducted through tourism certification schemes such as the Costa Rican Certification for Sustainable Tourism, there can be hesitancy on the part of the auditor to report damaging information for fear of compromising the business relationship between auditor and organisation.

In transcending problems related to codes of ethics in specific organisational contexts (e.g. vague standards, codes merely as window-dressing), multi-stakeholder initiatives (MSI) have recently developed in business in order to make firms more socially responsible (see Font & Harris, 2004). An MSI is a 'not-for-profit organisation comprising coalitions of companies, unions and NGOs that have developed specific standards for workplace conduct' (Mamic, 2004: 61). Examples of MSIs developed over the past few years include the Forest Stewardship Council, Fair Labor Association, the Ethical Trading Initiative, Social Accountability International, the Global Reporting Initiative, and the Marine Stewardship Council. In order for these entities to be successful, they have had to develop standards that are more stringent than standards found in corporate codes of ethics. MSIs often develop accreditation programmes for the purpose of auditing organisations and determining compliance to the standards of their code (see Chapter 2). The benefit to companies is the opportunity to advertise their certification in securing a greater market share. Some firms have even opted to be certified by more than one MSI, thereby increasing their legitimacy in the eyes of the consumer (see Rohitratana, 2002). Social Accountability International (SAI), for example, certifies in many different sectors. Its stakeholder representation includes NGOs, trade unions, socially responsible investors' and government, and industry; individual factories are certified; certification lasts for three years; and SAI publishes the locations of certified factories on its website, a list of complaints, corrective actions, and a monthly newsletter (Mamic, 2004).

While their benefits appear to be numerous, MSIs have been criticised on the basis of:

(1) the development of codes from a top-down fashion without input from workers;
(2) the implementation of codes and policies that sometimes prevent workers from joining unions;
(3) codes fail to reach far enough down the supply chain;
(4) concern over the privatisation of a function that should be performed by government; and
(5) a system powered by consumer preference (e.g. threats of consumer boycotts) will be subject to problems or issues of legitimacy (Mamic, 2004).

Enforcement

Parker (1999) suggests that enforcement is the last stage in the effort to implement policy, which entails controlling the actions of many different stakeholder groups or targets, including tourists and service providers. He also notes that enforcement is the weakest link in the policy chain because of problems related to funding, politics and the failure of organisations to be effectively coordinated. Enforcement, and the sanctions that may be imposed, refers to the consequences of non-compliance to the code of ethics. Sanctions can come in the form of warnings, if there are no large implications to the tourism unit, or they may be severe in the case of threats of termination to the business itself. In all cases, the sanction is designed to motivate the unit to avoid breaking its their commitment and to increase the likelihood that they will comply with the standards (see Sirakayal and Uysal (1997) for a discussion of the reasons why sanctions and deterrent measures failed to predict conformance behaviour of ecotour operators).

Dunfee (no date, cited in Fleckenstein and Huebsch, 1999), observes that the key to a successful code of ethics for an industry is how it is able to police itself. In any type of business there are at least seven key principles required for success: act in good faith, exercise due care, honour confidentiality, avoid conflicts of interest, willingly comply with the law, respect the liberty and rights of others, and respect human well-being. Kolk and Tulder (2002) found that financial involvements will have the effect of making firms more likely to adhere to a code of ethics. But the simple fact is that relatively few codes have such a financial mechanism built in. Only 14 of the 132 codes analysed by these authors had a financial inducement as part of the code enforcement process. In other research, Raiborn and Payne (1990) examined a study by the Conference Board of the US which found that 58% of companies surveyed specified punishments for acts contrary to their code of ethics, with dismissal being the most common punishment. Other noteworthy enforcement actions include suspension, probation, demotion, and negative comments on evaluations, many of which can be found in the following example of enforcement procedures of the Midwest Travel Writers Association (MTWA).

The MTWA is an organisation of travel professionals including writers, photographers, editors and broadcasters who report on travel and tourism. Their Code of Professional Responsibility is designed to protect travel writing as a profession, and more specifically to promote the exchange of ideas, encourage high professional ideals, foster communication between travel professionals and readers, and champion the cause of travellers from the Midwest. An important aspect of their code is an elaborate enforcement policy that details the protocol for evidence of unprofessional conduct (Box 3.6).

Box 3.6 The MTWA code enforcement policy

Section 1. Violations of the Code are to be made in writing, signed by the complainant (members or non-members of the MTWA), and mailed to the President.

(A) Signed complaints will be investigated by an appointee of the President. Within six weeks the appointee will conduct an investigation, and be free to contact either the complainant or the subject of the complaint for more information. If an investigation is deemed to be warranted, the appointee will be joined by two others appointed by the President in the creation of a Committee. Complainant and subject are to be informed of the Committee, with no further contact of these individuals with the Committee.

(B) The Committee will fully investigate the complaint, contacting as many sources deemed necessary, and deliver a report to the President who will carry the decisions out within 45 days.

(C) The decisions made by an Ethics Committee include:

    (a) Dismiss the complaint.

    (b) Issue a warning to the subject to cease the activity in question. This includes having the subject rectify any financial obligations within 30 days, providing proof of the actions.

    (c) Place the subject under probation not exceeding two years (on all MTWA-sponsored activities).

    (d) Expel the subject from the MTWA.

(D) The subject and the President must be informed immediately. Disciplinary action is also effective immediately.

(E) The President must also inform the subject of the Appeal process.

Section 2. The subject may request a review of the Ethics Committee's decision by an Appeal Panel within 45 days. The Chairperson of the Appeal Panel shall inform the President and subject of the panel's decision, which will be considered final.

Section 3. The subject may have a representative discuss the issue, at any stage of the process, with the President, Ethics Committee or Appeals Panel. The subject shall bear all costs associated with this contact.

Section 4. If expelled, the subject will not be allowed to re-apply for MTWA membership for at least four years.

Source: Adapted from MTWA (www.mtwa.org/Pages/0102ethics.html. Accessed 12.10.05)

The policy quite clearly articulates the options available to the Association, the offending party and the complainant. Decisions range from outright expulsion to less draconian measures including warnings and the dismissal of the complaint. Specific dates provide more rigour to the procedures in delineating deadlines in fulfilling obligations.

Conclusion

One of the main conclusions drawn from this chapter is the critical absence of information and research on code development and compliance in tourism. This finding in many ways parallels the work of the UNEP (1995) and Mason and Mowforth (1995), who reported such over a decade earlier. The same holds true for business in general. In her comprehensive overview of the social performance of businesses from an international perspective, Mamic (2004) concluded that, despite the many advances in codes at the international level, there was much to be done in the reorganisation of monitoring and compliance efforts. New advances are being made in environmental management systems and global/regional certification programmes, but the crossover to codes of ethics has not been explicit. In making such comparisons, readers are urged to examine Mamic's (2004) book on implementing codes of ethics in business, where many common themes can be seen that crossover amongst the gamut of emerging voluntary initiatives that currently exist in tourism. Another main conclusion is the fact that monitoring and enforcement efforts have been constrained by a critical lack of resources. Operators and associations need to dedicate more time and effort into better understanding the long-term impacts of their activities, which have been avoided because of short-term interests. Finally, if conventional mechanisms of behavioural control, such as codes of ethics and permits, are felt to be just as useful as more sophisticated mechanisms such as certification schemes (see Buckley, 2002a), then more effort should be placed into their planning, development, implementation, and evaluation in efforts to achieve sustainable outcomes.

Part 3

Meditative Thinking

Chapter 4

Mapping the Theoretical Terrain of Ethics

Introduction

A lasting tradition in tourism has been the reliance on impacts as the principal way by which to examine social, economic, and ecological problems. In many ways, however, a focus on impacts is decidedly reactive (i.e. we try to learn from our mistakes in doing things differently in the future). But what has been abundantly clear in the last few years is that reactive ways of looking at the world often fail to take into account the dynamic or chaotic nature of systems (Berkes & Folke, 2000). Dilemmas are different in space, time and circumstance, which suggests that the ability to learn from other case studies in a reactive capacity often provides little guidance in ameliorating current ones. Tourism industry dysfunctions have also been examined and explained at broad socio-economic and political levels. These can be found in almost every text on tourism (see, for example, Pearce, 1987 for a good description of tourism models), and include noteworthy contributions by Hills and Lundgren (1977) and Britton (1982). In the absence of a coherent non-linear tool to draw upon, and in acknowledgement of the tremendous gains made in understanding the tourism system at the broadest levels, in this chapter we choose to adopt the tradition of ethics as a guide to help tourism decision makers be more proactive in their attempts to establish ethical tourism programmes. In doing so, we briefly touch on the evolution of morality in humans, related theories of human nature, and later broaden the discussion into main traditions of ethical thought. The chapter also includes a brief overview of applied ethics as the essential bridge to theoretical ethics. Applied ethics is defined and examined through the lens of environmental ethics and moral standing – areas that are directly applicable to tourism.

The Nature of Morality

The propensity to follow impacts as the main path to meaning gives a rather incomplete picture of the overall nature of the tourism system. Often neglected or, worse yet, forgotten is the fact that tourism systems are the result of human agency. This fact was not lost on Przeclawski (1996), who aptly noted that we cannot effectively explain tourism without an understanding of 'man, the human being'. Taken to its logical end, what is it that we know about human beings and human nature in tourism? There is a world of knowledge outside the walls of tourism that would serve us well in better understanding the basic tendencies of tourists, local people and the other participants of the tourist trade. A causal link to human nature and tourism was made by Wheeller, who said that:

> All growth has costs and benefits. We are out for ourselves. It is a question of what is best for me and if someone, or somewhere, else pays the cost, then too bad as long as I get the benefits. Doesn't this 'devil take the hindmost' mentality realistically reflect mainstream consciousness? And isn't this Darwin's survival of the fittest? (Wheeller, 1994: 648).

Two thoughts emerge from this quote. The first is that theories we currently use in tourism have been generally unsuccessful at pinpointing the underlying reasons for what appears to be a universal propensity towards doing what is best for ourselves (for criticisms of social science theories, see Pinker, 2002; Saul, 1995, 2001,). As such, we can rationalise taking those extra photos, disregarding the bad press that the cruise industry gets, misleading tourists through unethical marketing, and so on, because in the end we get what we want. The second is that while most other disciplines have embraced the theory of evolution and associated more conventional theoretical spin-offs from it, we in tourism have not. So, although the quote above is accurate, we certainly have little in the way of context to put it into perspective. This is unfortunate because if there is any form of leisure behaviour that might substantiate perspectives on the survival of the fittest, it would surely be tourism. What do we know about self-interest in tourism? Why do we co-operate at some times but not others? What is altruism, and how does it weigh into the equations? If morality is seen as a uniform human condition, then there are evolutionary implications and theories that spawn from this over-arching perspective, and these must be drawn into the argument (Fennell, 2006a, 2006b).

Thomas Hobbes (1651/1957) argued that, before the existence of central authorities such as governments, the state of humanity was presided over by selfishness. War and general hostility were the manifestations of this inherent self-interest, where each attempts to obtain whatever he or she so desires, but at a cost to others. Only through a social contract, presided over by government, could this self-interest be surrendered. Hobbes felt there was no social driving force that compelled humanity to bind together in co-operative ventures, only the state which held the power to harness individual self-interest. By contrast, Kropotkin (1902/1972) argued much later in his book entitled *Mutual Aid: A Factor in Evolution* that it is only because of co-operation that humanity has managed to be successful. The more this co-operation takes form, the greater the chance for humanity to succeed.

It took until the 1960s and 1970s for sufficient light to be cast on the biological basis of self-interest and co-operation, through the work of Hamilton (1964) and Trivers (1971). These scientists developed two persuasive but controversial theories as to why animals are selfish. Both were based on the theory that organisms are designed, not to operate on the basis of what is right for themselves or for the group in which they are situated (group selection), but rather for their genes. Genes are not dedicated to the body in which they are housed, but rather to themselves and their ultimate longevity as passed on in other individuals. It is the gene, therefore, that is the unit of importance because genes pass on the characteristics of the individual. The two major theories that had their genesis grounded in this perspective are inclusive fitness and reciprocal altruism.

Inclusive fitness

If given the opportunity to help one of two people, a family member or a non-family member, whom would you choose to help? For example, if you are in a position to recommend someone for a job in another firm, and it just so happens that a close cousin is in competition with someone else for this job, whom would you recommend? Chances are you would recommend your cousin, because, as they say, 'blood is thicker than water'. It might even be said that among relatives, we might choose to aid a brother or a sister over a cousin, because the donor (you) and the recipient (in this case, your brother or sister) are more closely related.

This theory posits that those who share genes, like brothers, sisters, and parents, are more worthy of an agent's altruism, because the benefits that are accrued from the altruistic act would aid in the fitness of the donor individual. We help our own because these people share our genes, and the longevity of our genes, even in someone else's body, helps to carry forward our own genes into the future. In Hamilton's words, inclusive fitness is based on the following, 'Selection operates when carriers of some genes out-produce carriers of other genes. If altruistic behaviour were inherited, it would be more likely to spread if the altruism were directed at close relatives, because relatives share genes' (Hamilton, 1964: 38). From this perspective, we gain more of an appreciation as to why nepotism exists through situations, for example, where we hire members of our own family into prestigious positions in firms. Examples of such exchanges based on kinship are bound to be numerous in tourism. For example, children succeeding parents in the family business, cousins sending business to each other instead of competitors who are unrelated, and wealthy family elites controlling the industry in LDCs (lesser developed countries), and not sharing control and profits with others who might otherwise benefit. When we do things for those who are biologically related to us, we ultimately help ourselves.

Reciprocal altruism

Another form of aid that is prevalent in human and animal societies comes in the form of return favours between non-relatives. For example, it is no secret that politics is as much about human interaction (co-operation, manipulation, and so on) as it is about other aspects of leadership. In this regard, a former Canadian Prime Minister was famous for adhering to the basic tenet, 'Keep yours friends close and your enemies closer'. Politicians are rather adept at knowing who is trustworthy or not, who has helped in the past and is deserving of help in the future; and who has been deceitful in undermining the efforts of others. In fact, candidacies are won and lost on the shoulders of those who have given their time and resources to a candidate, who will someday down the road return a favour. It's a dirty game for the uninitiated, but it is a legal game, which further suggests that what is legal is not always moral.

Trivers (1971) observed that although people are generally self-interested, they will periodically demonstrate a willingness to co-operate with others. But this co-operation is far from altruistic, however, as there is the expectation of a reciprocal act in the future (you scratch my back, I'll scratch yours later). So this goes beyond inclusive fitness, as noted above, by including altruistic acts that may be extended to non-family members. The more frequently we engage in these acts of kindness, the greater the level of reciprocity in the future. This has manifested itself in the animal world, where there is a huge array of different species that help one another in situations involving protection, hunting and social bonding, but only if the beneficiary has demonstrated a willingness to do the same. Not surprisingly, the same also takes place in human societies. In commerce we often do favours for colleagues, with the expectation of a return in the future. The co-operation is meaningful to both parties because each can benefit at the times when they are most needy.

The psychological system that underlies this evolutionary set of adaptations has been outlined by Trivers (1971), who wrote that selection will favour:

(1) a complex system where people regulate their own altruism and cheating tendencies as well as the responses to these tendencies in others;
(2) tendencies to like others and to form friendships as the immediate emotional rewards motivating altruistic behaviour;
(3) injustice, unfairness and lack of reciprocity, which motivate human aggression and indignation;
(4) sensitivity to the costs and benefits of altruistic acts;
(5) a system whereby cheaters (defined as those who fail to reciprocate) pay for their transgressions by being cut off from all future acts of aid;
(6) the evolution of friendship, moralistic aggression, guilt, sympathy

and gratitude to regulate the system, and also to mimic these traits in order to influence the behaviour of others to one's advantage;

(7) the ability to detect subtle cheaters as well as the ability to distrust those who perform altruistic acts without the emotional basis of generosity (i.e. those who are insincere) (see Chapter 3);

(8) a mechanism for establishing reciprocal relationships, including performing altruistic acts towards strangers in inducing friendship;

(9) the formation of norms of reciprocal conduct; and

(10) the ability for reciprocal altruism to grow, learn, and be adaptive under a number of different circumstances.

The connections between tourism and reciprocal altruism are numerous. For example, in a study on ethical issues confronting travel agents, Dunfree and Black (1996) identified a various ethical concerns broadly categorised as: (1) issues involving the travel agency industry as a whole, (2) interactions between suppliers and travel agents, and (3) interactions between clients and travel agents. There is an undercurrent of reciprocal altruism in these interactions, where favouritism is contingent on co-operative relationships that have perhaps emerged over time supporting some agents and marginalising others. Given that travel agents cannot be effective travel information specialists if their word is not trusted by suppliers and clients, Dunfree and Black suggest that a code of ethics is the only way to develop standards that will be respected and internalised by individual travel agents. The American Society of Travel Agents' Code of Ethics embodies this commitment (Box 4.1).

Finkler and Higham (2004) found that the perception of impact on whales from whale-watching was dependent on location. Those watching from land-based platforms were significantly more concerned about the activities of boats on the whales (e.g. powerboat noise disturbing the whales' behaviour, and powerboats having an impact on the safety of the whales) than their water-based counterparts were. Finkler and Higham also discussed what has been termed 'the whale watcher's paradox' (see also Blewett, 1993: 1, as cited in Finkler & Higham, 2004). This is the feeling amongst whale watchers that, though there is an expressed need to get as close as possible to whales, they simultaneously know that doing will heighten the level of impact on the creatures. The attraction provides a degree of pull that is significant enough to compel tourists to suppress their own sense of what is good or right in the face of normative pressures (norms of reciprocal conduct). The same has been reported in safari tourism where, in return for better tips, vans often get closer to large mammals than standards permit (D. Smith, personal communication).

In Ecuador, cheating (defined as the failure to reciprocate, as noted above) often takes place amongst tourism service providers, who have

Box 4.1 The ASTA Code of Ethics

Preamble

We live in a world in which travel has become both increasingly important and complex in its variety of modes and choices. Travellers are faced with a myriad of alternatives as to transportation, accommodations and other travel services. Travellers must depend on travel agencies and others in the industry to guide them honestly and competently. All ASTA members pledge themselves to conduct their business activities in a manner that promotes the ideal of integrity in travel and agree to act in accordance with the applicable sections of the following Principles of the ASTA Code of Ethics. Complaints arising under this Code should be filed in writing with the ASTA Consumer Affairs Department.

ASTA has the following categories of membership: Travel Agency, Travel Professional, International, International Travel Professional, Allied Company, Allied Associate, Travel School, Senior, and Future Travel Professional.

Responsibilities of all travel agency, travel professional, international travel agency and international travel professional members:

(1) *Accuracy.* ASTA members will be factual and accurate when providing information about their services and the services of any firm they represent. They will not use deceptive practices.

(2) *Disclosure.* ASTA members will provide in writing, upon written request, complete details about the cost, restrictions, and other terms and conditions, of any travel service sold, including cancellation and service fee policies. Full details of the time, place, duration, and nature of any sales or promotional presentation the consumer will be required to attend in connection with his/her travel arrangements shall be disclosed in writing before any payment is accepted.

(3) *Responsiveness.* ASTA members will promptly respond to their clients' complaints.

(4) *Refunds.* ASTA members will remit any undisputed funds under their control within the specified time limit. Reasons for delay in providing funds will be given to the claimant promptly.

(5) *Co-operation.* ASTA members will co-operate with any inquiry conducted by ASTA to resolve any dispute involving consumers or another member.

(6) *Confidences.* ASTA members will not use improperly obtained client lists or other confidential information obtained from an employee's former employer.

(7) *Confidentiality.* ASTA members will treat every client transaction confidentially and not disclose any information without permission of the client, unless required by law.

(8) *Affiliation.* ASTA members will not falsely represent a person's affiliation with their firm.

(9) *Conflict of interest.* ASTA members will not allow any preferred relationship with a supplier to interfere with the interests of their clients.

(10) *Compliance.* ASTA members shall abide by all federal, state and local laws and regulations.

Responsibilities of all members:

(1) *Notice.* ASTA members operating tours will promptly advise the agent or client who reserved the space of any change in itinerary, services, features or price. If substantial changes are made that are within the control of the operator, the client will be allowed to cancel without penalty.

(2) *Delivery.* ASTA members operating tours will provide all components as stated in their brochure or written confirmation, or provide alternate services of equal or greater value, or provide appropriate compensation.

(3) *Credentials.* An ASTA member shall not, in exchange for money or otherwise, provide travel agent credentials to any person as to whom there is no reasonable expectation that the person will engage in a bona fide effort to sell or manage the sale of travel services to the general public on behalf of the member through the period of validity of such credentials. This principle applies to the ASTA member and all affiliated or commonly controlled enterprises

Conclusion

Adherence to the Principles of the Code of Ethics signifies competence, fair dealing and high integrity. Failure to adhere to this Code may subject a member to disciplinary actions, as set forth in ASTA's Bylaws.

Source: http://www.astanet.com/about/codeofethics.asp. Accessed 29.08.05

been sharply criticised for their lack of co-operation, and the associated effects of this self-interest on the social and ecological conditions of the region. In striving to capture a larger percentage of the market, service providers regularly undermine each other; they have been found to exploit agreements with indigenous federations by refusing to make contact before doing business in peripheral communities. Programme delivery also suffers as operators value profit above more intrinsic values, with the end result that the basic standards and philosophies of eco-tourism are compromised without hesitation (Garcia, 2000).

What makes reciprocal altruism even more attractive as a theoretical tool – and why it is so important to us here – is its connection to the evolution of morality. Theorists have gone so far as to suggest that reciprocal altruism explains how and why morality evolved in humans, as a necessary constraint on individuals' pursuit of their own well-being (Beversluis, 1987). The co-operative/self-interest dynamics within small communities is described as a function of size, stability, dependency and time. In other words, reciprocal altruism thrived in communities that were small and where stability was achieved through dependency and co-operation of repeated interactions over time. As observed by Pinker (2002), sympathy and trust, gratitude and loyalty, guilt and shame, and anger and contempt all evolved to balance cheating with co-operation. Millions of years of evolution have thus allowed humans to cross an evolutionary threshold, paving the road towards intelligence, anticipation, abstraction, and self-awareness. This has been observed by Ayala (1987), who writes that humans are ethical because we can (1) anticipate the consequences of our actions, (2) make value judgements, and (3) choose between alternative courses of action (see also Ehrlich, 2000). Mayr (1988) contends that the evolution of larger brains in association with larger social groups provided the foundation for morality. This led to selection rewards (in the biological sense) for the demonstration of unselfish traits that benefit the group, and to the evolution of ethical behaviour by choice and freewill – see Mayr (1988) for a discussion of how reciprocal altruism evolved as the basis for morality, and Marcus (2004) for a discussion of mental life in the context of gene–environment co-evolution.

This knowledge provides the basis from which to conclude that morality is a human universal (i.e. it is ingrained in each and all of us as a consequence of millions of years of evolution). But even so, we must be careful when we apply this reasoning to moral norms and codes of ethics. Although we have evolved with the capacity to be moral, the various normative approaches to ethics in existence around the world are variable from culture to culture (see Williams, 1993a for a good discussion on the biological and cultural co-evolution that have endowed us with the capacity to be ethical). So, the moral standards and ethical principles that we follow:

> constitute a structure of interlocking behavioural guidelines that have been growing organically since our ancestors first became human, if not earlier. We worked them out through a long and arduous evolutionary process marked by many wrong turns and much social discord. Indeed, the structure is still imperfect and we continue trying to make improvements. We are building a sense of humanity-as-a-whole as the ultimate in-group, which exists over and above our sense of national consciousness and whatever residual loyalties we retain from the earlier, culture-based periods. The need is increasingly urgent, for galloping technological change is forcing new global problems on us that demand global solutions. (Coon, 2005: 43–44)

Reciprocal altruism, cheating and co-operation, evolution, inclusive fitness, altruism and selfishness: these are all new terms in tourism studies. Their inclusion into the tourism vernacular is essential, however, if we are to understand the complete picture of why tourism continues to be plagued by impacts. Tourism is very much about freedom, which generally means the freedom to remove the moral cloak that regulates our behaviour in everyday life (Przeclawski, 1996). But, as noted above by Beversluis (1987) and corroborated by Midgley (1994), morality evolved at the crossroads of freedom and constraint. Although we have broken free of the chains of instinct through rational thought and action, too much freedom does not do us very well as a species at all. In this, Midgley writes:

If freedom and morality are indeed closely linked ... it is perhaps a rather paradoxical fact that the first effect of freedom should be to put us under these new constraints [impartiality, truthfulness, parsimony, and so on]. Our freedom is exactly what gives us these headaches, what makes possible this moral thinking, this troublesome kind of search for priority among conflicting aims. By becoming aware of conflict – by ceasing to roll passively from one impulse to another, like floods of lava through a volcano – we certainly do acquire a load of trouble. But we also become capable of larger enterprises, of standing back and deciding to make lesser projects give way to more important ones. That, it seems, may be why moralities are needed. (Midgley, 1994: 9)

It should come as no surprise, therefore, that the code of ethics is a limitation on the freedom to do as we please whenever we please. Indeed, the equilibrium of constraint and freedom is a natural expression of who we are at the deepest level of human nature. Seen from this perspective we argue that the code of ethics is simply a natural progression of who we are, and that such constraints are simply an expression of responsible citizenship. The principal concern for tourism is acknowledging that although we have purchased the 'right' to be hedonistic, this enjoyment is still subject to the dynamic tension that exists between freedom and constraint.

Ethics: What Should We Do?

Despite the fact that the study of ethics and morality has continued now in the Western world for perhaps 2500 years, the options for us remain much the same now as they did at the beginning. We have essentially three possibilities – to seek ends, means, and/or authenticity. To seek moral ends implies that the decision-maker reviews possible alternatives and selects that which has the greatest potential for goodness ... happiness. To seek moral means, one essentially is looking at proper duty and placing outcome as secondary. Finally, the search for authenticity, while not perceived by all as a moral endeavour, has been the focus of significant academic interest. In this chapter, each of these three moral options and some of their most interesting correlates will be discussed. While these theories themselves do not contain specific codes of ethics, they do or can form the underlying theoretical framework for codes. Therefore, an understanding of these ideas is essential to appreciate the nuance of existing codes and to prepare the code writer for the development of new codes of ethics.

While there are countless definitions of ethics, we have selected a somewhat Thomistic perspective (i.e. that of Aristotle and Aquinas) and defined ethics as the *rules, standards and principles that dictate right, good and authentic conduct among members of a society or profession* (examples are tourism ethics, medical ethics, sport ethics, business ethics and environmental ethics)

Morals, on the other hand, are perceived not to be a contextualised set of rules (e.g. a code of ethics), but rather the rational and natural inclinations of humanity to do good and avoid evil (e.g. preserving life, forming an ordered society and pursuing the truth). In the following section we discuss three general approaches to moral theory that could form the basis for ethical conduct and codes in tourism.

Seeking the end

There are two dominant approaches to seeking the moral end. The first has its roots in Aristotelian philosophy, in which the end we ought to seek is the Greek term, *eudaimonia*. The most accurate translation of this term is 'to flourish' rather than seeking simple happiness. Aristotle argues that there are many activities in a person's life that lead to various forms of so-called happiness – food, sex, popularity, etc. These forms of happiness are typically short lived and often require others for their actualisation (i.e. in order for me to be honoured, I need someone to honour me). They ultimately do not result in an individual tapping into his or her potential as a human as they require only lower order functions to satisfy them. For example, sex may make a human momentarily physiologically blissful as it would a primate. However, unless one contemplates the act philosophically (e.g. a union of psyche), then the primate and the human essentially share the same degree of physiological bliss. Sex, Aristotle would argue, is not a demonstration of the human's extraordinary capacity to reason but rather a satisfaction of a physical need shared with other animals. Aristotle suggests that there is a more profound form of happiness that we should have as our life's target – one that we do not share with other animals. This target can be hit only through the use of our capacity to reason.

Our rationality allows us to choose and (the potential) to choose well. If not for reason, we could not be decision-makers in the first place. If all we had were instinct and emotion, then nature would be choosing – not us! Reason then gives us the ability to think through options and to determine the quality of happiness we seek (this phrase will come back to haunt us below).

The target then is to flourish and any decision we make that does not lead instrumentally to our flourishing is a bad decision. Good or virtuous decisions aim us in the direction of eudaimonia. Virtuous decisions, Aristotle believes, are the result of selecting the mean between excess and deficit. In other words 'all things in moderation' or the 'golden mean' would be the watchword for Aristotelians. For example, the mean between being a coward and being rash is the virtue of courage; the mean between underdevelopment of a natural resource and scorched-earth policy would be the virtue of sustainable development.

Thus, for the human to be truly happy or rather to flourish, he or she must be making use of the capacity to think – to contemplate – to reflect. By reflecting we understand and will naturally choose the activities that lead to our eudaimonia (Figure 4.1). Aristotle makes this clear in the following:

> Every art and every inquiry, and similarly every action and pursuit, is thought to aim at some good; and for this reason the good has rightly been declared to be that at which all things aim ... Will not the knowledge of it, then, have great influence on life? Shall we not, like archers who have a mark to aim at, be more likely to hit upon what is right? (Aristotle, 1992: *Nicomachean Ethics*: Book I, 1094)

This approach is also known as virtue morality and is perceived to be universal in its application. Where simple forms of happiness can be relative and subjective according to the particular tastes of individuals and cultures, the target of eudaimonia is a universal and objective good (Figure 4.1).

A second approach to seeking the moral end is based on the pursuit of happiness in a way that is substantially different from Aristotle's view. This theory can be subdivided into two themes, one seeking individual pleasure and the other seeking the pleasure of the group.

Seeking pleasure and avoiding pain, as the end we should seek, is the moral view of the hedonists. While this approach doesn't hold a great deal of moral stock among philosophers, it is certainly an apparent basis for much of human behaviour – particularly with regard to the realm of tourism. Pleasure is the end to be sought; however the kind of pleasure to be sought varies considerably among hedonists. Perhaps the best-known hedonists were the Epicureans. Despite the fact that they have been much maligned as the primary philosophical source for drugs, sex and rock'n roll, they were actually promoters of life's most simple pleasures, including friendship and philosophical debate. The Cyreniacs have been equally accused of promoting immorality, however, they too argued in favour of higher and lower-order pleasures and suggested that none should obsess us. Hedonism in general is the basis for what we today may better under-

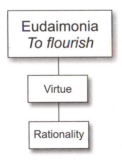

Figure 4.1 Eudaimonia

stand as relativism, which posits that what an individual or a culture perceives as pleasure is relative to that individual or particular culture and no external judgement of morality ought to be made. This subjectivist view is in obvious conflict with the objective and universal beliefs of Aristotle.

Group hedonism is the democratic expansion of individual hedonism. Seeking the greatest pleasure or happiness for the greatest number is the end that is coveted. Also known as utilitarianism, this moral school of thought has a number of variations. The earliest treatise written by Jeremy Bentham led the individual to believe that quality of pleasure was not an issue, only quantity (Long, 1977). In other words, if sex tourism resulted in more pleasure than ecotourism, for example, then the former would be the more obvious choice among decision-makers. These choices were made by way of the hedonistic calculus that is not unlike our contemporary rational decision-making process in which alternatives are weighed against a particular criterion (i.e. pleasure). The alternative that maximises the intended goal (i.e. greatest good for the greatest number) is the 'best' choice.

J.S. Mill followed Bentham's lead, however, he responded to the criticism of utilitarianism by distinguishing between qualities of pleasure. He argued, not unlike the misunderstood hedonists, that not all pleasures were of the same value (Mill, 1861/1957). The goal of the maximisation of happiness remained for Mill; however, higher-order pleasures are to be preferred over lower-order pleasures. Distinguishing between the two requires the wisdom of expert judges who have experienced both and will naturally choose the higher over the lower (i.e. eco-tourism over sex-tourism).

Criticism of the implicit denial of rights to the individual in favour of those of the group lead contemporary utilitarians to devise a somewhat hybrid version that incorporate rules into the calculus of ethical behaviour. Rule-utilitarianism suggests that an act is moral if it follows the *rule* that ultimately leads to the greatest goodness rather than placing emphasis upon the *act* that will bring about the greatest good. For example, let's look at the environmental impact of the periodic practice of oil tankers dumping their refuse into the ocean. Suppose that, in order to put an end to this practice, local officials board the next tanker that enters their waters (not knowing if they have polluted or not) and publicly execute the crew in an effort to establish a very powerful message and deterrent for other ships. While this extreme utilitarian act may result in the greatest good for the greatest number (i.e. pollution will come to an end), it also involves the denial of rights of those potentially innocent crew. Cultural relativism aside, the basic human right to live is generally regarded as a 'rule' that results in the maximisation of goodness. Therefore establishing laws that maintain this basic assumption would result in the utilitarian end mediated through a rule. Returning to our polluters, lopping off the heads of the crew may put an end to the problem of polluting waters; however, it may in turn cause a greater degree of collective pain if the public then becomes uneasy about the status of their basic rights (e.g. despite my innocence, I can lose my head if it serves the public good).

Another major criticism of utilitarianism in general (act or rule) is the vagueness of the end to be sought. What exactly is the greatest good, and who make up the greatest number? Is this goal set for our immediate goodness or that of the next generation? Do animals count? Does the environment count? While there have been attempts to rein in the notion of who's happiness is maximised (e.g. the culture, the society, the group, the organisation), it remains a contentious aspect of this approach to moral decision-making.

Utilitarianism is pervasive in our Western society as almost implicitly we seek to act or at least are encouraged to act for the greatest good for the greatest number. Hedonism, while in full bloom in many aspects of our life, is not the epitome of the moral life that most would proclaim. In many respects utilitarianism was an offspring of the age of science in which calculations of moral virtue seemed possible. It was also a rebellion against the firm grasp the Church had upon the decision-making ability of the masses. Utilitarianism took the process of moral choice out of the hands of the priest and into the control of the individual who was able then to consider the weight of various options in a secular manner. The Church's perspective of moral decision-making was and is based upon the followers' obligation to do their duty to God and to the Church. It is this sense of duty to follow rules that is our next focus.

Seeking duty: Seeking the means

Moral theories that are based on duty are formally termed *deontology*. From this perspective what is moral is that which abides by the rule or principle and not what results in a particular outcome. That I do my duty is enough. The obvious question is, 'what is the basis of my duty'? Some deontologists will argue that the principles based upon a religious source are the foundation of moral behaviour. For example, the Koran and the Bible provide devotees with the information required to live moral lives. Doing one's duty to abide by these rules can be perceived as a form of prayer or yoga (i.e. practice).

A second source of deontological behaviour is understood as social contract ethics. This secular perspective sees ethical behaviour as that which adheres to the rules, principles and norms that we as a civil society agree to uphold. The American Constitution, the Canadian Charter of Rights and Freedoms, the Australian Bill of Rights are all examples of social contracts to guide moral behaviour. From a micro view, codes of ethics in organisations and professional associations are rules and principles that have been formulated by stakeholders to guide and monitor ethical conduct – deontological tools for organisation.

A third source of deontology is intuitive. This is not the intuition of a hunch to buy a lottery ticket when I 'feel' lucky. This is based upon the capacity of reason that only human share. Immanuel Kant is the dominant proponent of this ethical perspective. He argues that because humans, regardless of their individualism based upon gender, ethnicity, age, etc., have the capacity to think, they can reach similar ethical conclusions. His intuitive rule is that ethical conduct must be universalisable (or, based on our definition, it must also be moral). He termed this global rule 'the categorical imperative' and described it like this: 'act only according to that maxim by which you can at the same time will that it should become a universal law' (1785/1988: 30). This rule implies then that, for a decision to be morally worthy, it must be suitable for all, not just for me in this particular instance. For example, promise keeping could be perceived as a universally desired law – we should all keep our promises and expect others to do so. If we do not, then when we make a so-called promise we could never be sure that it will be kept. The outcome would be the impossibility of making any sort of formal or informal agreements or contract between individuals, organisations, and nations. Theoretically, this seems reasonable – intuitively right in fact. However, when real life enters into the picture the ideal breaks down. For example, I am driving my car to the airport to meet my wife for our second honeymoon, an occasion we promised each other to keep. On the way, I notice an elderly woman sitting in a park being accosted by some young toughs. I have a decision to make, do I assist the woman and break my promise to my wife, or do I continue on in order to meet my soul mate? The strict Kantian would argue in favour of keeping the original promise; however such a decision strikes most of us as, on face value (or prima facie), the wrong action to take – we should help the elderly woman. W.D. Ross championed a more flexible deontological perspective, as presented in the following:

> If as almost all moralist except Kant are agreed, and as most plain men think, it is sometimes right to tell a lie or to break a promise, it must be maintained that there is a difference between prima facie duties and the actual or absolute [e.g. the categorical imperative]. (Ross, 1975: 104)

A second universal law, termed the *practical imperative*, is in some respect easier to handle. It states that you should never treat people simply as a means to an end, but rather as an end in themselves. This does not mean that you cannot use someone at all as we all must 'use' the skills and attributes of others to survive in any form of community. What is meant here is that while we do use others, we must also at the same time respect these others and accept them as individuals with dignity. For example, we use a tour guide to prevent us from being lost on a trek and at the same time, he or she uses us as a means for livelihood. As long as we treat the guide with respect and take a reasonable interest in his or her life (or life projects) and if he or she does the same with us, then all is well according to Kant. If, however, the guide perceives us only as a source of revenue and if we see the guide only as a means to our personal survival, then we both have failed to exercise Kant's practical imperative.

Seeking authenticity

Seeking authenticity has not been the private domain of existentialists, though it is their primary concern as a philosophical movement. While it is noticeably the most individualistic of moral perspectives it is also cosmopolitan in nature for when the existentialist chooses for him/herself, the choice is made for all. Though other moral theories are also universally geared, the real twist in the existentialist's world is that the decision-maker must take responsibility for all choices and their impact globally.

Existentialists as a group worry about the influence that society has over their pursuit to be true to themselves. Nietzsche called the public the 'herd' and Kierkegaard felt that the 'monstrous public' levelled us into becoming homogeneous and inauthentic. This tendency to become automatons was expressed in similar terms by Marx and Marcuse in their criticism of bureaucracy. Marcuse states that

> In the period of large scale industry, however, the existential conditions making for individuality give way to conditions which render individuality unnecessary. In clearing the ground for the conquest of scarcity, the technological process not only levels individuality but also tends to transcend it where it is concurrent with scarcity. Mechanised mass production is filling the empty spaces in which individuality could assert itself. (Marcuse, 1998: 61)

Despite this revulsion toward bureaucracies, crowds, society and systems, it is conceivable that existentialists can operate as profoundly 'moral' individuals within society. Furthermore, their overt behaviour may be remarkably similar to those of individuals promoting other moral orientation – what differentiates them is intention. For example, a teleologist may save a drowning man in order to gain reward; a deontologist may do the same in order to do his or her duty based on the categorical imperative; the existentialist may save the individual because to do otherwise would violate his or her self-made conception of universal care – it would violate her conscience. In each case, the drowning man is saved, but the rationale for the heroic act was different.

It is conceivable that existentialism has made its way into the world of art more than any other realm of human endeavour and this is unfortunate because it has much to offer other realms. The worlds of business and government have tended to steer clear of this philosophy. They have perceived it to breed chaos and excessive individualism in an environment in which solidarity, efficiency, effectiveness and productivity are the watchwords (Hodgkinson, 1996). Included here, of course, is the acceptance of organisational imperatives (e.g. Scott & Hart, 1979) that dictate that the survival and growth of the organisation supersedes the survival and eudaimonia of the individual.

There is room in our practical world, however, for existentialism other than the acknowledgement of angst we all suffer from time to time in our jobs. Rules, systems and obligations can be accepted, followed – even created by existentialists – the key is that they are carried out in good faith. Good faith implies that choices are made and action taken as a function of the individual's own will. So, if I am required to abide by certain restrictions on my behaviour as a tour guide, I may accept them in good or bad faith. In good faith I will read these rules, assess their validity and their resonance with my principles and follow them if I can be true to myself while at the same time being an agent to the organisation for whom I work. Or, I may accept these rules of conduct in bad faith. This would imply that I abide by them, not because of a congruence with my authentic self, but because I was told to follow them or because I fear I will lose my job or because everyone else follows them and therefore I feel I should in order to conform or because I simply follow orders because its my duty to do so. While both choices end up in the same place – following the rules – one is based upon good faith and the other is based upon bad faith. Does it matter? Teleologists in general and pragmatists (a philosophical approach with its home in the United States) in particular would say, 'no, it doesn't matter – only the outcome is of concern'. The Hindus and modern existentialists would vehemently argue that it does in fact matter – one's authenticity is pre-eminent. Consider the following quotations that express this line of thinking:

From the *Bhagavad Gita*:

> Be focused on action and not on the fruits of action. Do not become confused in attachment to the fruit of your actions and do not become confused in the desire for inaction. (*Bhagavad Gita*, 1972: 2, 47)

From the existentialist, Sartre,

> In fact, in creating the man [woman] that we want to be, there is not a single one of our acts which does not at the same time create and image of man [woman] as we think he [she] ought to be. (Sartre, 1957: 17)

Let's have a look at this concept in tourism. I decide to visit Costa Rica because I have a personal interest in the country's folk music and wish to see and *experience for myself* local musicians performing their distinctive style of singing and story-telling (e.g. Cateras). This would be good faith tourism. On the other hand, if I make the decision to visit this location as a result of convincing marketing strategies (I would be 'cool' and 'party' with beautiful tanned people on the endless beaches) or by friends who would pressure me to vacation with them, then I would be acting as a bad faith tourist – there but for the wrong reasons.

In this brief section, we have provided the reader with an overview of three very different ways to view moral and ethical conduct. Philosophers from ancient Greece to our present age have more or less agreed that moral conduct is based upon ends, means or authenticity. While these views do express different perspectives, they may not necessarily be mutually exclusive.

Moral Development

Where morality and ethics tell us what we ought to do, the psychology of moral development tells us why we do what we do. This field of study has its roots in the early work of the child psychologist Jean Piaget (1948), who found a progression in the complexity of moral reasoning as a child matures. Laurence Kohlberg, an educational psychologist at Harvard, expanded this early work to include adolescents and adults. Through empirical investigation, he found that complexity of moral reasoning about ethical dilemmas moves through three general phases subdivided into six stages. The first phase, termed pre-conventional, is hedonistic in nature, focusing on seeking pleasure and avoiding punishment for the individual. In the second phase an individual's rationale for action is based upon seeking approval from others (i.e. significant others or society in general). The third and most advanced phase deals with universal principles that are developed by the individual as a function of experience, education and introspection. This final phase is existential in nature as it appeals to the individual's sense of authenticity and responsibility.

A criticism of this model is that it is justice-oriented and thus the dominant moral orientation of men and not women. In response to this model, Carole Gilligan (1982), also of Harvard, proposed a model of moral development that focuses on females. Her model is based upon the morality of care as opposed to justice. She describes this perspective in the following: 'Judgement remains psychological in its concern with the intention and consequence of action, but now it becomes universal in its condemnation of exploitation and hurt' (Gilligan, 1982: 492). As with Kohlberg, she perceives three major phases of moral development. However, the emphasis at each stage is not upon rules or a sense of justice, but rather upon caring for oneself, others, and all of humanity. Between phases 1 and 2 and phases 2 and 3, she identifies transitions in which the woman has begun to identify the significance of the content of the next level. For example, at the conventional level in Gilligan's model, the female is caring for all her relationships with the exception of the relationship with herself – she is selfless. The transition from this phase to the next suggests that the woman has begun to see that exploitation and hurt can certainly include her own self-neglect, and the 'goodness of altruism' is in harsh contrast with the principle of universal non-violence. In other words, the woman can and should care for others as well as herself. One moves through these various stages and levels as one's cognitive complexity becomes more and more advanced. This complexity is the result of education as well as of experiencing the perceptions of others and juxtaposing them with one's own. The cognitive challenge to personal views may lead to more advanced perspectives of moral reasoning.

As an example, let's look at John, a single 31-year-old man with a keen interest in sex tourism. He travels to location X, a well-known sex-tourism locale, and is an active consumer for a week and then returns home to his 'normal' life. He reasons that he is paying for a service that is not illegal in this particular country and therefore he is doing nothing wrong. One day, John and a co-worker enter into a tourism conversation and begin to exchange stories of their last trip. His friend, Immanuel, is an ecotourist and travelled last to the Antarctic to view the penguin rookeries and cried for most of the trip home thinking about global warming. He is nothing short of apoplectic when John tells him of his escapades in X. John is totally dismayed at the reaction and asks for an explanation. Immanuel goes on at length about the exploitation of women and children as means and not as ends, and explains the concepts embedded in the universal principles of the categorical and practical imperatives and the ethic of care. John's response is initially predictable, suggesting that he is one of thousands who partake in this kind of tourism and that in fact he is helping the country's economy by spending his money there. The conversation ends, and John begins to reflect. Immanuel's comments have not only embarrassed him but also caused him to consider the negative impact of what he has been doing – he is considering the existence of others as ends in themselves. His cognitive worldview has been questioned – his complexity in evaluating this situation has been heightened because of the intellectual and moral challenge from his co-worker Immanuel.

Values

Value has been defined in many ways; however, one of the most succinct definitions can be found in the work of Christopher Hodgkinson (1983: 36) who used this concept to understand behaviour in organisational contexts.

He suggests that a value is 'a concept of the desirable with a motivating force'. This definition implies the following:

(1) A value is an abstraction (i.e. a concept). It is imposed by humans on something that may have no inherent value (e.g. diamonds).
(2) A value is something that is socially acceptable (i.e. desirable) as opposed to individually desired. For example, sadism may be desired by some but not by most.
(3) A value pushes us into action (i.e. motivating force). Another way to see this is that our behaviour is a manifestation of what we value.

This is a rather powerful definition that renders much of what we say rather impotent if it does not translate into action. If I say that I value the environment, yet freely pollute it with an SUV (when I could reasonably walk to my destination), then this value is rhetoric.

George England, in his seminal work on organisational values (England *et al.*, 1974), suggested that values can be understood hierarchically from weakest to strongest. Weak values are those we say we value but do not translate into action of any sort, as in the example provided above. Adopted values are those put into action based only on context – they are not internalised. These may be the values I am forced to uphold in my work context, but are abandoned once I leave the building. Intended values are those that I truly believe – they are personally relevant and I do as best I can to put them into action. However, there are some circumstances in which I may let these values fall by the wayside. I may walk to the store to do my bit for the environment, however when it is minus 40 degrees in a Canadian January, I may opt for my polluting car to keep me warm. Finally, operative or core values are those that are not compromised by context. These values do result in action – they have a significant force to motivate my behaviour.

Hodgkinson (1996) also argues in favour of a values hierarchy. He believes that a value can be held from four disparate levels. At the base level, we value something because we simply like it. Little cognitive thought is present in this almost instinctual level of *preference*. I enjoy tea and not coffee simply because prefer the taste – nothing more. The next level incorporates the preferences of the collective or *consensus*. I make my choice to value something based upon the activity of others – a democracy of value so to speak. So I drink tea at this level, not because I personally like it, but because others seem to drink it. Kohlberg would argue that I am drinking tea for conventional reasons. The third level is much more robust in its cognitive activity. Here one's values are the *consequence* of valuing. In other words if, through a rational/logical assessment of the outcome of valuing X, I determine that it has a positive benefit for society or the environment, then I will value it – otherwise I will not. I drink tea and promote tea drinking because I know through my empirical research that it is better for one's health than drinking coffee. At the highest level of valuing I base my behaviour not upon what I like, or what others like, or what science tells me, but upon a transrational and authentic *principle*. I may well consider these levels of valuing; however, my deepest sense of valuation comes from this sense of personal will, genuineness and faith. I drink tea at this level because I am a Buddhist and it is part of an expression of my transcendental practice or prayer or yoga. Of all that we do value, only a tiny minority will be based upon the highest level of principle (Table 4.1).

This hierarchy can be applied to anything we value – honesty, religion, work, volunteerism, etc. What application this has for daily practice is the recognition of why one values at all. Performing a value audit using this model can make explicit what is latent and provide tools for self-reflection and cognitive challenge to existing scheme. Perhaps I value vacations simply because they are fun and constitute a break from the rigour of thinking. Or, I may vacation in order to seek out experiences that will be catalysts for personal and or spiritual development. In the first instance I may sit on a beach in Cancun drink, play volleyball, and ride the inflatable banana. In the second instance I may visit Calcutta and attend an ashram for two weeks or cloister myself with Buddhist monks in Kamakura, Japan. If nothing else, these two models provide a means to assess what drives us to do what we do. It may not cause us to vary our behaviour, however, we will recognise – at least – why we do what we do.

Table 4.1 The value paradigm

Value type	Grounds of value	Psychological orientation	Philosophical orientation
1	principle	• the will • conation	• existentialism • religion/faith • Kantianism
2	consequence	• cognition • reason • thinking	• pragmatism • utilitarianism
3	consensus		• democracy • liberalism
4	preference	• affect • emotion • feeling	• hedonism • behaviourism • positivism

Source: Hodgkinson (1983)

Applied Ethics

Applied ethics is the division of ethics that investigates the specific moral issues of the day. In the past 30 years it has been subdivided into a number of different areas, including bioethics, legal ethics, environmental ethics, and so on (see Figure 4.2). It is widely accepted that there are two main features that render an issue 'applied'. In the first case, the issue must be controversial enough to have spawned enough support from both sides (i.e. those in favour of it and those against it). For example, hunting generates both support and opposition depending on a range of variables including socio-economic status and urban versus rural residency. Of course there are those who simply may or may not form an opinion on an issue like hunting, but this is not to say that the issue does not exist. Secondly, for an issue to be applied it must have universal applicability and thus not be of a localised nature (e.g. bylaws and zoning). In this regard, there is nothing immoral about allowing children to sell lemonade in front of the house, because it generally does not offend the average person (acknowledging perhaps the envy of other children!). In this case, moral relevance at a broader level is a key determining factor as to whether an issue qualifies as an applied one. Van Zyl (2002) provides a similar commentary on the nature of applied ethics, by noting that there are specific logics that frame its applicability. These include: (1) the standards of right action, (2) a sensitivity to the complexity of moral life in multicultural and pluralistic societies, (3) the acceptance of the principle of universality as a necessary property of ethical theory, and (4) the provision of a non-egoistic justification and explanation of universal rules and principles.

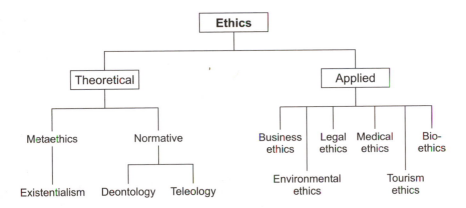

Figure 4.2 A framework of moral philosophy

Adapted from Honderich (1995)

In reference to tourism and the need for change, Tearfund notes that *fundamentally* (our italics) tourism is an ethical issue. In substantiating this, and linking with the discussion above on applied ethics, Tearfund notes that

> Tourism is not just an economic transaction or a series of activities which can be isolated from everyday life or from their impact on people. The very fact that we travel to another culture and come into direct contact with the people there raises a number of ethical issues. (Tearfund, 2000: 5)

Many of these ethical issues, which are considered to be some of the most entrenched and distasteful in tourism, include sex tourism, the displacement of local people as a consequence of tourism development, and the exclusion of local people from basic resources and amenities for health and well-being (Holden, 2003).

The link between theoretical and applied ethics takes place when we attempt to resolve the applied issue by consulting any one of a number of different normative theoretical perspectives, as noted in the previous section. The problem with this is that these theories often yield different and opposing results. This means that it may or may not be possible to use just one theory to resolve ethical issues that are so comprehensive and many-sided. This has prompted theorists to employ pluralist strategies that include the use of more than one ethical realm in attempting to resolve the issue. Fennell and Malloy (1995) used this strategy in the development of a comprehensive ethical model for ecotourists, ecotourism operators and local people. They argued that stakeholders should consider the application of deontological, teleological and existential perspectives in striving for morally sound outcomes in ecotourism.

Environmental ethics

One of the forms of ethics most familiar to tourism scholars is eco- or environmental ethics, which has been expressed as 'concern over redefining the boundaries of obligation to the environment and evaluating the human position towards it' (Holden, 2003: 97). In a similar vein, Miller (1991: 12) writes that 'eco-ethics ... attempts to create a conceptual framework for human interaction with the environment, a framework that can assist us in holding our own lives together and enable us to act with discipline, understanding, and reverence toward the natural world'.

Rolston III (2000, 1986) observes that environmental ethics was virtually unknown until the mid-1970s. Although philosophers had thought about human–environment relationships for millennia, it was left to Aldo Leopold to lay down the basic tenets of this ethic in 1949, and another 25 years for this ethic to be articulated into a meaningful, cohesive movement. Leopold's *A Sand County Almanac* (Leopold, 1949/1991) is seminal in that it helped to ignite a form of environmentalism that was more dedicated and philosophical than previous efforts (Johnson, 1984). In reference to an ecological ethic, Leopold (1949/1991: 238) wrote that it 'is a limitation on freedom of action in the struggle for existence'. In bridging this philosophy to the broader ecological community, Leopold (1949/1991: 239) wrote, 'The land ethic simply enlarges the boundaries of the community to include soils, waters, plants, and animals, or collectively: the land' which ' ... changes the role of *Homo sapiens* from conqueror of the land-community to plain member and citizen of it. It implies respect for his fellow-members, and also respect for the community as such' (Leopold, 1949/1991: 240).

The establishment of a framework for environmental ethics has necessi- tated an analysis of the root causes of environmental problems. Lynn White (1971) has traced such problems back through the ages, with Western reli- gion acting as a catalyst for mankind's dominance over nature. The indus- trial revolution has also been cited as a contributing factor to the disassociation between people and commerce on the one hand and the natural world on the other. But even more deeply seated is what Ehrenfeld (1981) terms the 'arrogance of humanism', spurred on by the Enlighten- ment, and characterised by the supreme overriding belief in human reason as the terminus for solving all the world's problems (see Mason & Mowforth, 1996; Holden, 2003).

In general, environmental ethics is based on two ends of a broad spec- trum. The first, anthropocentrism, literally means 'man-centred'. The opposite end of the spectrum is ecocentrism, and is described by Aiken (1984) as a position that places value in systems at the broadest level. It is therefore holistic in its orientation rather than atomistic. Aiken (1984: 268) observes that it is both evolutionary, and ecologically oriented, such that 'everything is connected and that the good of the parts is dependent on the good of the whole'. Even so, those who champion the eco-centric stand- point are not universally in agreement on the extent to which it ought to be operationalised. For example, Aiken (1984) identified three different eco-centric positions organised along an extreme/moderate continuum, as noted below:

- *Eco-holism.* The biotic community at large is the unit given most value. Human rights are not considerable, because all species should have the same rights. The land ethic of Aldo Leopold is taken literally to the point where human presence is really not required at all for the overall health and balance of the biotic community.
- *Eco-compatibilism.* Seen as the mid-point of eco-centrism, this position advocates more love and care for non-humans. Disruption to ecology is seen as unfortunate, but every effort is made to minimise these disturbances. As such, and in an attempt to be as free as possible from

conflict with the natural world, actions are deemed right if they promote harmony, integration and co-operation.

- *Eco-humanism.* Gives priority to human interests and argues that self-conscious creativity and awareness of the future are traits which provide the grounds for granting greater significance to the human species. This perspective allows our species to remain as humanists (placing the primary value on humans) but not to the extent that we would be anthropocentric in our actions. It is therefore a compromise between eco-holism and anthropocentrism.

Anthropocentric ethics, in the context of the environment, are premised on the belief that environmental policies need to be constructed exclusively on the basis of how they affect people. Ethicists would thus say that humans are the only beings or entities that are morally considerable. Everything else does not count. Norton (1993), however, argues that an ethic based on weak anthropocentrism should be favoured over other non-anthropocentric theories of environmental ethics. He argues that anthropocentrism should be differentiated on the basis of preferences. A felt preference is a need that can be satisfied by some specifiable experience of the individual. By contrast, a considered preference is any need that takes place only after careful deliberation with reference to the need and a rationally adopted world view; in other words, the need is examined in the context of broadly-based issues that are subject to theories and moral ideals. From this, Norton (1993: 288) defines two types of anthropocentrism:

- *Strong anthropocentrism* takes unquestioned felt preferences of human individuals as a determining value. There is no internal check on the felt preferences in this value system.
- *Weak anthropocentrism* recognises that felt preferences can be either rational or not. It provides a basis for criticism of value systems that are purely exploitative in nature.

Weak anthropocentrism provides the basis from which to formulate different types of values that might offer alternative ways to criticise preferences that are exploitative in nature. Norton favours weak anthropocentrism over eco-centric theories because it does not get caught up in the debate on intrinsic values, which he feels has constrained these other approaches.

It is also important to recognise that environmental ethics is different from the other forms of ethics because of the centrality of the natural world, representing a major paradigmatic shift in moral philosophy (Callicott, 1984). In other realms (e.g. business ethics) people sit at the centre of the equation. While the focus of these other disciplinary perspectives is human–human, there is the recognition that these interactions unfold in broader environments. So the challenge that exists in environmentalism lies in the types of values that we need to embrace if we are to contribute to a larger whole. Coles (1993) says that the reasons for advocating new values are based on instrumental reason, meaning that values are ultimately grounded in the self (the self in individual and social contexts). If we place ourselves at the epicenter of decision-making, or as the locus of concern, there can be little we can do to actualise an ethic of care for the larger whole. Everything is connected and this, today, more than at any other time in our history, is glaringly apparent.

Moral standing

Williams (1993b) observed that efforts to apply ethics (e.g. codes of ethics) in and for tourism represent the formal acknowledgment that the industry has impacts. And although we have known this for quite some time, the development of codes places a great deal more reinforcement into the need for positive change. We might also say that a code of ethics provides tangible evidence that other beings and physical entities have moral standing.

In his work *Respect for Nature*, Taylor (1936: 16–17) writes that, 'all moral agents are moral subjects, but not all moral subjects are moral agents'. Moral agents include beings (e.g. people) that have the ability to treat others rightly or wrongly. These individuals are said to have duties and responsibilities towards others. By contrast, a moral subject is someone or something that can be treated rightly or wrongly by agents. This latter group may or may not have rights. Moral agents, therefore, have the potential to act benevolently towards a moral subject (i.e. to better the conditions of that being's existence) or conversely to act malevolently towards the other and thus be detrimental to his or her well-being. Taylor further maintains that moral agents have the ability to make judgements on how various moral subjects ought to be treated, and that all moral subjects have a good of their own. This includes all living organisms, but not inanimate objects like stones, sand, water, ice and air. But although air, for example, is not considerable as a moral subject, moral agents still have duties and responsibilities towards it and to the organisms that rely on it for survival.

One of the most recognisable faces of the debate on moral standing is the animal liberation platform, which has been dominated by two main groups: utilitarian-oriented advocates, and rights-based advocates. The utilitarians (e.g. Peter Singer) argue that because animals are able to experience pain and pleasure, and since it is wrong to cause pain to another being on utilitarian grounds without justification, it is unacceptable to do so. Singer has coined the term 'speciesism', to identify the different values that people place on non-human plants or animals. He defines it as, 'a prejudice or attitude of bias towards the members of one's own species and against members of other species' (Singer, as cited in Gunn, 1984: 307). The speciesist therefore undervalues other species from the perspective of calculating how they may be able to increase the fitness of the human individual or human groups. In the same way sexism or racism de-values women or minorities; speciesism accords no intrinsic value to other beings. On the other hand, those (such as Tom Regan) who advocate the rights-based perspective representing the deontological theoretical perspective, suggest that, because animals have rights or ought to have rights, it is morally wrong to kill them, make them suffer, or interfere with their interests (such as the right to graze or suckle their young).

Elliot (1995) identifies three forms of ethics in terms of what is and is not morally considerable. These include human-centred ethics, animal-centred ethics, and life centred ethics, representing a move away from the individual human out to the broadest level. As regards the second level, animal ethics, although animals are morally considerable they may not be ranked equally. This means that humans range in their treatment of animals from a direct obligation to restrict the use and treatment of animals for the sake of the animals themselves (Benjamin, 1985). This tiering of animal standing has been addressed by Hughes (2001), who identifies three scales of moral considerability with regard to animals: environmental ethics, animal welfare and animal rights. The first, supported by the Aldo Leopold school of thought, is premised on the belief that the ecosystem as a whole is worthy of moral consideration, and not necessarily the individual parts. At this scale it would be morally acceptable to kill an animal if that action did not have a direct overall effect on the ecosystem. Animal welfare advocates argue that it is not acceptable to impose any form of threat or suffering to individual animals. However, while suffering is not acceptable in this context, it does not mean that animals deserve the same treatment as people under the same conditions, which implies that it is acceptable to use animals for human preferences and interests (Regan, 2004). The third scale, animal rights, takes the position that any act whatsoever which affects the welfare of an animal is morally wrong. So we should not use animals as a means to an end, as in traditional farming, as these practices could cause physical and/or psychological pain to the beast.

The application of calculative vs. meditative thinking introduced at the beginning of this book is applicable here through the example of the human use of whales. Birch (1993) says that saving whales is now a moral question (meditative) rather than an empirical one (calculative). There are no resources that whales give us today that cannot be made in some other way. As such, whales ought to have moral considerability, not because of some cost–benefit calculation based on use values, but rather on intrinsic grounds above all. It should also be noted that the way we use animals is a much different mind set than the way animals interact amongst themselves. Although it is often a difficult perspective to envision, nothing in nature counts morally (Rolston III, 2000). What this means is that animal interactions like predator–prey relationships exist without any rational thought as to whether such behaviour on the part of both parties is right or wrong. Taken one step further, the killing of one's own species is not morally wrong, because such behaviour is seen as a frequent fitness technique to preserve one's own good or the population in general. In this way it is not morally wrong for a male lion to kill the offspring of another male, as this behaviour provides a biological function within the population.

An application of the animal rights platform in tourism is observed in the work of Hughes (2001) in regards to the structural change that has taken place in the UK dolphin-viewing industry. Over the course of the past decade there has been a change from an industry based on viewing captive dolphins in dolphinaria, to one which is geared towards viewing dolphins in the wild only. In this case, the animal rights and welfare lobby against dolphinaria was so intense that it very quickly demonstrated that the industry which supported captive dolphins was morally unacceptable owing to the many effects that it had on individual animals and family groups. The lobby was able to show that moral considerability could be extended to individual animals, and not just to the species or to the level of an ecosystem.

We should extend moral standing not only to the plants, animals and physical and cultural resources of the planet for tourism and other purposes, but also to the space environment, as we are fast discovering. Williamson (2003) argues thatm if outer space is to be treated as an extension of our terrestrial business environment, than it should be subject to the same protective measures that we employ on Earth. This means that space should be afforded intrinsic value. Williamson suggests that a code of ethics is one of the most logical protractions of this value and devised with both philosophical and operational postulates. The space code might serve as a precursor to more formal legislation to be developed at a date sometime well into the future.

Conclusion

In this chapter we have explored the foundations of morality not only from an historical context, but also from an evolutionary one. While the latter explains why we are moral beings, the former describes the three main conceptual tools needed to understand the grounding for ethical codes and ethical behaviour in tourism. Virtue ethics, hedonism and utilitarianism are three approaches to seeking the moral end; religious principles, social contract ethics and Kantian intuition represent the main perspectives of seeking moral means, while seeking authenticity is the realm of existentialism. Important in framing these various theoretical perspectives was the discussion on moral development and values, especially the notion that values are not static, but can be held from a number of different levels. We also argued that theoretical ethics is one side of the coin shared by applied ethics. Both are essential in tourism for the purpose of better understanding the depth and diversity of tourism problems. One of the most recognisable forms of ethics in tourism – environmental ethics and moral standing – was used as a platform to better contextualise applied ethics. In light of the need for a change in mindset to foster acceptance of animals and of the broader environment in general, the question is, 'How do we go about fostering an ethical awareness that will translate into ethically sound behaviour?' One option is the formal documentation developed by the organisation to address ethics at many different levels. The following section provides the foundation from which to articulate more broadly- based values that have resonance beyond self-interest.

Part 4

Synthesis

Chapter 5

Codes-in-Action: Theory and Practice

Introduction

In this chapter we examine values – concepts that are desirable which motivate us to act in a particular manner. If values are deeply held by the individual and are shared in the context of the organisation in which that individual exists, then a certain level of congruence will prevent the violation of such standards. Key works in the business literature are scrutinised for the purpose of illustrating levels of commitment to values and codes of ethics, how this commitment corresponds to behaviour and decision-making, and the organisational and individual conditions that need to be firmly in place in order to engender consistency. The chapter ends with a look at the bigger picture of international codes of ethics and social contract theory, and more specifically at the UN World Tourism Organisation's Global Code of Ethics in Tourism.

Commitment to a Code: The Individual and the Organisation

Individual behaviour is a function of what we value. Our values push us – motivate us to do something. If they don't inspire action, then they are not values we actually hold. Among the many functions of codes of ethics, the primary purpose is to inspire ethical behaviour, and the primary criticism is that they are platitudes (Vinton, 1990; Wheeller, 1994). In other words, the individual must value the code if it is to serve its purpose. Herein lies the dilemma: how does the organisation instil this sense of value?

Levels of valuation

If we return to the theory proposed in Chapter 4, we can identify four levels of valuation. The lowest level is based upon feeling, the next on consensus, then outcome, and the highest on principle. Each ascending level inspires a heightened level of commitment (Lang, 1986) to the value, which in our case is the code of ethics. The application of this model to codes of ethics would look something like the following, in ascending order:

(4) I value the code because I like it – it makes me feel content/secure just knowing its there to guide and protect me (Adams *et al.*, 2001);

(3) I value the code because everyone else does – I am socialised or pressured to conform by the organisation;

(2) I value the code because I actually see the positive outcome of the code in terms of heightened awareness and ethical behaviour;

(1) I value the code because it coalesces with my personal values and those I genuinely believe everyone should follow.

Clearly levels 2 and 1 demonstrate the most profound degrees of commitment. Codes held at these levels will result consistently in ethical behaviour as a function of logic and faith/authenticity respectively. Codes held at levels 3 and 4 are at the whim of individual and group preference and as a result may be relatively unstable and situational. Let's explore these levels further.

Level 4 rationale: Preference

At the base level of valuation, we value because we like it. Little if any cognitive energy is exerted – we react – accept or reject. Often our choices at this level are based upon our sense of pleasure and pain – seeking and avoiding. Thus in terms of a code of ethics, I may follow it because I have a sense that if I do I will be praised – which is pleasurable. Or I may follow the code because if I don't I have a programmed sense that I will get into trouble – I will be punished. This level of valuation results in the weakest long-term commitment because an individual's feeling may change often and quickly. Clearly code adherence should be held at a higher level.

Level 3 rationale: Consensus

This level, as you will recall, concerns the will of the group. Its power lies in the individual's desire for acceptance and susceptibility to conform to external locus of control (i.e. peer pressure). I value because others do and I fear not being part of the herd. This is a potent tool to instil a level of commitment to any organisational policy not the least of which is the code of ethics. If an individual wishes to conform, and the research on this is voluminous – from Stanley Milgram to Laurence Kohlberg[1] – then to socialise members to adopt a code is a relatively easy process if the organisation has the power to exclude those who don't fit. As most of us seek external validation for our actions, then if we are provided with a code of ethics we have a relatively easy and effective tool to assist us in decisions. Thus our valuation of the code becomes not one of pain or pleasure but one of adherence to the perceived norm. This is workable as long as the group continues to garner 'pleasure' from it – once its utility for the group is on the wane (for whatever reason) – it will be discarded.

Level 2 rationale: Consequences

Logic enters hard and cold at the level of consequence. Things and concepts valued are known to have a role to play in creating positive outcome and this is why they are, in fact, valued. The individual does not *feel* this to be true, he or she *knows* it to be true as a function of science, empirical investigation, and/or logical deduction. A code is then valued at this level because the individual has enough evidence to suggest that following the code results in a positive outcome. The individual has tangible evidence that demonstrates that the code changes behaviour in a preferred manner. Should the code no longer be effective in modifying behaviour, it must be revisited. As long as it is effective and efficient, it will be held strongly.

Level 1 rationale: Principle

The most complex and perhaps misunderstood level of valuing is that based upon principle. This is principle not imposed by others, but principle that is reached through one's own experience, travels, education and – most importantly – through one's own will. Things and concepts valued at this level are inextricably linked with the individual's sense of himself/herself. Values at this level are held authentically and supersede logic, the collective will, and simple emotion. As a result commitment to what one values is imperative to the essential fabric of the individual's personhood. Thus a code of ethics is adopted at this level because the principles and rules it promotes coalesce with those of the individual. The code is not imposed externally; rather it matches what has already been established as morally worthy. Furthermore the code is not situational – it is universal and not subject to change.

From an organisational perspective, it would seem that the higher the level of commitment to the code of ethics, the better in terms of stability and consistency in ethical decision-making. Despite this intuitive logic, organisations tend to focus on the lower levels – reward and punishment (level 4) and/or peer pressure (level 3) – to instil a sense of code adherence. The emphasis on level 3 and level 4 rationale is most likely a function of the resources available to foster higher levels of commitment. It is a rather simple and short-term effective strategy to create a sense of fear and non-conformity in an individual (see note 1): *Follow the code or you're fired; follow the code if you wish to be part of our corporate 'family'*, etc. The resources required to demonstrate effectiveness of a code or to facilitate self-actualisation (or *eudaimonia* – see the brief discussion on Aristotle in Chapter 4) through the code are significant despite the fact that organisational efforts to do so may well result in higher levels of commitment to the code, and thus a greater likelihood for ethical behaviour.

Wood and Rimmer (2003) suggest that there are five aspects required to foster commitment at a higher level than fear and blind conformity:

(1) The code must be part of the day-to-day operations of the organisation. It must form part of the decision-making matrix. 'It should not be an ornament of the organisation, but the catalyst for an entire program

of business ethics within organisations that engenders better practices in the marketplace' (Wood & Rimmer, 2003: 191).

(2) The code must be developed from the input of as many stakeholders as possible. Employees need a sense of 'buy-in' in order for it to be internalised.

(3) The organisation needs a comprehensive method of education/socialisation about all aspects of the code for current employees and those new to the organisation.

(4) The code must be communicated both internally and externally to demonstrate the organisation's transparency and public commitment to the code.

(5) The organisation must be explicit about its own valuation of the code. What is its rationale? For example, if it is type 4, then the organisation values the code because it fears public backlash or seeks simple public approval; if it is type 3, then the organisation values the code because it is industry standard behaviour (everyone else is doing it); if it is type 2, then the organisation has explored the effect of the code on employee perception and behaviour; or if it is type 1, then the organisation values the code because it believes that by adhering to it, all members will be able to understand and enhance their own sense of ethical awareness and conduct.

Values, commitment and behaviour

The ultimate point of a code is to influence behaviour. Behaviour is a function of what one truly and deeply values. Here, we revisit the work of George England, who suggested that we have four levels of obligation to what we value (England *et al.*, 1974. We can *say* that we value something, yet fail to act on it (weak valuation – a platitude). We can value something in certain contexts and then abandon it in others (adopted valuation – see Derry, 1989). We can intend to value something yet allow other obstacles to prevent us from carrying through with our valuation. Finally, we can follow through with our intent to value regardless of the obstacles placed before us (core values). In this last case our behaviour is truly a manifestation of what we say and intend to value. Generally speaking, adopted valuation is the norm in organisational contexts as it is the essence of the bureaucratic system. Workers are encouraged to be value free or at least value neutral as they walk through the doors of the organisation and then adopt the values promoted by the organisation. Once the individual leaves work at the end of the day, he or she is then free to resume authentic values. While this may work as long as someone is willing to be a moral automaton, the ideal – the existential ideal – would be for the individual's core values to match the organisation's core values. This is not to suggest the 'borg' mentality of *Star Trek* fame or a 'cult' in which all individuals march to the same imposed beat, but rather that behaviour is guided by shared principles that have been internalised - independent of coercion.

In order to accomplish this aim, senior management needs to invest time and resources in a comprehensive educational system that has the code of ethics as a central feature of all operations. The code needs to be central to all hiring practices, promotions, merit awards and terminations.

Code content and ethical decision-making

Codes of ethics can be effective tools that impact upon actual behaviour, as noted in Chapter 3 and the section on, 'The Language of Codes', but it appears that much depends on the readiness of the reader and the nature of his or her valuation of the code. Therefore, in order to achieve maximum utility, it is imperative to design the code content and its form appropriately. The key to effectiveness is to know the audience and, as seen in the previous discussion, the audience is the individuals who have not yet formed core values relative to the workplace and seek guidance as well as those individuals whose values are loosely held and can be swayed with incentive (reward or punishment).

To appeal to this first group (i.e. those needing or seeking ethical guidance), the code must be written in a manner that explains fully why a preferred mode of behaviour is sanctioned. Unfortunately, far too many codes are written without rationale for expected behaviour (Malloy & Fennell, 1998a; Malloy *et al.*, 2002; Murphy, 1995; Weaver, 1995). As a consequence, those who are open and thirsty for explanation (rather than the recipients of a dictum) are left wanting. For example, in one study, Malloy and Fennell found that an overwhelming number of ethical codes in tourism were lacking any sort of explanation for the preferred behaviour:

> This general trend toward deontology suggests that codes of ethics, as they are currently designed, fail to provide the decision maker with the rationale for abiding by a particular code. The assumption, presumably, is that an explanation of consequence is unimportant to the tourist or organisational member. (Malloy & Fennell, 1998a: 457)

Malloy *et al.* (2002) argue that failure to provide rationale for expected professional behaviour results in the document being ineffective as an educational tool for the membership. Assuming of course that the intended purpose of the code is to educate and guide behaviour, the importance of clear rationale for statements in an ethical code seems obvious.

A number of studies have been conducted that have explored the implicit theoretical content of codes of ethics (e.g. Malloy *et al.*, 2002; Malloy *et al.*, 2006). This body of research has made use of content analysis methodology to determine the extent to which a code is based in teleological or deontological ethical theory. Statements that are teleological provide the reader with the consequence of action, whereas those that are deontological rely on the reader's sense of duty to follow – no justification is required other than one ought to. Here is an example taken from Malloy and Fennell:

> Maintaining and promoting natural, social and cultural diversity *is essential for long term sustainable tourism, and creates a resilient base for the industry.* (Malloy & Fennell, 1998a: 456)

as opposed to the following:

> Maintain and promote natural, social and cultural diversity.

The first statement is teleological in nature; the second is deontological. The first gives the reader a clear indication why he or she should be cognisant of diversity (*do this because it will result in ...*), the second is a dictum (*do it!*). To provide the rationale for required behaviour not only would appear, in the long run to be more effective in establishing a value set for the individual, but also represents a sense of respect, justice, and dignity according to Murphy (1995: 371), who suggests that '[b]y satisfying this demand [i.e. to provide a rationale for decision allocation] an organisation shows its willingness to treat people justly, and shows that its actions [and codes] are not merely arbitrary'. In other words, treating individuals with respect involves providing them with the rationale for the requirements for various standards of ethical behaviour.

Organisational conditions

The obvious organisational variable necessary for success is an environment of willingness and readiness for ethical conduct. Clearly, if the organisation's purpose in establishing a code lies predominantly in public relations, then it is doubtful that it will function to modify behaviour and decision-making among the employees. Employees easily sniff platitudes out. However, if ethical conduct is truly valued at the level of consequence and/or principle (Chapter 4), then the foundation is laid for potential success.

Part of an organisation's measure of commitment to ethical conduct and to a code is the extent to which senior administration publicly supports it and actually lives and works by it. Theoretical and empirical research suggests that the dominant factor in employees' ethical conduct is the behaviour of the senior administration (O'Boyle & Dawson, 1992: role-set configuration references). Thus the code manifested in the behaviour of leadership is critical to the members' adherence. The psychological rationale for this adherence can be found in the classic work of Milgram and Kohlberg, above, that is, the vast majority will follow external cues (i.e. leader behaviour, rules and regulations). Ford and Richardson (1994: 216) stated that, 'an individual's ethical beliefs and decision making behaviour will increasingly become congruent with top management's belief as defined through their words and actions as rewards provided for compliance congruency are increased'. Fritzsche (1997) concludes that:

> both peers and top management appear to influence significantly the ethical behavior of managers, with top management wielding the greatest influence. Ethical behaviour can be encouraged and unethical behaviour can be discouraged by the actions of top management and of peers. Unfortunately, the converse is also probably true. (Fritzsche, 1997: 66)

If this first condition (i.e. the public sanction by leaders) has been met, then developing the code is an obvious next step. More will be said about the content and form of code construction below, so let's assume we have organisational support and we have a code. The next step is the communication and operationalisation of the document. Codes that are platitudes are written, bronzed and slapped on the wall of the coffee room and perhaps tucked away somewhere on a web page should anyone wish to search for them. These codes will not impact on behaviour. Codes that will be functional are those that are communicated to all employees on a regular basis through written material (i.e. newsletters, performance criteria documents, on the back of identification tags, etc.), workshops, public speeches, hiring committees, employee orientations and so on. The bottom line is when everyone knows that there is a code and everyone is aware of its content, as well as the reward and reprimand for following or avoiding the code. Additionally, while codes of ethics have been shown to increase ethical conduct in the organisations, research has also shown that the process of developing the code itself is enough to increase ethical awareness of certain issues (Adams *et al.*, 2001).

Cohen (1998) suggests that the idea behind the creation of a code of ethics for the organisation lies in trust through ethical empowerment. Superiors are empowering subordinates with the authority to make ethical decisions. Trust is built not only from this top down approach but also through the willingness and ability of subordinates to prove that they are capable of exercising good judgement. This reciprocal arrangement provides a dynamic tension between all levels of the organisational hierarchy in an effort to build co-operation amongst all group members. The absence of continued acts of reciprocal exchange (see Chapter 4), based on the expected behaviours as outlined in a code of ethics, opens the door to the possibility of cheating – the failure to reciprocate – at many levels of the organisational hierarchy (Fennell, 2006a, 2006b; Plummer & Fennell, in press).

Knowing that a code exists and knowing its content is still not enough. The employee must be aware of how the code is put into daily action. Therefore the communication of the code must be focused not only on simple awareness, but also on implementation (see Chapter 3). For example, the code may be designed to be used as a decision screen through which the individual must assess the ethical capacity of various alternatives and be led to the ethical ideal. Employees must understand how this is done and see that it is a part of the 'way the organisation does its business' to the degree that it becomes habitual (e.g. Aristotle's notion of habitual virtue is that it becomes a lifestyle and not an occasional behaviour used when others are watching). For example, let's say that the organisation stands by three values X, Y and Z and develops its code based upon these three. When decisions are being made (i.e. decisions with ethical intensity such as policy rather than simple office choices), final selection of alternatives must satisfy the conditions or criteria of X, Y and Z – otherwise they fail the ethical test based upon the code.

All of this is of course contingent upon the employee being aware of the code, understanding its content, and accepting the direction the code gives toward ethical conduct. In the next section the individual variable is discussed.

Individual conditions

The individual decision maker has a set of core values (as does the organisation) that form the impetus for action. Recall that a value is a 'concept of the desirable with a motivating force' (Hodgkinson, 1996: 110) – our actions are the result of what we truly value. These core values are essential to the authentic self – they won't be violated. The ideal scenario is when individual core values align with organisational core values as represented in the code of ethics. When this occurs, there is no conflict between expected and actual behaviour. However, this may work in reverse when the individual's core is in direct conflict with the organisation's core (e.g. sustainable tourism vs. profit for shareholders). The third scenario occurs when there is an absence of core values relative to the workplace (i.e. someone whose work moral development is relatively immature); the fourth occurs when intended individual values conflict with the organisation's core values. These scenarios can be viewed in Table 5.1.

In these four scenarios, it is interesting to note that in only the third and fourth cases is a code of ethics of potential influence. In scenario 1, there is no need for a code, as the individual will already display preferred behaviour with or without a code. In scenario 2, the individual's core values or those held at the principled level, will prevent him or her from adopting a conflicting set of organisational values regardless of what the punitive outcome may be. In the third scenario a code is of practical use as it can provide the information about ethical conduct that the decision-maker lacks. And finally in scenario 4, the code provides guidance and incentive

Table 5.1 Code effectiveness and preferred behaviour

Value-based scenarios*	Code of ethics is effective	Preferred organisational behaviour manifested
1. Individual core values are congruent with organisational core values.	No. The individual will act in the preferred manner regardless of the existence of the code.	Yes
2. Individual core values are in conflict with organisational core values.	No. The individual will ignore the code.	No
3. Individual values as they relate to the organisation are weakly held or are adopted (i.e. they are situationally held).	Yes. The individual is seeking guidance to form values and the code provides this resource.	Yes
4. Individual values are intended yet in conflict with organisational core values (i.e. the decision-maker intends to act on the value but, because of other factors, may not.	Yes. If there is sufficient incentive to overrule individual intended values.	Yes

*The assumption here is that the organisation is aware of its own core values and has expressed them clearly in its code of ethics.

for the individual to overlook his or her intended values and adopt the organisational values (see Lere & Gaumnitz, 2003).

Now let's go back to our decision maker in scenario 3. This individual is ready and willing to be guided towards ethical behaviour because he or she lacks a commitment to a work-related core value due perhaps to inexperience (task-relevant maturity). Is it not reasonable to assume that the more information the organisation provides this individual, the more apt he or she is to implement this information in organisational behaviour? Further, should not the content of the code address issues of moral intensity that are outside the range of the decision-maker's core values? The point being made here is that statements in the code that are perceived to be societal 'givens' do not impact behaviour as they are already ingrained in the morally healthy person. If the intent of a code is to impact behaviour, then it must provide information that is unknown or at least ambiguously known by the individual, and therefore the code makes the preferred behaviour unambiguous. For example, let's say Pat has recently been hired by an ecotourism organisation having recently graduated from a local university's recreation programme. Let's also suppose that while Pat did take a course in tourism, it involved only one lecture in ecotourism. Pat is generally a nice person with strong family and religious values, however, other than working summer sports camps, she has never held a full-time position (i.e. her task-relevant moral maturity is relatively low). Unless Pat is given a code of ethics that clarifies the unknown or the ambiguous, then she will be forced to seek guidance informally from other sources (e.g. family and friends) or make uninformed choices based on unexamined values. If, on the other hand, a code is provided that avoids vague platitudes and gives her a clear rationale for adherence, then it will effectively have made an impact on Pat's decision-making behaviour.

The individual in scenario 4 is different, as he or she is in value conflict. However, the conflict is between individual intended values and organisational core values, and thus incentive is required to overcome intended values. In this case it is vital that the code has some teeth. It must have the power to reward and to punish, and this incentive must be meaningful to the individual. In other words, employment or professional membership must mean more (possibly a core value for the individual) than the intended value currently in conflict with the organisation. Further, the threat of loss of employment is a significant incentive if and only if there is an opportunity for comparable re-employment elsewhere. The incentive must be an explicit part of the code, of hiring and firing practices as well as policies surrounding promotion and awards of merit. As a result, if an individual in scenario 4 is aware of the consequences of code adherence and neglect, then the calculus is simple.

To conclude, we provide the following recommendations to organisational leaders who are developing or revamping their ethical code:

(1) A willingness and readiness for an ethical organisation must exist.
(2) Senior leadership must be willing to show public support for an ethical climate and must be capable of actually demonstrating this in their day-to-day decision-making.
(3) The code of ethics must be consistent with senior leadership behaviour.
(4) The code must be widely communicated through a variety of media (including those that are interactive).
(5) The communication of the code must result in awareness of the code and its content.
(6) The socialisation of the code must result in the members being able to implement it in their daily decision-making practices.
(7) The code should be geared to those organisational members who lack task-relevant moral maturity and require guidance.
(8) For those members whose values may not link with those of the organisation, the code should provide strong incentive for adherence.
(9) The code should be written in such as way that it provides rationale for the expected behaviour in order for members to fully understand why the code is necessary, to demonstrate that ethical statements are not

arbitrary, and to show that the organisation respects the members enough to provide full disclosure.

International Codes and Integrative Social Contract Theory

The mere thought of establishing an international code of ethics in any sector is daunting. In the realm of tourism, which by definition involves explicit desire for experiences with other religions, cultures and social systems, this task becomes exceptionally intimidating as a function of the complex needs and rights of the many stakeholders involved. This problem is particularly acute in a global society that is increasingly more tolerant of diversity and cultural relativism. Is it possible, regardless of where we are located geographically, culturally, religiously or philosophically, that we could agree to conduct our business by a common set of ethical principles? In this chapter we explore this possibility through the discussion and application of social contract theory.

Social contract theory has its roots in Plato's *Republic* and extends through to the contemporary work of John Rawls (1971). Included in this long history are Thomas Hobbes (1651/1957) and Jean-Jacque Rousseau (1762/1979). Hobbes argued that the sovereign (king or other forms of government including democracy) represents the people and the laws handed down by this authority are ultimately in everyone's best interest. Further, he suggests that without the structure that laws provide, chaos and war will be the norm and the result will be 'no Arts; no Letters; no Society; and which is worst of all, continuall feare, and danger of violent death; And the life of man, solitary, poore, nasty, brutish, and short'(Hobbes, 1651/1957: 108).

Rousseau (1762/1979) developed this notion further to include the hedonistic altruism of choosing to live under self-imposed laws. He argued that forfeiting certain liberties in the name of a safe and structured society demonstrates the nobility of humanity and the capacity of individuals to freely choose to abide by external laws. He states

> Although in civil society man surrenders some of the advantages that belong to a state of nature [i.e. a state of complete individual freedom], he gains in return greater ones ... Man acquires with civil society, moral freedom, which alone makes man the master of himself; for to be governed by appetite alone is slavery, while obedience to a law one prescribes to oneself is freedom. (Rousseau, 1762/1979: 65)

In other words, we agree to abide by rules that in the long run are mutually beneficial to all members of society.

John Rawls (1971) approached the social contract and social justice from the perspective of obtaining the maximum justice to the least advantaged.

He proposed that in the creation of the ideal society, we conduct a 'thought experiment' in which we place ourselves behind a 'veil of ignorance' regarding our future role (i.e. advantaged/disadvantaged, rich/poor, educated/uneducated, etc.). Assuming that we may personally end up in the disadvantaged position in this new society, Rawls predicted that we would naturally choose principles that will provide the best possible outcome for those in the worst possible situation. Thus a code of ethics designed from a Rawlsian perspective would ensure that the least advantaged stakeholder in the organisation's sphere of influence was protected (e.g. the junior level employee in a hotel located in a tourist destination of a developing country).

These approaches to social contract ethics are deeply theoretical (as are the deontological and teleological theories of Kant and Mill, respectively) and cause a significant amount of cognitive stress when attempts are made to use them in practical contexts. One relatively recent attempt to overcome this intellectually mind-numbing task has been proposed by professors Donaldson and Dunfee (1994) who developed a contemporary formulation of the social contract approach to global organisational ethics. Their Integrative Social Contract Theory (ISCT) consists of macro and micro social contracts that include universal, global and community norms which, when addressed under the assumption of bounded moral rationality (i.e. in practice, we can't always know all the moral answers or variables) can result in unified sense of moral propriety regardless of the particular culture or societal context in which we find ourselves.

Donaldson and Dunfee (1994: 260) pose the following question that they argue would establish the macro social contract: 'What general principles, if any, would contractors who are aware of the strongly bounded nature of moral rationality in economic affairs choose to govern economic morality?' They suggest that four general principles would emerge in the context of economic morality:

(1) Local economic communities may specify ethical norms for their members through micro social contracts.
(2) Norm-specifying micro social contracts must be grounded in informed consent buttressed by a right of exit.
(3) In order to be obligatory, a micro social contract norm must be compatible with hypernorms.
(4) In case of conflicts among norms that satisfy principles 1 to 3, priority must be established through the application of rules consistent with the spirit and letter of the macro social contract.

Let's discuss each of these four principles as they might apply to the tourism context.

The first principle appeals to the notion of moral free space to operate in the unique context of industry norms and in the particular cultural, social, religious and philosophical environment in which the tourist organisation is situated. Each industry has its own particular culture and values, which may or may not link with other industries or even with the broader social context. This is acutely true in the world of sport in which physical violence is not only condoned but encouraged (e.g. tackling in rugby or punching in boxing). These behaviours could not take place outside the athletic arena. In the same manner some industry practices seem questionable to outside observers, yet are completely acceptable within the confines of the economic sphere of business. The vendor in Bangkok's night market does not expect the tourist to pay the listed price for any item. The expectation is to barter. However, when the same individual orders a coffee at Starbuck's in Tokyo, there is an expectation that the list price is the final price – there is no negotiation. As long as the individual is aware, explicitly, of the expecta-tion of the moral variation in industry or cultural practice (i.e. the microsocial contract), then he or she is prepared to do business informed transactions. In the same manner, this is true of the person who steps into a boxing ring, prepared to be hit. [If this first principle is causing you some anxiety due to its moral relativism, relief lies ahead in principle 3.]

The second principle deals with the freedom and awareness of each party to exit from the relationship if these principles are violated. Donaldson and Dunfee (1994: 262) state, 'consent to the microsocial contract is binding only when it is informed'. Thus, if an individual enters into a relationship in which key components of the micro social contract are hidden, then he or she has the right to exit from the agreement. This problem exists in tourism where we often fail to know the rules of exchange across cultures. Tourists, for example, either accept at face value the rules of exchange without truly knowing, and risk being cheated – in the context of reciprocal altruism – or transfer accepted rules of exchange from their home country in socio-economic transactions, leading to the potential for a break-down in co-operation.

The third principle establishes the moral limits regarding the accept-ability of the micro social contracts. In other words, economic or cultural relativism can only go so far and these hypernorms or metavalues provide the boundaries. Donaldson and Dunfee (1994: 265) define hypernorms as, 'principles so fundamental to human existence that they serve as a guide in evaluating lower level moral norms ... we would expect them to be reflected in a convergence of religious, philosophical, and cultural beliefs'. They go on to describe their perception of the most basic hypernorms as being the following:

> Core human rights, including those of personal freedom, physical security and well-being, political participation, informed consent, the

ownership of property, the right to subsistence; and the obligation to respect the dignity of each human person. (Dunfee (1994: 267)

If we, for argument's sake, accept this portrayal of moral universality, then if any local practice in tourism contravenes any part of these two hypernorms, the individual has the right and perhaps the obligation to withdraw from the agreement/partnership. For example, suppose you were interested in establishing a joint venture with a tourism organisation in country X. You travel there to finalise an agreement to promote the location and its accommodations and once you arrive you realise that the hotel is catering to clientele interested in prostitution. Clearly contravening the hypernorm of, 'respecting the dignity of each human person', you return to your home country and cancel the memorandum of agreement.

Finally, the fourth principle concerns the participants' need to be aware of the process to follow in order to arbitrate and resolve conflicts among principles 1 to 3. Donaldson and Dunfee (1994: 269–270) suggest the following:

(1) Transactions solely within a single community, which do not have significant adverse effects on other humans or communities, should be governed by the host community's norms.
(2) Community norms indicating a preference for the way in which conflict-of-norms situations should be resolved, so long as they do not have significant adverse effects on other humans or communities.
(3) The more extensive or more global the community that is the source of the norm, the greater the priority which should be given to the norm.
(4) Norms essential to the maintenance of economic environment in which the transaction occurs should have priority over norms potentially damaging to that environment.
(5) Where multiple conflicting norms are involved, patterns of consistency among the alternative norms provide a basis for prioritisation.
(6) Well-defined norms should ordinarily have priority over more general, less precise norms.

To summarise, the ISCT provides four general principles to guide the moral activity of individuals and organisations who are entering into joint ventures from disparate cultural, religious, social and philosophical contexts. While joint ventures of this nature generally tend to focus upon the economic obligations of just partnerships (see the comments on calculative thinking in the Preface), they rarely, if ever, discuss the moral obligations of their endeavours (i.e. meditative thinking). The ISCT raises the participants' awareness of the complexity of international agreements (i.e. beyond the basic economics of the deal) and in turn may enhance the degree of trust between them. At this point, it may be worthwhile to test the logic of the Integrative Social Contract Theory on a current effort to guide global tourism behaviour, namely, the Code of Ethics of the United Nations World Tourist Organisation (UNWTO) – set out in Appendix 2. But first we need some background.

WTO's Global Code of Ethics for Tourism

D'Sa (1999) writes that the UNWTO was developed in 1975 with a mission to, 'develop tourism as a significant means of fostering international peace and understanding, economic development and international trade'. However, D'Sa observes that the chief goal of the UNWTO has been to promote tourism for profit and that there is little evidence that the organisation is concerned with values such as 'peace' and 'understanding'. For example, while the Manila Declaration of 1980 sought to re-think the underlying nature of tourism profit in the face of cultural and ecological dislocation, the first UNWTO-sponsored conference for government and industry elites was also in Manila at this time but with the mandate of increasing tourism receipts.

In 1999, the UNWTO moved to better address issues of peace and understanding through the development of a global code of ethics for tourism (see Appendix 2), as one of many new initiatives. Over a two-year period, this organisation requested input from all the various sectors of the tourism industry, and this culminated in the approval of a document at the 13th session of the General Assembly at Santiago, Chile, in 1999. In July of 2001, the United Nations Economic and Social Council (ECOSOC) adopted a draft resolution of the Code and called on the UN General Assembly to recognise it. The official recognition by the UN General Assembly of the Global Code of Ethics for Tourism came on 21 December 2001, through its resolution A/RES/56/212 (http://www.unwto.org/code_ethics/pdf/UN res.56.pdf; accessed 04.12.06) by which it further encouraged the UNWTO to promote an effective follow-up of the code. The Secretary General of the World Tourism Organisation, Francesco Frangialli, issued the following statement in support of the code:

> The Global Code of Ethics for Tourism sets a frame of reference for the responsible and sustainable development of world tourism. It draws inspiration from many similar declarations and industry codes that have come before and it adds new thinking that reflects our changing society at the beginning of the 21st century.

> With international tourism forecast to nearly triple in volume over the next 20 years, members of the World Tourism Organisation believe that the Global Code of Ethics for Tourism is needed to help minimise the negative impacts of tourism on the environment and on cultural heritage

while maximising the benefits for residents of tourism destinations. (http://www.tourismpartners.org/globalcode background.html; accessed 12.12.06)

As illustrated in Figure 5.1, the code includes 10 articles built around a number of broad themes or hypernorms (see Donaldson & Dunfee, 1994), including respect, fulfilment, sustainable development, cultural heritage, economic well-being, tourism development, rights of tourists, liberty of tourist movement, rights of workers in tourism and the implementation of the principles. The ten articles outlined in the WTO provide the basis for a macro contract which more or less covers each of the four 'rules of engagement' from the ITSC (see above). Finally, though the micro-contract is not detailed in the WTO's code, there is a general indication of the particular stakeholders to which the code is directed.

The implementation of any one code at the global level will obviously be subject to a great deal of scrutiny. In the context of human resource development, Russ-Eft and Hatcher (2003) argue that there are essentially three major issues that need to be addressed in the debate over the merits of a global code of ethics. These are: (1) the questionable status of 'social responsibility' as a main principle (i.e. hypernorm) for the development of a code of ethics, (2) the predominance of developed nations in various codes of ethics, and (3) the role of differing cultural values in such a code. Code development, Russ-Eft and Hatcher argue, should take place only as a result of agreement over shared norms or hypernorms that in turn might be realised only in the context of a 'stabilised world'. Hofstede's (2001) work is indeed salient in this regard with respect to recognised differences in the developed and lesser developed countries based of power distance, uncertainty avoidance, individualism and collectivism, masculinity and femininity, and long-term versus short-term orientation. Low power distance cultures hold that, 'all should have equal rights'. Conversely, high power distance cultures would assert that, 'power holders are entitled to privileges'. Therefore, the manner in which these two cultures interpret respect for rights and dignity would be quite different, making the inclusion of such a statement in a global code of ethics (or its enforcement if it did exist) problematic.

These issues have been recognised by D'Sa (1999), who feels that a universal global code of ethics is inappropriate because of the massive impasse between market values (e.g. competition, profits, survival of the fittest, individualism) and family and community values, which focus on sharing of wealth, co-operation, support for the weakest, spirituality and harmony with nature. A code of ethics cannot hope to bridge this gap, because the problem is lies more deeply in a bed of profit that has no room for social costs. In addition D'Sa notes that the UNWTO is virtually

Hypernorms

['Hypernorms' are foundational principles to be followed in any partnership regardless of culture, religion, or organisational typology.]

UNWTO: '... to promote responsible, sustainable and accessible tourism in the framework of the right of all persons to use their free time for leisure pursuits or travel with respect for the choices of society of all peoples...the world has much to gain by operating in an environment that favours the market economy, private enterprise and free trade...'

Macro social contract

[This contract provides the basis for the unique conditions of micro contracts established between partners at the community level (i.e. ethnic, professional, economic, government, non-profit, for-profit partnerships)].

Article 1 – Tourism's contribution to mutual understanding and respect between peoples and societies;

Article 2 – Tourism is a vehicle for individual and collective fulfilment;

Article 3 – Tourism is a factor of sustainable development;

Article 4 – Tourism, a user of the cultural heritage of mankind and a contributor to its enhancement;

Article 5 – Tourism, a beneficial activity for host countries and communities;

Article 6 – Obligations of stakeholders in tourism development:

Article 7 – Right to tourism;

Article 8 – Liberty of tourist movement;

Article 9 – Rights of the workers and entrepreneurs in the tourism industry; and

Article 10 – Implementation of the principles of the Global Code of Ethics for Tourism (including clause #3 that states ' ... any disputes concerning the application or interpretation of the Global Code of Ethics for Tourism for conciliation to an impartial third body known as the World Committee on Tourism Ethics').

Micro social contract

[Inter-organisational partnerships fall into the realm of micro social contracts in which one 'community' enters into a partnership with another 'community'. Though both are guided by their unique community norms (i.e. micro social contracts), they are also obliged to respect the 'hypernorms' and the conditions set by the macro contract]

Stakeholders:

(1) national, regional and local administrations, enterprises, business associations;

(2) workers in the sector;

(3) non-governmental organisations and bodies of all kinds belonging to the tourism industry, as well as host communities;

(4) the media; and

(5) tourists themselves.

Figure 5.1 ISCT and the UNWTO Code of Ethics

unknown to small local communities (the places that need assistance because there is no dialogue with them), but rather only with the local elite, who have the largest stake in tourism enterprises. The importance of community values is reinforced by Ryan (2002), who identifies gaps in Article 6 on the obligations of stakeholders in tourism development. Missing is any mention of the local community as a stakeholder and tourists themselves. Fleckenstein and Huebsch (1999) have also directed criticism at the document by who identify five main issues in international tourism that will be problematic for any code of ethics. These include bribes, political issues, government intervention, customs clearance, the questionable transfer of funds and cultural and business practice differences.[2]

The difficulty in developing and implementing a meaningful global code (as opposed to a platitudinous one) should come as no surprise. Agreeing on a set of hypernorms is certainly logical as far as process goes, and conceptually correct as far as theory goes; however, making assumptions about global practice may be much more complex than anticipated. As D'Sa (1999) has pointed out, implicit ontological assumptions (such as the profit motive) may be unquestioned truisms for some, yet antithetical to global behaviour to others. This is certainly not to say that a global code of ethics for tourism is impossible. Rather, we would argue that making hypernorms universal is a critical first step that drives the remainder of the ethical decision-making process and their selection cannot be taken lightly – false assumptions will always sink an argument. Donaldson and Dunfee's (1994) Integrative Social Contract Theory serves as an excellent model with which to ground the UNWTO code of ethics in ensuring that both macro and micro social contracts are represented consistently in its application.

Conclusion

Critics (see Wheeller, 1994) suggest that codes of ethics are merely platitudinous statements that have no real impact. In this chapter we have attempted to conceptualise codes from the perspective of values. In doing so, we hope to have made a firm connection between the importance of the code of ethics not just as an organisational expression of ethics, but also from the perspective of commitment, which must exist from the broadest to the lowest levels within the organisation. We can value codes of ethics because we are told to (i.e. to avoid punishment and pain), or we can value them based on principle (i.e. values held authentically and universally). Furthermore, in order for codes of ethics to be effective, agents must be receptive to the code in achieving maximum utility. Knowing the audience is of obvious importance, as is the empowerment and authority to make ethical decisions. Another factor in eliciting receptivity is how codes are structured. In this context, research suggests that codes, although deontological by nature, should have a consequential aspect tied to them in order to give the reader a clear indication of why they should be followed. We used the UNWTO Global Code of Ethics as an example of how to contextualise Donaldson and Dunfee's contemporary formulation of the social contract approach to global organisational ethics through their Integrative Social Contract Theory (ISCT). This model consists of macro and micro social contracts that include universal, global and community norms which, when addressed under the assumption of bounded moral rationality (i.e. in practice, we can't always know all the moral answers or variables), can result in a unified sense of moral propriety regardless of the particular culture or societal context in which we find ourselves.

Notes

1. Milgram is the author of the infamous experiments (Milgram, 1974), in which students were asked to administer electrical shocks to a subject when errors were made in various memory tests. The researchers found that two thirds of the students were willing to administer lethal levels of punishment when asked to do so by an authority figure – the students were unaware until after the protocol was complete that the subject was an actor and no harm was actually done. Laurence Kohlberg (1969) and a generation of researchers using his work have found that the vast majority of individuals seek external cues from significant others or from society at large to arrive at their own ethical choices.
2. See Mamic (2004) for a discussion of global standards and the inclusion of prohibitions against forced labour and child labour, freedom to bargain collectively, support for non-discrimination and equal remuneration, as well as health and safety, minimum wages, job security, hours and overtime, benefits, training, adherence to labour laws, and family leave, environmental stewardship, disclosure of information, competition, taxation, bribery and corruption, science and technology, and consumer protection.

Chapter 6

Conclusion

This book emerged in response to what appears to be increasing acceptance and utilisation of codes of ethics in the tourism industry. This acceptance has taken place based on sustained efforts to generate sustainable and ethical approaches to tourism development through conferences (Manila in 1980, AIEST in 1992 and Rios in 1992), academic publications (Krohn *et al.*, 1991; Lea, 1993), tourism operator co-operative efforts, and countless community initiatives. The level of interest in tourism codes of ethics has evolved steadily, yet somewhat cautiously, over the past 15 years, for example, through comprehensive works by the UNEP (1995) and Mason and Mowforth (1995), and through empirically-based works that attempt to understand the place of codes in tourism from a theoretical perspective (Malloy & Fennell, 1998). One of the most enduring trends in studies on tourism codes of ethics is the link to sustainability, noted quite effectively in the work of Johnston and Twynam (2001), who suggest that the principle-based approach to sustainability (including codes of ethics) will continue to garner interest and support the world over. Although inroads have been made, what is strikingly evident is that the effort put into understanding codes of ethics in tourism is rather insignificant when compared with what is taking place in business in general, both from practical and research viewpoints, where there has been a flurry of activity over the past two decades.

As such, codes of ethics are now part of the business firmament, where organisational accountability is a 'front page' issue in large part due to a number of recent major scandals, most notably involving Enron and Worldcom at the turn of the century. In response, the US Sarbanes-Oxley Act and the Securities and Exchange Commission Rule of October 22, 2002, require companies to disclose details around the implementation of a code of ethics. While it is not mandatory that companies adopt a code of ethics, theorists argue that it is expected that the market would react strongly and adversely to the absence of such a code (Grunfeld, 2002; Brincat & Wike, 2000). This essentially compels a company to adopt a code of ethics in the interests of financial viability and trust. In addition, the proposed rules brought forward by the SEC and the Sarbanes-Oxley Act include, among other stipulations:

(1) bringing conflicts of interest to the attention of a company compliance officer;

(2) a system of reporting violations of the code of ethics to compliance officers; and

(3) a mechanism for enforcing codes of ethics within the company, including sanctions for violation.

Academe has kept pace with the momentum behind codes of ethics in business, where there has been a profusion of academic work in recent books (e.g. Carroll & Buchholtz, 2000) and journals such as the *Journal of Business Ethics* (see Beversluis, 1987; Cassell *et al.*, 1997). At the heart of this body of research is the investigation of ways that businesses might be more ethical. For example, Swenson (2000) writes that the organisation should adhere to the following four steps in efforts to be more socially responsible:

(1) the elevation of corporate ethics awareness through training and codes of ethics;

(2) aggressiveness directed towards the incorporation of ethics into university curricula, especially in business schools;

(3) the active encouragement of organisations to develop and apply broad-based core value systems to screen for unethical behaviour; and

(4) hold employees accountable for violating the corporate codes of ethics.

Yet in a sphere of life (business) that is so strongly guided by competition and the will to achieve at any cost, and influenced by irresponsibility and convenience, it is no wonder that profit takes precedence over social and ecological factors (see Tinkler, 2005).

The importance of stimulating an ethical culture in university curricula, as noted above, has been addressed by Vallen and Cosado (2000), who support the belief that all students in hospitality programmes should be required to study ethics as part of the curriculum. The argument is that if ethical principles are internalised during the time of a student's formal education, they will spill over into their managerial practices and procedures. This was confirmed through Vallen and Cosado's analysis of managers of lodging properties in the US, who were asked to rank perceptions of ethical issues in the industry. Managers were consistent in their belief that employees routinely lie, deceive, and regularly seek personal over organisational benefits. The findings of such studies make it easy to recommend the same emphasis on ethics for students in tourism studies, who regularly learn about ethical dilemmas through the voluminous work available on social, economic, and ecological impacts. Ethics provides the opportunity to recast these dilemmas in a more proactive fashion (Fennell, 2006a). (See Box 6.1; Hay & Foley, 1998; Tribe, 2002; Klonoski, 2003, and O'Halloran, 1991, for more information on teaching ethics in tourism and hospitality.)

What has emerged quite clearly in this work is that our behaviour, as

Box 6.1 Teaching codes of ethics: Developing case studies

In our teaching experience, one of the most effective ways of demonstrating the relevance of theory to practice is through the use of case studies. We take this one step further by suggesting that students not only evaluate and apply theory and pragmatism to the case but also develop the cases themselves. In this way students become fully engaged in the act of putting theory into practice and evaluating its effectiveness. In the following section we provide a brief outline of how an instructor might develop a major project for groups of students studying codes of ethics in tourism.

Philosophy. The first class dealing with codes of ethics could focus on the philosophical orientation of the organisation – what does the organisation stand for? In this lecture the instructor may wish to discuss the constellation of purposes that tourism organisations have – from raw capitalism to religious enlightenment. Knowing why the organisation exists is critical to developing a code of ethics that is congruent with the overriding purpose. Let's say, for argument's sake, that an organisation proposes that it is in the ecotourism paradigm philosophically – how ridiculous for the code of ethics to remain silent on issues related to the environment. As a class assignment, the students (in groups) could develop hypothetical organisations representing the broadest array and have them develop statements of organisational philosophy. These statements and case studies can then be used in subsequent lectures dealing with specific code development.

Organisational dynamics. Knowing what an organisation stands for is the first step towards developing a code of ethics; the next step is to understand the organisational structure and culture. Organisations that are highly bureaucratic and centralised will require formal codes that will differ markedly from those that are less officious and laissez-faire. Further, organisations that are culturally market-driven will be distinguished from non-profit tourism organisations in the manner in which they *'do things around here'*. Therefore the next step for the students is to further develop their hypothetical organisations' culture to include statements of belief, what their organisation values, what behaviours are expected, etc. A suggested reading for this exercise is 'Ecotourism & ethics: Moral development and organisational culture' (Malloy & Fennell, 1998).

Ethics. Now that the students have a sense of their organisational purpose and culture, they can begin to develop codes of ethics that are congruent with implicit and explicit philosophy. As discussed in Chapter 4, there are at least three options when developing an ethical rationale for codes: deontology, teleology and existentialism – see also 'Ethics and ecotourism: A comprehensive ethical model (Fennell & Malloy, 1995). Lectures and discussions of the merits and disadvantages of each should occur at an early point in the semester to ensure that students have a sound theoretical basis and the necessary tools to use in debates and discussion throughout the course.

A veil of ignorance. One interesting approach to help students understand how codes might be developed is to employ the 'thought experiment' used by John Rawls (1971). Rawls (see Chapter 5) suggests that when we are trying to create the ideal social contract, we imagine that we place ourselves behind a veil of ignorance with regard to our particular role in an ideal society or, in our case, an ideal (or terrible) tourist location or organisation. So, in this thought experiment, we imagine that we could be employed in a tourist organisation as the CEO or as part of an oppressed housekeeping staff. Or, we also assume that we might be tourists with money to spare or a student staying in a flea-infested youth hostel or a child forced to sell trinkets on the beach to tourists. Based on our 'ignorance', what rules or codes of ethics would we want to see if we could be thrown into any one of these scenarios? Rawls suggests that we usually make our decisions based upon the belief that we would be in the least preferred position and then create codes that would allow for the best possible circumstance for the least empowered.

Once this 'veil of ignorance' is explained to the class, the instructor could challenge the students with the task of developing a code of ethics that would best serve the least empowered in their particular tourism organisation (i.e. their hypothetical case study). Students would develop these codes with a keen awareness of the implicit ethical theory upon which each statement is based.

Linguistic rationale. When students have developed a code of ethics that is intentionally based in ethical theory and satisfies the Rawlsian criteria, it is time to re-evaluate the grammatical form of these statements to ensure that the linguistic style fits the intent of the code, of the culture, of the organisational philosophy (see Chapter 3).

Hierarchy. It can be a very interesting exercise to have students attempt to form a hierarchy among code statements or groupings of code statements. To do this we recommend overview and discussion focusing on the value paradigm proposed by Christopher Hodgkinson (Chapters 1 and 5). See also the Canadian Psychological Association's Code of Ethics (http://www.cpa.ca/; accessed 15.12.06) and Malloy & Hadjistavropoulos (1998).

Linkage with decision-making processes and organisational behaviour (praxis). A penultimate exercise and test of relevance for the students' code is to determine how it will be employed in the maintenance and/or enhancement of ethical decision-making and behaviour in general in process of the organisation. This would, of course, include how it will be evaluated and monitored (Chapter 5).

The students then submit this group project to the instructor for initial evaluation. It should include at least the following:

(1) introductory rationale of the organisation's existence;
(2) a description of the nature of the organisation:
 (a) structure;
 (b) culture;
(3) ethical statements:
 (a) based upon ethical theory;
 (b) written with explicit linguistic intent;
(4) description, intent, and implication for the code's hierarchy;
(5) description of how the code will be put into daily practice by the organisation;
(6) conclusion.

The capstone exercise occurs once the instructor has provided the groups with feedback, and the documents are re-distributed randomly to each group with a hypothetical dilemma attached. In other words, each group is given someone else's code and asked to apply a dilemma to it. For example, a housekeeper must be fired for stealing jewellery from a guest's room or a manager has 'fudged' an expense claim, etc. This final task is to see if the code provides decision-makers with enough guidance to resolve the dilemma. If the code does not, what needs to be included in order to make the code more effective? This work is best presented orally as well as in written form as the final project for this course or this section of a course.

individuals and as organisations, is a function of what we value (i.e. values inspire us to act). If we value codes on the basis of outcome and principle then we can expect to have a higher degree of commitment, then if we value them because everyone else does or simply because, 'I'm happy because the code is in place'. Commitment on the basis of preference and consensus will at best be situational and unstable. Furthermore, those values that are held most deeply (core values) are those that we follow despite the innumerable obstacles that might come into play (e.g. bribes, coercion, personnel conflicts). As noted in Chapter 5, organisational leadership that emphasises the importance of adhering to core values is essential if workers are to place value in the code. Codes will not be adhered to if the audience (employees) have not been adequately socialised in the workplace. This holds true for new workers, as well as for more seasoned employees whose value set is loosely held and swayed by rewards or punishments. What contributes to the erosion of individual values is too much of what has been termed the, 'bureaucratic ethos' (Garofalo & Geuras, 1999), which is thought to be much more instrumental than the contrasting democratic ethos, and where workers succumb to centrally positioned decision makers who mould their values according to the needs of the organisation (see Jos, 1988; Hodgkinson, 1996).

In motivating employees and other stakeholders to value the code of ethics, it is imperative that codes be well developed to explain why a preferred mode of behaviour is endorsed. In the case of tourists, Malloy and Fennell (1998) found that codes of a deontological nature were found to be less effective in educating tourists about preferred behaviours than teleological codes. Stating the consequences of actions or inactions was deemed essential in educating a tourist group (e.g. ecotourists) who were eager not only for ecological knowledge but also for information on how to be a 'good' tourist. Implementation was also said to be critical in allowing the employee to be aware of how the code is put into daily use. Knowing that it exists and understanding its content is not enough. The collective must believe in the code of ethics, and exercise it in day-to-day operations of the organisation, to the degree that it becomes a habitual way of doing business. As such, ethics – codes and other ethical devices – should become part of the routine and not an occasional behaviour – suggesting that ethics is not just for heroes and saints, but rather like our muscles which need to be regularly exercised (Saul, 2001). And just as muscles atrophy without regular use, behaviour may follow the same depreciative path without continual exposure to that which is deemed moral.

An understanding of values also helped us to better appreciate the reasons why people are motivated to act differently – on the basis of profit, preservation, co-operation, and so on. But this was not enough. We also needed to explain why we are endowed with the capacity to be ethical through a brief look at evolution (i.e. how is it that we are ethical by nature?). Inclusive fitness (altruism as an expression of relatedness) and especially reciprocal altruism (co-operation with those not related) were instrumental in making this connection. Reciprocal altruism, or return benefits between agents over time in building co-operation, is said to act as the springboard for ethics (Mayr, 1988; Pinker, 2002). This form of altruism ('I scratch your back, you scratch mine') lies at the heart of human co-operation explaining why we detect guilt, sympathy, gratitude, cheating, punishment aggression, trust and suspicion in our interactions with others. Theorists have also argued that ethics evolved at the intersection of freedom and constraint (Midgley, 1994). Too much freedom sets us up for a load of trouble, in Midgley's words, while too much constraint stifles us in exploring or realising the human potential. (In connecting thoughts here, Mamic (2004) suggests that codes of ethics create somewhat of a paradox, by limiting the power of the organisation that creates it, which is a different way of expressing what Midgley observes in reference to freedom and constraint.)

This innate ethical capacity, however, is not simply instinct, but has provided us with the ability to derive innumerable culturally distinct ethical tools, like codes of ethics, which serve to meet situational and locational demands. The universality of codes of ethics has been discussed by the ethicist Peter Singer who writes that:

> Every human society has some code of behaviour for its members. This is true of nomads and city-dwellers, of hunter-gatherers and of industrial civilisations, of Eskimos in Greenland and Bushmen in Africa, of a tribe of twenty Australian aborigines and of the billion people that make up China. Ethics is part of the natural human condition. (Singer, 1981: 23)

Singer further argues that we are becoming more ethical as time goes on through what he describes as an expanding circle of morality. Here, and increasingly, moral value is placed on individuals or entities (people, plants, animals) where before it failed to exist. Tourism, as part and parcel of normal, everyday life (at least for the lucky few who travel regularly) must be influenced by general societal trends. We see the subtle emergence of society's influence in tourism through investigations of what has been termed the 'new tourism' (Poon, 1993) and, more recently, an increasing body of literature that says that there is demand, however marginal, for ethical programmes in tourism, as illustrated by the Tearfund group. (A key question surrounds the notion of whether or not the apparent need for more ethically-based products is a function of calculative or meditative thought.) The other side of the debate is that codes of ethics and the moralisation of tourism are merely window-dressing ploys to cover up the real essence of tourism: profit and self-interest (Wheeller, 1994; Butcher, 2003).

Seeking the proverbial silver lining in this debate, we feel that the exchange of ideas is essential if we are to forge ahead in gleaning further enlightenment in regards to ethics and codes of ethics.

Having argued for a sustained debate on ethics, we feel that the division between the two camps (those who support an ethical agenda in tourism and those who believe it is more difficult to realise) is held constant by a critical lack of theoretical, conceptual and empirical knowledge that would prove helpful in clearing much of the fog. By this we mean that there is simply not enough known about codes of ethics in tourism to definitively take one side or the other. While critics suggest that little progress has been made to date, it would seem equally warranted to criticise their work because of a lack of evidence pointing to the failure of codes of ethics in tourism. Sethi (2000) refers to the two opposing sides of the codes debate as 'an unintentional and unholy alliance'.

Yet, in examining the literature outside tourism, we see numerous studies that legitimise codes of ethics as valuable tools that help make organisations, through employee behaviour, more ethical. For example, Ferrell & Skinner (1988: 107) write that, 'the existence and enforcement of codes of ethics are associated with higher levels of ethical behaviour'. But if there is anything we can take a way from the critics, it is that we should not accept codes of ethics as a panacea to the many problems we face in tourism. Codes of ethics are perhaps one option – an extremely important option we would argue – for the planning and development of an ethical tourism industry, which might effectively complement other methods like regulations (Mamic, 2004). Management strategies should thus be the culmination of a variety of different techniques that are specific to space, time and resources (Valentine, 1992; Johnston & Hall, 1995; Genot, 1995). Added to this is the belief that codes exist as just one ethical vehicle that we can use to make decisions. Veatch (2003) argued that cases, codes, normative theory and meta-ethics are all important in helping us to arrive at the right decision. This is corroborated by many other theorists including Hay and Foley (1998), who suggest that we ought to use a variety of theories and methods which allow for informed, critical thought. In this way codes of ethics and other similar mechanisms are but one of many different approaches that may be used to develop sustainably based products in tourism.

A main task of ours was to address some of the many difficult questions related to codes of ethics in tourism in an effort to move the discussion forward. What has been most helpful in this attempt is the incorporation of ethical theory in providing a 'groundedness' based on the rich history of debate on ethics spanning some 2500 years. Here we found rich fodder for the nexus of theory and tourism codes based on the means–ends dichotomy (from the normative context), as well as the more subjectivist existentialism mindset. The benefit of keeping an open mind in problem solving was championed by Socrates. His notion of the 'examined life' is based on the premise that we should not act: (1) out of habit alone; (2) on our own desires; (3) on the basis of an authority figure; or (4) on the basic normative principles that we get from our immediate environment (Beversluis, 1987). Instead, Socrates felt it was the individual's responsibility to examine, be aware and evaluate various normative beliefs (e.g. deontology) through a state of fallibilism – the half-way point between dogmatism (no possibility of being mistaken) and scepticism (we can never know the truth), with the emergence of a tension that forces ongoing examination. The Socratic examined life acknowledges that while some normative principles need to be adopted in making decision-making possible, we must always be open to new evidence that may allow for change in our principles.

Theory was also helpful to us in the earliest stages of the book through Heidegger's views on calculative and meditative thinking. This was important because we feel, as many others do, that the code of ethics should make individuals consider their actions in a philosophical manner. The use of Heidegger's philosophy in conclusion seems equally warranted for the purpose of stimulating further research and education on the merits of ethics and codes of ethics for a more responsible and sustainable tourism industry.

Adoption of the calculative mindset forces us to value nature, other people, and the world in general on a functional basis (i.e. rational decision making that is efficient and effective, and based on science). Such thinking has proven to be short-term, lacking in sufficient grounding, and foundational to many of the serious negative consequences that we experience in tourism. For example, if hotel developers see no reason why communities shouldn't be displaced in order to facilitate tourism, then it is not hard to envision the associated socio-cultural implications that might stem from such an approach.

By contrast, meditative thinking, or the search for meaning, is logically grounded in philosophical rationale that enables us to frame our actions in the context of the broader horizon. The deontological nature of codes of ethics, if carefully constructed, opens the door to the possibility of realising meditative thinking in tourism. Aspects such as tradition, culture, integrity, common sense, and so on, may be preserved through this mindset which emphasises 'rootedness'. Using the example of hotel development above, meditative thinking allows us to see the broader picture beyond the immediate short-term, cost–benefit calculation: families, memories, history, reverence for place, and rights. It would then be a matter of deciding collectively, and in full view of human rights, ecological parameters, and so on, a more ethical action to follow. Having championed the meditative mindset, however, we readily acknowledge the difficulty in thinking this way. Foremost in the minds (and actions) of many who participate in the tourism trade is one prime directive: to make money. Elevating self-interest to such a lofty height, has a tendency to blur all other values that might be used to provide a balanced approach to human–human and human–ecology inter-actions.

Although we could find no other reference to Heidegger's work on rootedness in tourism, this is not to say that similar theoretical views have not been considered. Hultsman (1995), for example, argued that a code of ethics (the operational side of ethics, in his terms) needs to be more firmly grounded in a more paradigmatic foundation. And while we can develop a code of ethics without this foundation, the inclusion of a stronger theoret-ical knowledge in codes of ethics eliminates the problems caused by 'zealous but ignorant moral reformers' (Johnson, 1974, cited by Hultsman, 1995: 554). This means that a little knowledge on the theoretical side of ethics may provide the needed expertise to better address issues that continue to plague the tourism industry. Hultsman took as the foundation for his ethical framework for 'just' tourism the concept of the land ethic developed by Aldo Leopold (1949/1991). Leopold's land ethic is a limita-tion on the freedom to do what we want as individuals (see Midgley, 1991), in favour of actions that are in the best interests of the community. What Hultsman is referring to is essentially a _spirit_ of tourism services delivery, based on the adage 'do no harm', that provides tourists with an opportunity to find meaning and benefit in their travels. The notion of spirit and meaning are further developed in Hultsman's work through his efforts in contrasting activities that are dichotomised as either intrinsic or extrinsic. When tourism becomes an activity grounded in profit and economy alone – say, for service providers – it loses its intrinsic worth, which further leads to the trivialisation of ethical concerns along socio-cultural and ecological lines.

A thought-provoking paper by Tribe (2002; see also Jamal, 2004) provides an excellent link between the intrinsic/extrinsic nature of behav-iour and codes of ethics. Tribe argues that so much rule following (i.e. adherence to codes) has taken place without recognition of the intrinsic nature of good, in the Aristotelian fashion. That is, being virtuous (virtues defined by Rachels, 1999, as traits of character that make one a good person), if cultivated through good habits, allows us not only to do things correctly, but most importantly to do them for the right reasons. This may be accomplished through Aristotle's notion of phronesis, or the develop-ment and exercise of practical wisdom, which may contribute to more responsible approaches to tourism development and management. Studies of this nature serve to further illustrate the benefits of thinking in a philo-sophical manner about the actions of tourism industry stakeholders.

Astride theory and philosophy, one of the most glaringly perceptible conclusions drawn from this work is the critical lack of practical examples to use in better understanding the processes behind code development, compliance and enforcement. There are simply too few readily available sources that can be used as examples in moving forward. Added to this is the finding that, sectorally speaking, most of the research on codes (not on the development of codes themselves) has tended to focus on cetaceans over other forms of tourism. However, even in the marine sector there is no clear standard ethical path, nor are there any definitive answers. For example, even though cetacean operators are presented with various regulatory devices, there is still a persistent failure to comply with these in the day-to-day operations of the provider – presumably in order to maximise profit (see Lusseau, 2004). Furthermore, the directives most likely to be followed by operators are those developed by the industry itself through cooperative ventures among like-minded parties (Gjerdalen & Williams, 2000). If this is the case, it seems logical to conclude that codes of ethics, if desired and meaningful, must come at the hands of those most likely to be impacted. This fits well with the concept of positive affect discussed in Chapter 3, whereby participants, if given a role to play in the development of programmes, are found to have more enriching experiences. The research on social dilemmas (Ostrom, 2003) could also prove useful in understanding the dynamic that exists between various tourism stakeholders and the resources that they share.

Another area of potential interest to researchers and practitioners is the identification of unique Aboriginal or Eastern codes of ethics and how these may be used to control tourism – in a pure form or merged with the Western approach to codes. In Canada, the Quebec Aboriginal Tourism Authority (STAQ) has completed what has been referred to as the first (at least in Canada) Aboriginal tourism code of ethics and standards (ATTC, 2002). Bullock (2004) writes that the intersection of Western scientific and Eastern indigenous knowledge is complementary in the development of ecotourism. This was found to be the case in Yunnan, China, where both world views often yielded similar conclusions. Theerapappisit's (2003) investigation of ethics in the Greater Mekong Sub region yielded interesting contrasts between the development practices of the Western world when immersed in a Buddhist culture (which seeks to balance problems with benefits). Theerapappisit (2003: 49) argued for a return to a 'sufficiency economy', defined as 'a philosophy that stresses the middle path as the overriding principle for appropriate conduct by the populace at all levels'. The application of Buddhist ethics in a tourism context was represented at three levels: individual, community and inter-organisational. These levels were said to be affected by the following six Buddhist ethical principles:

(1) *morality* – balancing altruism with greed;
(2) *wisdom* – balancing impartiality with bias;
(3) *holism/dynamism* – balancing interdependence with disconnection;

(4) *sufficiency* – balancing self-reliance with unlimited growth;
(5) *non-violence* – balancing co-operation with competition; and
(6) *causality* – balancing adaptive systems with rigid systems.

In operationalising these concepts, Theerapappisit observed that economic policy issues continue to be favoured over policies which are holistic and future-focused. The six Buddhist principles serve as a code of ethics to bring the various stakeholders in tourism together for the purpose of minimising conflict.

On the back of these studies in tourism and the many cited here from other fields so vitally important to the development of ideas in this book, we hope that this work stimulates further discussions on the topic of codes of ethics in tourism. The diffuse nature of tourism in theory and practice, especially on a topic that is only just emerging, has presented a unque challenge. Having said this, we can't help but be optimistic about the prospects for an amplified focus on codes of ethics in tourism because of the myriad social, economic and ecological issues that have come to the fore. As we continue to look for solutions that make us more communicative, responsible, knowledgeable, accepting of an ethical climate, rooted, value conscious, cooperative, inclusive, and forward looking, to name a few, the code of ethics continues to hold promise as a tool to achieve a suitable balance.

Sources of Further Guidance

There are several web sites that may prove helpful to both researchers and practitioners interested in the growing number of codes of ethics currently available in tourism. The accommodation site 'VISIT', lists environmentally-friendly accommodations in Europe, dozens of definitions, codes of conduct, legislation, environmental seals and awards, ecotourism criteria, and projects and publications for the purpose of educating tourists (http://62.250.6.250/visit/green-visit/pagina_gb.asp; accessed 4.12.06). Another helpful site is the Big Volcano Ecotourism Resource Centre, which lists many accreditation and certification programs, as well as codes of conduct, practice and operational guidelines for places and programmes around the world. Examples of codes of ethics include Antarctic Tour Operator Guidelines, Codes from Tourism Concern, and the Australian Natural Heritage Charter (http://www.bigvolcano.com.au/ercentre/ercpage.htm; accessed 4.12.06).

The Isbell Hospitality Ethics unit in the School of Hotel and Restaurant Management, Northern Arizona University, provides a wealth of information on past studies on hospitality and tourism ethics. In particular, Jaszey's (2001) review of ethics articles in hospitality journals lists several titles and their associated research forums (www.nau.edu/hrm/ahrrc/isbell_center. html; accessed 4.12.06). The Centre for the Study of Ethics in the Professions,

Illinois Institute of Technology, provides a good general database of articles on codes of ethics (www.ethicsweb.ca/codes/articles.htm; accessed 4.12.06) and how to create a code of ethics for your organisation (www.ethics web.ca/codes/; accessed 4.12.06). In addition, a few of the major tourism organisations have developed programmes or networks on various aspects of the tourism industry. For example, the WTTC in concert with the European Commission has developed ECoNETT (European Community Network for Environmental Travel and Tourism). Their website specifies information on good practice, codes of ethics, and various related organisations (http:// www.wttc.org/; accessed 4.12.06). In 1999, the ECoNETT site listed 55 codes of ethics which were posted for the purpose of providing information to ecotourism operators (ECoNETT, 1999; Shephard & Royston-Airey, 2000). Rainforest Alliance has a good site for a range of sustainable tourism tools, including codes of ethics and certification (http://www.rainforest- alli-ance.org/programs/tourism/tour-operators/codes-of-conduct.html; accessed 4.12.06); while the Global Development Research Centre lists a number of charters, declarations, codes, tools, strategies, checklists, and reports on ecotourism and sustainable tourism (http://www.gdrc.org/uem/eco- tour/ eco-tour.html/; accessed 4.12.06). Aside from these sources, those interested in ethics and tourism need only do a web search using the keywords 'Ethical travel' to discover a huge number of resources that will provide guidance on how to be a conscientious traveller. These sources deal with specific regions and topics, as well as a variety of general suggestions on travel and tourism.

Glossary

Accreditation A voluntary fee-based and audit-based quality control mechanism designed to improve tourism programmes and services according to industry standards. Logos are awarded to service providers for the purpose of achieving competitive advantage. Accreditation and certification are terms that have become synonymous.

Applied ethics The division of ethics that investigates the specific moral issues of the day. Applied ethical issues have two features, including: (1) suffcent controversy to gain support from those who do and do not support the issue in question; and (2) universal applicability.

Auditing A process a business goes through to identify and confirm benchmarks, to provide accreditation with reliability and validity, and to measure and verify best practice.

Awards Conferred or bestowed upon persons or agencies in cases where they have satisfied the requirements of a programme (e.g. certification), or if they have somehow made an outstanding contribution (Webster, 2002). The Responsible Tourism Awards recognise individuals, companies and organisations in the travel industry that are making a significant commitment to the cultures and economics of local communities and are providing a positive contribution to biodiversity conservation (see Hammond, 2005).

Benchmark A point of reference allowing for the systematic comparison of one entity (e.g. a tourism organisation) against another.

Best practice Practices that are considered the most effective and efficient at the time. This is a management approach to operations and customer service that demands the highest standard of performance at all times.

Bill of Rights A formal summary of those rights and liberties considered essential to a person or group of people. The original Bill of Rights of 1689 set the conditions upon which the British throne was offered to King William and Queen Mary (Cook, 1995). The Tourism Bill of Rights and Tourist Code (1985) developed standards of conduct for states, tourists and service providers with reference to the sexual exploitation of target groups (e.g. children).

Canons General laws, rules or principles; a basic standard by which something is judged (*The Globe Modern Dictionary,* see Weber, 1984). The Air Line Pilots Association Code of Ethics is based on five tenets, all of which are supported by a number of canons. With reference to the tenet on the responsibility for the safety, comfort and well-being of passengers (see *Tenets*), five canons are offered. These include 'He will never permit external pressures or personal desires to influence his judgement, not will he knowingly do anything that could jeopardise flight safety'; and 'If disaster should strike, he will take whatever action he deems necessary to protect the lives of his passengers and crew'.

Certification See *Accreditation*, above.

Code of conduct Specific measures designed to ensure that signatories (e.g. members of an organisation) adhere to its principles according to moral expectations.

Code of ethics A systematised set of standards or principles that defines ethical behaviour appropriate for a profession. The standard and principles are determined by moral values (Ray, 2000; see also Little *et al.*, 1973).

Code of practice A systematic collection of rules relating to a particular subject (*The Globe Modern Dictionary*, Weber, 1984).

Code, corporate Codes of ethics are developed in recognition of the moral and legal responsibilities of the company, including all those who work within it, i.e. to affect the behaviour of those employees who work within the firm. Internal responsibility and external pressures are central factors that motivate firms to develop codes (see Raiborn & Payne, 1990; Higgs-Kleyn & Kapelianis, 1999).

Code, professional Codes of ethics designed to guide the behaviour of members of an association and to provide standards to use in making ethical judgements (Tucker *et al.*, 1999). Codes are intended to enhance professionalism, i.e. what is prohibited and what is accepted (Coughlan, 2001), and may include punitive measures such as loss of membership for certain violations. Frankl (1989) lists three different kinds of codes of professional ethics:

(1) aspirational, where the focus is on realising human achievement over notions of right and wrong;

(2) educational, where commentary and interpretation are central with an effort to deal with ethical problems; and

(3) regulatory, which include detailed rules to govern professional conduct, including adjudication, monitoring and sanctions.

Although distinct, Frankl argues that any single code could contain features of all three types.

Codify The process of arranging principles into a formal code.

Compliance Actions that conform to requests, commands or regulations – in the context of this book, actions that conform to a tourism code of ethics. Viewed more broadly, compliance is a term that encompasses implementation, monitoring, reporting, auditing, verification and enforceability of codes of ethics.

Credos (Vision statements) A general statement of belief. In the organisational context, the credo signifies in what the organisation believes.

Declarations An explicit, formal announcement, either oral or written (Weber, 1984). Examples include the United Nations Declaration of Human Rights, adopted by the UN General Assembly resolution 217A (III) of December 10, 1948 (www.un.org; accessed 15.12.06), the Manila Declaration on World Tourism (1980), and The Hague Declaration on Tourism. The world conference on sustainable tourism (1995) in Lanzarote, Canary Islands, Spain, established that all areas of tourism including the international community, governments, public authorities and institutions chose to adopt the principles and objectives of the following declaration that follows:

> Tourism development shall be based on criteria of sustainability, which means that it must be ecologically bearable in the long term, as well as economically viable, and ethically and socially equitable for local communities. Sustainable development is a guided process, which envisages global management of resources so as to ensure their viability, thus enabling our natural and cultural capital, including protected areas, to be preserved. As a powerful instrument of development, tourism can and should participate actively in the sustainable development strategy. A requirement of sound management of tourism is that the sustainability of the resources on which it depends must be guaranteed. (INSULA.org, 2005:1)

Deontology What is deemed to be 'right' is a function of following universal principles and duty, cultural and ecological norms and law.

Ethics The branch of philosophy concerned with the examination of that which contributes to living a good life. Determining what is good or right often comes from the consideration of a systematic set of rules that define behaviour (see *Code of ethics*).

Existentialism Behaviour that is authentic, self-determined, freely chosen. Existentialists reject universally valid objective standards of ethics and values.

Guidelines Any suggestion or rule that should be followed (*The Globe Modern Dictionary*, Weber, 1984). Citing Stonehouse (1990), Mason (1997) suggests that guidelines are based on precepts that indicate a course of action, together with the reasoning behind the actions.

Inclusive fitness Altruism extended to those who share genes (like brothers, sisters, and parents) because the benefits that accrue from the altruistic act aid the fitness of the donor individual, as measured by the expression of genes in future generations.

Mission statement Like a credo, the mission tends to be aspirational but, unlike the credo, it tends to be more specific to the purpose of the organisation. It provides the public and the organisational member with a brief sense of organisational direction and intent.

Morals The broad values upon which ethical directives are established.

Non-compliance Actions that do not conform to requests, commands or regulations – in the context of this book, actions that fail to adhere to a code of ethics.

Norms Sets of standards or criteria that are held by different groups or within certain bodies of thought.

Precept Commands, maxims or moral instructions (Concise Oxford Dictionary, 1976).

Principles Principles imply truism and provide the basic philosophical groundwork or foundation upon which other more specific statements can be generated. With reference to codes of ethics, Johnston and Twynam (2001) make little distinction between guidelines and principles, but note that codes act as a mechanism for implementing guidelines and principles by specifying expected behaviour of participants in various situations (see Jamal, 2004).

Reciprocal altruism Altruism directed towards another with the expectation of a return favour somewhere down the road for the purpose of increasing one's own fitness.

Regulation Referred to as 'a big stick' or authoritarian manner of control, where the actions of a group (e.g. service providers) are subject to restrictions enforceable by law.

Standards Standards are defined by Saura (2000: 555) as, 'the norms with which products or services must comply'. These norms are generally specified through objectives that need to be met to satisfy the needs, desires and expectations of a target group. It helps if these objectives are simple, relevant and easily understandable. Standards are wide-ranging in tourism (e.g. quality, safety), and have application in such devices as: codes of ethics (where there is no verification or measurement); benchmarking (where companies can measure and compare their performance against an industry-wide set of prescribed indicators); and certification and award schemes where companies are evaluated independently for the purpose of attaining an award that demonstrates their success in meeting environmental or social standards (Roe *et al.*, 2003; see also Vorley *et al.*, 2002).

Strategy There are four different meanings:

(1) a plan for getting from 'here' to 'there';

(2) a pattern in actions over time;

(3) a position for offering products to particular markets; and

(4) a perspective, i.e. a vision or direction.

An example of a tourism strategy is the 1990 Action Strategy for Sustainable Tourism Development developed at the Globe '90 Conference in British Columbia, Canada.

Teleology Behaviour that is focused on the ends or consequences of our actions. 'Good' behaviour seeks to develop virtues, the greatest good for the greatest number, and the greatest good for the individual.

Tenet Any opinion, principle or doctrine believed by an organised group or profession (Dervaes, 1992). The Air Line Pilots Association's Code of Ethics, originally written in 1956 and updated in 1977, has five main tenets. The first of these states that, 'An Airline Pilot will keep uppermost in his mind that the safety, comfort and well-being of the passengers who entrust their lives to him are his first and greatest responsibility' (http://cf.alpa. org/internet/ethics.html, accessed 04.12.06). Each of the five tenets is followed up by a number of canons which help to further develop the rationale of the tenet (see *Canons*).

Theoretical ethics In the context of this book, includes normative theories such as deontology and teleology, and also the subjectivist theory of existentialism.

Values A concept of the desirable with a motivating force (Hodgkinson, 1983: 36), or behaviour as the outward manifestation of what we, internally, find to be of worth.

Value statements Public insights into the motivational force behind an organisation's behaviour.

Voluntary initiatives Social, ecological or economic measures that target a number of different groups or sectors (e.g. accommodation, food and beverage, operators, transportation) where the initiator is not obliged by law to run the initiative, and where the target groups are not required to join (WTO, 2002). Examples include eco-label and certification schemes, prizes, awards, environmental management systems, self-commitments, charters and declarations and codes of ethics.

Appendix 1

San Martin de los Andes

CRISTINA LAZOS[1]

Background to the Environmental Code of Conduct for San Martin de los Andes

Tourism is the main socioeconomic activity of the city of San Martin de los Andes, a small destination in Patagonia, Argentina. This region is noted for its exceptional natural resource base, which provides the foundation for a variety of outdoor activities, including skiing, rafting, fishing, and hiking. The 108-year-old city is one of the main gateways to Lanín National Park, which is comprised of 380,000 hectares of forests, mountains and lakes.[2]

The execution of these activities and the development of tourist services has increased the degree of interaction with the natural world, as much in the city as in the natural areas. Recognising this, both government and community have been involved in the development of a sustainable tourism strategy for the purpose of: (1) environmental education, (2) helping to communicate the conservation and preservation actions that are needed for the region, (3) endorsing the environmental best practices of the accommodation sector, and (4) promoting active participation of tourists during their visit. A code of ethics (below) was felt to be the most effective way to communicate these broad values, while ensuring that visitors respect the natural and cultural characteristics of the vicinity

Code of Environmental Conduct

The development of the code was not a straightforward process. Initially, organisations with different objectives, and working independently, created guidelines that best suited their own needs. Recognising the problems with this system, they agreed to unify the disparate messages into a more universal document, which included many different components of the environment, such as the forest, lakes and rivers, the ground, the sun, the roads and the people. It was also important to elaborate on the environmental dynamics for each component, its contribution to quality of life, the behaviours expected for its conservation, and contacts with corresponding authorities. Organisers of the code felt it was important to include recommendations to protect tourists – many of whom come from urban areas – from potential harm while spending time in nature. Examples include information on the coldness and deepness of lake waters, the harmful effects of the solar rays at certain times of the day, driving on mountain roads, and preventative measures against Hanta disease.

The code of environmental conduct for tourists is communicated on the region's sustainable tourism website,[3] in brochures in the Municipal Tourist Office, and through accommodation that supports and adheres to the environmental best practice programme. Furthermore, some aspects of the code like waste management

157

are posted frequently, especially in the national park urging tourists to return their waste to the city where a more adequate waste management system exists.

Survey research amongst tourists[4] has yielded a considerable range of data on environmental quality and participation in best practice. Results indicate that: (1) tourists choose attractions/destinations that they perceived to have high environmental quality; (2) tourists care that the municipality is concerned with the environment; and (3) amongst other good practices, about two-thirds of the participants carry out their waste from the natural areas. These results suggest that, by following the environmental code of conduct, tourists are doing their part to conserving the resources of San Martin de los Andes and helping to establish this beautiful region as an emerging sustainable tourism destination.

Notes

1. Cristina Lazos, Department of Tourism, San Martin de los Andes (c.lazos@ smandes.gov.ar)
2. The Municipal Tourism Secretary of the city has recently certified the Excellence in Tourism Destination Management Organisations (DMOs). WTO Sbest.
3. On WWW at http://www.sanmartindelosandes.gov.ar (accessed 16.12.06).
4. Municipal Tourism Secretariat, Summer Tourism Survey 2006.

The Code of Environmental Conduct for San Martin of the Andes
(translated from Spanish)

Welcome!

Each area possesses unique features.

The behaviour of tourists and residents can either maintain or alter the delicate balance in these areas. So that everyone can fully enjoy this marvellous natural environment, this community presents the following code of conduct that you are expected to follow, based on: 'Preserving for a better life'.

Our Forests

Our forests invite us to travel through them, but we must be committed to enjoying them responsibly.

If you want to make a bonfire, construct a small one only in an appropriate place. Carelessness can cause irreparable damage to our forests.

The fire that unites can also destroy.

Fire can be put out only with abundant water.

The ashtray of your car is the best place for matches and cigarette ends. The conservation of forest flora and fauna is a gift to the future.

Emergencies: Forests Dept (02972) 427097; Lanin National Park (Fire): 210; Fire Brigade: 100; Civil Guard: (02972) 491281

Our Lakes and Rivers

They are the ideal environment for sport fishing. Respect the rules of the game!

Acquire a fishing license.

Do not let the fish become exhausted.

Conserve these natural environments, as trout do not survive in degraded environments.

If you are going to enjoy the water, do not forget that:

- water is often colder and deeper than it seems. Look after your children constantly and respect the buoyed areas for bathing;
- if you are going to sail, carry all the security equipment required by the Prefectura Naval (lake, river and sea police);
- let the authorities know your destination and time of navigation.

Rivers, streams and river banks are a reservoir for humanity.

Emergencies: Prefectura Naval Argentina: 106; National Gendarmerie: 134

The Ground

Do not dirty the space you choose to enjoy. Mountains, beaches and streams cannot process rubbish.

Carry a marked bag or a box for waste and take it back with you to an urban zone, where there is an adequate disposal system.

Keep rubbish in its place – this will also keep away rodents.

The Andean region, like most others, contains various species of wild rodents. Two of these can transmit the Hanta virus to man. Here are some suggestions for avoiding contact with the virus:

- the virus persists only in closed and poorly-ventilated places, for this reason it is not recommended to enter or to occupy sheds or abandoned refuges;
- on walks, use only open paths and well-travelled ways;
- try to maintain a clean campsite.

Some waste products are especially dangerous for us and for nature (batteries, detergent, disposable nappies, plastic and bottles). We must be careful with them!!

Emergencies: Environmental Guards: 103/105; Hospital: 107

The Sun

The ozone layer protects us from UV rays that can be harmful to health. We should, therefore, take extra precautions.

Prolonged exposition to high doses of UV rays, year after year, can result in premature ageing of the skin, the appearance of wrinkles and an increased probability of skin cancer.

In mountain regions, UV radiation increases in relation to the altitude. It is advisable to take proper precautions during walks. Take care of your family:

- using SPF of no less than 15, with periodic reapplication;
- wearing sunglasses with a UV filter;
- wearing caps, hats or parasol and white clothes;
- avoiding exposure to the sun between 11:00am and 3:00pm.

Emergencies: Hospital: 107

Our Roads

The journey is an important part of travel.

The National Park offers access to its marvellous landscapes via roads that are mostly unpaved, so we must change our way of driving:

- use seat belts;
- on long straight stretches, maintain speed and do not make abrupt manoeuvres;
- do not underestimate bends, reduce speed in anticipation;
- do not overtake on bends or slopes with poor visibility;
- it is common to find animals (cows, horses, goats, etc) on the road. Drive with caution;
- on steep slopes, do not go down in neutral gear using only brakes;
- remember that priority is given to vehicles going uphill.

Our People

The host community has its own norms of conduct. *There are many things you can do to make yourself feel part of that community.*

- ask for permission before taking photos of houses or local people. People may feel uncomfortable;
- try to adopt local customs regarding clothing and traffic;
- a resident that greets you will expect you to answer his or her greeting;
- by hiring services and buying local products, you encourage the development of the local economy;
- take from our region only photos and good memories, do not forget that we expect you to return.

Emergencies: Police: 101; Tourist Information: (02972) 425500 – 427347 / 695

Appendix 2

UNWTO Global Code of Ethics for Tourism

ARTICLE 1: Tourism's contribution to mutual understanding and respect between peoples and societies

(1) The understanding and promotion of the ethical values common to humanity, with an attitude of tolerance and respect for the diversity of religious, philosophical and moral beliefs, are both the foundation and the consequence of responsible tourism; stakeholders in tourism development and tourists themselves should observe the social and cultural traditions and practices of all peoples, including those of minorities and indigenous peoples and to recognise their worth.

(2) Tourism activities should be conducted in harmony with the attributes and traditions of the host regions and countries and in respect for their laws, practices and customs.

(3) The host communities, on the one hand, and local professionals, on the other, should acquaint themselves with and respect the tourists who visit them and find out about their lifestyles, tastes and expectations; the education and training imparted to professionals contribute to a hospitable welcome.

(4) It is the task of the public authorities to provide protection for tourists and visitors and their belongings; they must pay particular attention to the safety of foreign tourists owing to the particular vulnerability they may have; they should facilitate the introduction of specific means of information, prevention, security, insurance and assistance consistent with their needs; any attacks, assaults, kidnappings or threats against tourists or workers in the tourism industry, as well as the wilful destruction of tourism facilities or of elements of cultural or natural heritage should be severely condemned and punished in accordance with their respective national laws.

(5) When travelling, tourists and visitors should not commit any criminal act or any act considered criminal by the laws of the country visited and abstain from any conduct felt to be offensive or injurious by the local populations, or likely to damage the local environment; they should refrain from all trafficking in illicit drugs, arms, antiques, protected species and products and substances that are dangerous or prohibited by national regulations.

(6) Tourists and visitors have the responsibility to acquaint themselves, even before their departure, with the characteristics of the countries they are preparing to visit; they must be aware of the health and security risks inherent in any travel outside their usual environment and behave in such a way as to minimise those risks.

ARTICLE 2: Tourism as a vehicle for individual and collective fulfilment

(1) Tourism, the activity most frequently associated with rest and relaxation, sport

and access to culture and nature, should be planned and practised as a privileged means of individual and collective fulfilment; when practised with a sufficiently open mind, it is an irreplaceable factor of self-education, mutual tolerance and for learning about the legitimate differences between peoples and cultures and their diversity.

(2) Tourism activities should respect the equality of men and women; they should promote human rights and, more particularly, the individual rights of the most vulnerable groups, notably children, the elderly, the handicapped, ethnic minorities and indigenous peoples.

(3) The exploitation of human beings in any form, particularly sexual, especially when applied to children, conflicts with the fundamental aims of tourism and is the negation of tourism; as such, in accordance with international law, it should be energetically combated with the co-operation of all the States concerned and penalised without concession by the national legislation of both the countries visited and the countries of the perpetrators of these acts, even when they are carried out abroad.

(4) Travel for purposes of religion, health, education and cultural or linguistic exchanges are particularly beneficial forms of tourism, which deserve encouragement.

(5) The introduction into curricula of education about the value of tourist exchanges, their economic, social and cultural benefits, and also their risks, should be encouraged.

ARTICLE 3: Tourism, a factor of sustainable development

(1) All the stakeholders in tourism development should safeguard the natural environment with a view to achieving sound, continuous and sustainable economic growth geared to satisfying equitably the needs and aspirations of present and future generations.

(2) All forms of tourism development that are conducive to saving rare and precious resources, in particular water and energy, as well as avoiding so far as possible waste production, should be given priority and encouraged by national, regional and local public authorities.

(3) The staggering in time and space of tourist and visitor flows, particularly those resulting from paid leave and school holidays, and a more even distribution of holidays should be sought so as to reduce the pressure of tourism activity on the environment and enhance its beneficial impact on the tourism industry and the local economy.

(4) Tourism infrastructure should be designed and tourism activities programmed in such a way as to protect the natural heritage composed of ecosystems and biodiversity and to preserve endangered species of wildlife; the stakeholders in tourism development, and especially professionals, should agree to the imposition of limitations or constraints on their activities when these are exercised in particularly sensitive areas: desert, polar or high mountain regions, coastal areas, tropical forests or wetlands, propitious to the creation of nature reserves or protected areas.

(5) Nature tourism and eco-tourism are recognised as being particularly conducive to enriching and enhancing the standing of tourism, provided they respect the natural heritage and local populations and are in keeping with the carrying capacity of the sites.

ARTICLE 4: Tourism, a user of the cultural heritage of mankind and contributor to its enhancement

(1) Tourism resources belong to the common heritage of mankind; the communities in whose territories they are situated have particular rights and obligations to them.

(2) Tourism policies and activities should be conducted with respect for the artistic, archaeological and cultural heritage, which they should protect and pass on to future generations; particular care should be devoted to preserving and upgrading monuments, shrines and museums as well as archaeological and historic sites which must be widely open to tourist visits; encouragement should be given to public access to privately-owned cultural property and monuments, with respect for the rights of their owners, as well as to religious buildings, without prejudice to normal needs of worship.

(3) Financial resources derived from visits to cultural sites and monuments should, at least in part, be used for the upkeep, safeguard, development and embellishment of this heritage.

(4) Tourism activity should be planned in such a way as to allow traditional cultural products, crafts and folklore to survive and flourish, rather than causing them to degenerate and become standardised.

ARTICLE 5: Tourism, a beneficial activity for host countries and communities

(1) Local populations should be associated with tourism activities and share equitably in the economic, social and cultural benefits they generate, and particularly in the creation of direct and indirect jobs resulting from them.

(2) Tourism policies should be applied in such a way as to help to raise the standard of living of the populations of the regions visited and meet their needs; the planning and architectural approach to and operation of tourism resorts and accommodation should aim to integrate them, to the extent possible, in the local economic and social fabric; where skills are equal, priority should be given to local manpower.

(3) Special attention should be paid to the specific problems of coastal areas and island territories and to vulnerable rural or mountain regions, for which tourism often represents a rare opportunity for development in the face of the decline of traditional economic activities.

(4) Tourism professionals, particularly investors, governed by the regulations laid down by the public authorities, should carry out studies of the impact of their development projects on the environment and natural surroundings; they should also deliver, with the greatest transparency and objectivity, information on their future programmes and their foreseeable repercussions and foster dialogue on their contents with the populations concerned.

ARTICLE 6: Obligations of stakeholders in tourism development

(1) Tourism professionals have an obligation to provide tourists with objective and honest information on their places of destination and on the conditions of travel, hospitality and stays; they should ensure that the contractual clauses proposed to their customers are readily understandable as to the nature, price and quality of the services they commit themselves to providing and the financial

compensation payable by them in the event of a unilateral breach of contract on their part.

(2) Tourism professionals, insofar as it depends on them, should show concern, in co-operation with the public authorities, for the security and safety, accident prevention, health protection and food safety of those who seek their services; likewise, they should ensure the existence of suitable systems of insurance and assistance; they should accept the reporting obligations prescribed by national regulations and pay fair compensation in the event of failure to observe their contractual obligations.

(3) Tourism professionals, so far as this depends on them, should contribute to the cultural and spiritual fulfilment of tourists and allow them, during their travels, to practise their religions.

(4) The public authorities of the generating States and the host countries, in cooperation with the professionals concerned and their associations, should ensure that the necessary mechanisms are in place for the repatriation of tourists in the event of the bankruptcy of the enterprise that organised their travel.

(5) Governments have the right and the duty – especially in a crisis, to inform their nationals of the difficult circumstances, or even the dangers they may encounter during their travels abroad; it is their responsibility however to issue such information without prejudicing in an unjustified or exaggerated manner the tourism industry of the host countries and the interests of their own operators; the contents of travel advisories should therefore be discussed beforehand with the authorities of the host countries and the professionals concerned; recommendations formulated should be strictly proportionate to the gravity of the situations encountered and confined to the geographical areas where the insecurity has arisen; such advisories should be qualified or cancelled as soon as a return to normality permits.

(6) The press, and particularly the specialised travel press and the other media, including modern means of electronic communication, should issue honest and balanced information on events and situations that could influence the flow of tourists; they should also provide accurate and reliable information to the consumers of tourism services; the new communication and electronic commerce technologies should also be developed and used for this purpose; as is the case for the media, they should not in any way promote sex tourism.

ARTICLE 7: Right to tourism

(1) The prospect of direct and personal access to the discovery and enjoyment of the planets resources constitutes a right equally open to all the worlds inhabitants; the increasingly extensive participation in national and international tourism should be regarded as one of the best possible expressions of the sustained growth of free time, and obstacles should not be placed in its way.

(2) The universal right to tourism must be regarded as the corollary of the right to rest and leisure, including reasonable limitation of working hours and periodic holidays with pay, guaranteed by Article 24 of the Universal Declaration of Human Rights and Article 7d of the International Covenant on Economic, Social and Cultural Rights.

(3) Social tourism, and in particular associative tourism, which facilitates widespread access to leisure, travel and holidays, should be developed with the support of the public authorities.

(4) Family, youth, student and senior tourism and tourism for people with disabilities, should be encouraged and facilitated.

ARTICLE 8: Liberty of tourist movements[1]

(1) Tourists and visitors should benefit, in compliance with international law and national legislation, from the liberty to move within their countries and from one State to another, in accordance with Article 13 of the Universal Declaration of Human Rights; they should have access to places of transit and stay and to tourism and cultural sites without being subject to excessive formalities or discrimination.

(2) Tourists and visitors should have access to all available forms of communication, internal or external; they should benefit from prompt and easy access to local administrative, legal and health services; they should be free to contact the consular representatives of their countries of origin in compliance with the diplomatic conventions in force.

(3) Tourists and visitors should benefit from the same rights as the citizens of the country visited concerning the confidentiality of the personal data and information concerning them, especially when these are stored electronically.

(4) Administrative procedures relating to border crossings whether they fall within the competence of States or result from international agreements, such as visas or health and customs formalities, should be adapted, so far as possible, so as to facilitate to the maximum freedom of travel and widespread access to international tourism; agreements between groups of countries to harmonise and simplify these procedures should be encouraged; specific taxes and levies penalising the tourism industry and undermining its competitiveness should be gradually phased out or corrected.

(5) So far as the economic situation of the countries from which they come permits, travellers should have access to allowances of convertible currencies needed for their travels.

ARTICLE 9: Rights of the workers and entrepreneurs in the tourism industry

(1) The fundamental rights of salaried and self-employed workers in the tourism industry and related activities, should be guaranteed under the supervision of the national and local administrations, both of their States of origin and of the host countries with particular care, given the specific constraints linked in particular to the seasonality of their activity, the global dimension of their industry and the flexibility often required of them by the nature of their work.

(2) Salaried and self-employed workers in the tourism industry and related activities have the right and the duty to acquire appropriate initial and continuous training; they should be given adequate social protection; job insecurity should be limited so far as possible; and a specific status, with particular regard to their social welfare, should be offered to seasonal workers in the sector.

(3) Any natural or legal person, provided he, she or it has the necessary abilities and skills, should be entitled to develop a professional activity in the field of tourism under existing national laws; entrepreneurs and investors – especially in the area of small and medium-sized enterprises – should be entitled to free access to the tourism sector with a minimum of legal or administrative restrictions.

(4) Exchanges of experience offered to executives and workers, whether salaried or not, from different countries, contributes to foster the development of the world tourism industry; these movements should be facilitated so far as possible in compliance with the applicable national laws and international conventions.

(5) As an irreplaceable factor of solidarity in the development and dynamic growth of international exchanges, multinational enterprises of the tourism industry should not exploit the dominant positions they sometimes occupy; they should avoid becoming the vehicles of cultural and social models artificially imposed on the host communities; in exchange for their freedom to invest and trade which should be fully recognised, they should involve themselves in local development, avoiding, by the excessive repatriation of their profits or their induced imports, a reduction of their contribution to the economies in which they are established.

(6) Partnership and the establishment of balanced relations between enterprises of generating and receiving countries contribute to the sustainable development of tourism and an equitable distribution of the benefits of its growth.

ARTICLE 10: Implementation of the principles of the Global Code of Ethics for Tourism

(1) The public and private stakeholders in tourism development should co-operate in the implementation of these principles and monitor their effective application.

(2) The stakeholders in tourism development should recognise the role of international institutions, among which the World Tourism Organisation ranks first, and non-governmental organisations with competence in the field of tourism promotion and development, the protection of human rights, the environment or health, with due respect for the general principles of international law.

(3) The same stakeholders should demonstrate their intention to refer any disputes concerning the application or interpretation of the Global Code of Ethics for Tourism for conciliation to an impartial third body known as the World Committee on Tourism Ethics.

Note

1. 'The liberty to move' is a right that should be balanced with the more contemporary view of restricting travel in efforts to combat global warming. How this ought to be done, concerning whom and on what scale, is open to debate.

Bibliography

ATTC (2002) *Aboriginal Tourism Team Canada Newsletter*, Volume 1 (2).

Adams, J.S., Tashchian, A. and Stone, T.H. (2001) Codes of ethics as signals for ethical behaviour. *Journal of Business Ethics* 29, 199–211.

Ahmed, Z.U., Krohn, F.B. and Heller, V.L. (1994) International tourism ethics as a way to world understanding. *The Journal of Tourism Studies* 5 (2), 36–44.

Aiken, W. (1984) Ethical issues in agriculture. In T. Regan (ed.) *Earthbound: New Introductory Essays in Environmental Ethics* (pp. 263–280). New York: Random House.

Amaro, B. (1999) Ecotourism and ethics. *Earth Island Journal* 14 (3), 16–17.

Ashcroft, (1993) One hundred and one dull machinations. *Journal of Sustainable Tourism* 1 (2), 346.

Aristotle. (1992) Nichomachean ethics (W.D. Ross, trans.) In R. McKeon (ed.) *Introduction to Aristotle* (pp. 319–579). New York: The Modern Library.

Ayala, F.J. (1987) The biological roots of morality. *Biology and Philosophy* 2, 235–252.

BBVS (1996) *Banff-Bow Valley: At the Crossroads*. Banff-Bow Valley Task Force technical report prepared for the Hon. Sheila Copps, Minister of Canadian Heritage, Ottawa: BBVS.

Barenberg, M. (2004) Forward. In I. Mamic *Implementing Codes of Conduct: How Businesses Manage Social Performance in Global Supply Chains* (pp. 10–11). Sheffield: Greenleaf.

Bart, C. K. (2002) Building mission statements that matter. *Provider* 26, 41–42, 44.

Beckmann, L. (1994) Marine conservation in the Canadian Arctic. *Northern Perspectives* 22 (2–3), 33–39.

Bendell, J. and Font, X. (2004) Which tourism rules? Green standards and GATS. *Annals of Tourism Research* 31(1), 139–156.

Benjamin, M. (1985) Ethics and animal consciousness. In M. Velasquez and C. Rostankowski (eds) *Ethics: Theory and Practice* (pp. 491–499). Englewood Cliffs, NJ: Prentice-Hall.

Berkes, F. and Folke, C. (2000) *Linking Social and Ecological Systems: Management Practices and Social Mechanisms for Building Resilience*. Cambridge: Cambridge University Press.

Berrow, S.D. (2003) An assessment of the framework, legislation and monitoring required to develop genuinely sustainable whale watching. In B. Garrod and J. Wilson (eds) *Marine Ecotourism: Issues and Experiences* (pp. 66–78). Clevedon: Channel View Publication.

Beversluis, E.H. (1987) Is there 'no such thing as business ethics'? *Journal of Business Ethics* 6, 81–88.

Bhagavad Gita (1986) *The Bhagavad-Gita: Krishna's Counsel in Time of War* (B. Stoler Miller, trans.) New York: Bantam Books.

Birch, C. (1993) *Regaining Compassion for Humanity and Nature*. Kensington: New South Wales University Press.

Blewett, C. (1993) A survey of *Orcinus orca* whale watching in Haro Strait and possible application in the rewriting of federal whale watching guidelines. Unpublished paper presented at the Killer Whale Ecology Summer Satellite Course, School for Field Studies, Northeastern Universities, Boston.

Bolt, R. (1974) *A Man for All Seasons*. Agincourt, ON: Bellhaven House Limited.

Boo, E. (1990) *Ecotourism: The Potentials and Pitfalls* (Vol. 1). Washington, DC: WWF.

Brincatt, C.A. and Wike, V.S. (2000) *Morality and the Professional Life: Values at Work*. Upper Saddle River, NJ: Prentice Hall.

Britton, S.G. (1982) The political economy of tourism in the Third World. *Annals of Tourism Research* 9 (3), 331–58.

Brookes, L.J. (1991) Codes of conduct for business: Are they effective, or just window-dressing? *Canadian Public Administration* 34 (1), 171–176.

Buchholz, W.J. (2004) Deciphering professional codes of ethics. *Proceedings of the Conference on Corporate Communications: Issues and Practices* (pp. 13–31). Madison, NJ: Fairleigh Dickinson University (originally published in 1988). On WWW at http://cyber.bentley.edu/faculty/wb/printables/codes.pdf. Accessed 30.11.04.

Buckley, R.C. (2001) Major issues in tourism ecolabelling. In X. Font and R.C. Buckley (eds) *Tourism Ecolabelling: Certification and Promotion of Sustainable Management* (pp. 19– 26). Wallingford: CABI.

Buckley, R.C. (2002a) Tourism ecocertification in the International Year of Ecotourism. *Journal of Ecotourism* 1 (2/3), 197–203.

Buckley, R.C. (2002b) Tourism ecolabels. *Annals of Tourism Research* 29 (1), 183–208.

Buckley, R.C. (2005) In search of the narwhal: Ethical dilemmas in ecotourism. *Journal of Ecotourism* 4 (2), 135–140.

Bullock, G. (2004) Creating positive synergies in mountain-based ecotourism development: Case studies from the Yunnan Rivers Project. On WWW at www. cbik. ac.cn/cbik/resource/articles/72%20Graham%20Bullock.pdf. Accessed 26.11.04.

Burns, J.M. (1978) *Leadership*. New York: Harper & Row.

Burns, P. (1999) Dealing with dilemmas. *In Focus* (33), 4–5.

Butcher, J. (2003) *The Moralisation of Tourism: Sun, Sand... and Saving the World?* London: Routledge.

Callicott, J.B. (1984) Non-anthropocentric value theory and environmental ethics. *American Philosophical Quarterly* 21 (4), 299–309..

Canadian Psychological Association (1991) *Canadian Code of Ethics for Psychologists*. Ottawa: Author.

Carlson, C. (2001) A review of whale watching guidelines and regulations around the world. Report for the International Fund for Animal Welfare. Yarmouth Port: International Fund for Animal Welfare.

Carroll, A.B. and Buchholtz, A.K. (2000) *Business and Society: Ethics and Stakeholder Management*. Cincinnati, OH: South-Western College Pub.

Carter, R.W., Whiley, D. and Knight, C. (2004) Improving environmental performance in the tourism accommodation sector. *Journal of Ecotourism* 3 (1), 46–68.

Cassell, C. Johnson, P. and Smith, K. (1997) Opening the black box: Corporate codes of ethics in their organisational context. *Journal of Business Ethics* 16, 1077–1093.

Clarke, J. (2002) A synthesis of activity towards the implementation of sustainable tourism: Ecotourism in a different context. *International Journal of Sustainable Development* 5 (3), 232–249.

Coccossis, H. (1996) Tourism and sustainability: Perspective and implications. In G.K. Priestley, J.A. Edwards and H. Coccossis (eds) *Sustainable Tourism? European Experiences* (pp. 1–21). CABI: Wallingford.

Cohen, S. (1998) General principles and specific codes: Tension and interrelation. *Professional Ethics: A Multidisciplinary Journal* 6 (3), 5–18.

Coles, R. (1993) Ecotones and environmental ethics: Adorno and Lopez. In J. Bennett and W. Chalouphe (eds) *The Nature of Things: Language, Politics and the Environment* (pp. 226–249). Minneapolis: University of Minnesota Press,

Coon, C. (2005) The architecture of ethics. *Humanist* 65 (1), 43–45.

Cook, C. (1995) *Pears Cyclopedia* (104th edn) London: Pelham Books.

Coughlan, R. (2001) An analysis of professional codes of ethics in the hospitality industry. *International Journal of Hospitality Management* 20 (2), 147–162

Crabtree, A., O'Reilly, P. and Worboys, G. (2002) Sharing experience in ecotourism certification: Developing an international ecotourism standard. Paper presented at the World Ecotourism Summit, Quebec City, May 19–22.

D'Amore, L.J. (1992) Promoting sustainable tourism: The Canadian Approach. *Journal of Tourism Management* 13, 258–262.

Davis, P.B. (1999) Beyond guidelines: A model for Antarctic tourism. *Annals of Tourism Research* 26 (3), 516–533.

Delta Airlines (1998) Gene Autry's cowboy code. *Sky Magazine,* August edition.

Derry, R. (1989) An empirical study of moral reasoning. *Journal of Business Ethics* 8, 855–862.

Dervaes, C. (1992) *The Travel Dictionary* (p. 45). Tampa, FL: Solitaire Pub.

Donaldson, T. and Dunfee, T.W. (1994) Toward a unified conception of business ethics: Interactive social contracts theory. *Academy of Management Review* 19, 252–284.

D'Sa, E. (1999) Wanted: Tourists with a conscience. *International Journal of Contemporary Hospitality Management* 11 (2/3), 64–68.

Dunfree, T.W. and Black, B.M. (1996) Ethical issues confronting travel agents. *Journal of Business Ethics* 15, 201–217.

Echtner, C.M. and Jamal, T.B. (1997) The disciplinary dilemma of tourism studies. *Annals of Tourism Research* 24 (4), 868–883.

ECoNETT (1999) World Travel and Tourism Council. On WWW at www.wttc.org. Accessed 30.06.00.

Edgell, D.L. (1999) *Tourism Policy: The Next Millennium.* Champaign, IL: Sagamore.

Edginton, C.R., Jordan, D.J., DeGraaf, D.G. and Edginton, S.R. (1995) *Leisure and Life Satisfaction: Foundational Perspectives.* Toronto: Brown & Benchmark.

Ehrenfeld, D. (1981) *The Arrogance of Humanism.* Oxford: Oxford University Press.

Ehrlich, P.R. (2000) *Human Natures: Genes, Cultures and the Human Prospect.* New York: Penguin.

Elliot, R. (1995) *Environmental Ethics.* Oxford: Oxford University Press.

England, G.W., Dhingra, O.P. and Agarwal, N.C. (1974) *The Manager and the Man: A Cross-Cultural Study of Personal Values.* Kent, OH: Kent State University Press.

Farrell, H and Farrell, B.J. (1998) The language of business codes of ethics: Implications of knowledge and power. *Journal of Business Ethics* 17 (6), 587–601.

Fayos-Solá, E. (1996) Tourism policy: A midsummer night's dream? *Tourism Management* 17 (6), 405–412.

Fennell, D.A. (2002) *Ecotourism Programme Planning.* Wallingford: CABI.

Fennell, D.A. (2003) *Ecotourism: An Introduction* (2nd edn) London: Routledge.

Fennell, D.A. (2004) Deep ecotourism: Seeking theoretical and practical reverence. In T.V. Singh (ed.) *New Horizons in Tourism: Strange Experiences and Stranger Practices* (pp. 109–120). Wallingford: CABI.

Fennell, D.A. (2006a) *Tourism Ethics.* Clevedon: Channel View Publications.

Fennell, D.A. (2006b) Evolution in tourism: The theory of reciprocal altruism and tourist–host interaction. *Current Issues in Tourism* 9 (2), 105–124.

Fennell, D.A. and Ebert, K. (2004) Tourism and the precautionary principle. *Journal of Sustainable Tourism* 12 (6), 461–479.

Fennell, D. A. and Malloy, D.C. (1995) Ethics and ecotourism: A comprehensive ethical model. *Journal of Applied Recreation Research* 20 (3), 163–183.

Ferrell, O.C. and Skinner, S.J. (1988) Ethical behavior and bureaucratic structure in marketing research organisations. *Journal of Marketing Research* 25, 103–109.

Finkler, W. and Higham, J. (2004) The human dimensions of whale watching: An analysis based on viewing platforms. *Human Dimensions of Wildlife* 9, 103–117.

Fleckenstein, M.P. and Huebsch, P. (1999) Ethics in tourism-reality or hallucination. *Journal of Business Ethics* 19, 137–142.

Font, X. (2001) Regulating the green message: The players in ecolabelling. In X. Font and R.C. Buckley (eds) *Tourism Ecolabelling: Certification and Promotion of Sustainable Management* (pp. 1–17). Wallingford: CABI.

Font, X. (2002) Environmental certification in tourism and hospitality: Progress, process and prospects. *Tourism Management* 23, 197–205.

Font, X. and Harris, C. (2004) Rethinking standards from green to sustainable. *Annals of Tourism Research* 31 (4), 986–1007.

Ford, R.C. and Richardson, W.D. (1994) Ethical decision making: A review of the empirical literature. *Journal of Business Ethics* 13, 207–224.

Forsyth, T. (1993) *Sustainable Tourism: Moving from Theory to Practice*. Godalming: WWF.

Frankfurt, H.G. (2005) *On bullshit*. Princeton: Princeton University Press.

Frankl, M.S. (1989) Professional codes: Why, how and with what impact? *Journal of Business Ethics* 8, 109–115.

Fritzsche, D.J. (1997) *Business Ethics: A Global and Managerial Perspective*. New York: McGraw-Hill.

Garofalo, C. and Geuras, D. (1999) *Ethics in the Public Service: The Moral Mind at Work*. Washington, DC: Georgetown University Press.

Garcia, J.C. (2000) Industry competition meets indigenous culture in Ecuadorian Amazon. *Tourism Concern* Bulletin 2 (Autumn), 4–5.

Garrod, B. and Fennell, D.A. (2004) An analysis of whale-watching codes of ethics. *Annals of Tourism Research* 31 (2), 334–352.

Garrod, B., Wilson, J. and Bruce, D. (2001) Planning for marine ecotourism in the EU Atlantic area: Good practice guidance. Project Report. Bristol: University of the West of England, Bristol.

Genot, H. (1995) Voluntary environmental codes of conduct in the tourism sector. *Journal of Sustainable Tourism* 3 (3), 166–172.

Gilligan, C. (1982) *In a Different Voice*. Cambridge, MA: Harvard University Press.

Gjerdalen, G. and Symko, C. (1999) The Johnstone Straight code of conduct for whale watching: Factors encouraging compliance. In P.W. Williams and I. Budke (eds) *On Route to Sustainability: Best Practices in Canadian Tourism* (pp. 15–19). Burnaby, BC: The Centre for Tourism Policy and Research, Simon Fraser University.

Gjerdalen, G. and Williams, P.W. (2000) An evaluation of the utility of a whale watching code of conduct. *Tourism Recreation Research* 25 (2), 27–37.

Glacier National Park (1999) *Glacier National Park Backcountry Guide*. West Glacier, MT: National Park Service.

Goodall, B. (1995) Environmental auditing: A tool for assessing the environmental performance of tourism firms. *Geographical Journal* 161 (1), 29–37.

Goodwin, H. and Francis, J. (2003) Ethical and responsible tourism: Consumer trends in the UK. *Journal of Vacation Marketing* 9 (3), 271–284.

Government of Canada (1998) *Voluntary Codes: A Guide for their Development and Use.* A joint initiative of the Office of Consumer Affairs, Industry Canada and the Regulatory Affairs Division, Treasury Board Secretariat. Ottawa: Distribution Services Communications Branch.

Gramann, J. and Vander Stoep, G. (1987) Prosocial behaviour theory and natural resource protection: A conceptual synthesis. *Journal of Environmental Management* 24, 247–257.

Green Globe 21 (2001) The Green Globe path. Online at www.greenglobe.org/index_cp.html. Accessed 03.06.02.

Grundy, S. (1987) *Curriculum: Product or Praxis.* Sussex: Falmer Press.

Grunfeld, R.S. (2002) Enforcing a written code of ethics: Well ingrained guidelines, given high priority, encourage executives to do the right thing. *New York Law Journal*, November 18. On WWW at www.clm.com/pubs/pub-1129630_1.html. Accessed 15.10.04.

Gunn, A.S. (1984) Preserving rare species. In T. Regan (ed.) *Earthbound: New Introductory Essays in Environmental Ethics* (pp. 297–332). New York: Random House.

Gunningham, N., Grabowsky, P. and Sinclair, D. (1998) *Smart Regulation: Designing Environmental Policy.* Oxford: Clarendon Press.

Hadjistavropoulos, T., Malloy, D.C., Douaud, P. and Smythe, W.E. (2002) Ethical orientation, functional linguistics and the code of ethics of the Canadian Nurses Association and the Canadian Medical Association. *Canadian Journal of Nursing Research* 34 (2), 35–51.

Hall, C.M. (1994) *Tourism and Politics: Policy, Power and Place.* Chichester: John Wiley & Sons.

Hamilton, W.D. (1964) The genetical evolution of social behaviour (I and II). *Journal of Theoretical Biology* 7, 1–52.

Hammond, R. (2005) Reaping the rewards. *Geographical* 77 (2), 97–102.

Harris, R. and Jago, L. (2001) Professional accreditation in the Australian tourism industry: An uncertain future. *Tourism Management* 22, 383–390.

Hawkes, S. and Williams, P. (1993) *From Principles to Practice: A Casebook of Best Environmental Practice in Tourism.* Burnaby, BC: Centre for Tourism Policy and Research, Simon Fraser University.

Hay, I. and Foley, P. (1998) Ethics, geography and responsible citizenship. *Journal of Geography in Higher Education* 22 (2), 169–183.

Heckel, G., Espejel, I. and Fischer, D.W. (2003) Issue definition and planning for whale watching management strategies in Ensenada, Mexico. *Coastal Management* 31, 277–296.

Heidegger, M. (1966) *Discourse on Thinking.* New York: Harper Torchbooks.

Higgs-Kleyn, N. and Kapelianis, D. (1999) The role of professional codes in regulating ethical conduct. *Journal of Business Ethics* 19, 363–374.

Hills, T. and Lundgren, J. (1977) The impact of tourism in the Caribbean: A methodological study. *Annals of Tourism Research* 4 (5), 248–267.

Hobbes, T. (1651/1957) *Leviathan.* New York: Oxford University Press.

Hobsbawm, E. (1994) *The Age of Extremes: A History of the World.* New York: Pantheon.

Hodgkinson, C. (1983) *The Philosophy of Leadership.* Oxford: Basil Blackwell.

Hodgkinson, C. (1996) *Administrative Philosophy.* New York: Pergamon Press.

Hofstede, G. (2001) *Culture's Consequence: Comparing Values, Behaviours, Institutions and Organisations across Nations.* Thousand Oaks, CA: Sage.

Holden, A. (2003) In need of a new environmental ethics for tourism? *Annals of Tourism Research* 30 (1), 95–108.

Honderisch, T. (ed.) (1995) *The Oxford Companion to Philosophy.* Oxford: Oxford University Press.

Honey, M. (2001) Setting standards: Certification programs in the tourism industry. *The International Ecotourism Society Newsletter* (1st and 2nd quarters), 1–4, 11.

Honey, M. (ed.) (2002) *Ecotourism and Certification: Setting Standards and Practice.* Washington, DC: Island Press.

Honey, M. (2003) Protecting Eden: Setting green standards for the tourism industry. *Environment* 45 (6), 8–22.

Honey, M. and Rome, A. (2001) *Certification and Ecolabelling.* Washington, DC: Institute for Policy Studies.

Hughes, P. (2001) Animals, values and tourism: Structural shifts in UK dolphin tourism provision. *Tourism Management* 22 (4), 321–329.

Hultsman, J. (1995) Just tourism: An ethical framework. *Annals of Tourism Research* 22 (3), 553–567.

Insula (2005) Online at http://www.insula.org/tourism/charte.htm. Accessed 06.05.05

Issarverdis, J-P. (2001) The pursuit of excellence: Benchmarking, accreditation, best practice and auditing. In D.B. Weaver (ed.) *The Encyclopedia of Ecotourism* (pp. 579–594).Wallingford: CABI.

Jafari, J. (2000) *Encyclopedia of Tourism.* London: Routledge.

Jamal, T.B. (2004) Virtue ethics and sustainable tourism pedagogy: Phronesis, principles and practice. *Journal of Sustainable Tourism* 12 (6), 530–545.

Jamal, T.B., Borges, M. and Stronza, A. (2006) The institutionalisation of ecotourism: Certification, cultural equity and praxis. *Journal of Ecotourism* 5 (3), 145–175.

Jaszay, C. (2001) *An Integrated Research Review of Ethics Articles in Hospitality Journals 1990 to 2000.* Northern Arizona University: Flagstaff.

Johnson, E. (1984) Treating the dirt. In T. Regan (ed.) *Earthbound: New Introductory Essays in Environmental Ethics* (pp. 345– 360). New York: Random House,

Johnson, O.E. (ed.) (1974) *Ethics.* New York: Holt, Rinehart and Winston.

Johnston, M. and Hall, C.M. (1995) Visitor management and the future of tourism in Polar regions. In C.M. Hall and M. Johnston (eds) *Polar Tourism: Tourism in the Arctic and Antarctic Regions* (pp. 297–313). Chichester: John Wiley and Sons.

Johnston, M.E. and Twynam, G.D. (1999) Evaluation of 1998 pilot projects: Linking tourism and conservation. Unpublished report submitted to WWF International.

Johnston, M.E. and Twynam, D.G. (2001) Evaluating achievement of sustainable tourism principles: The WWF Arctic Tourism Guidelines Initiative. In S.F. McCool and R.N. Moisey (eds) *Tourism, Recreation and Sustainability: Linking Culture and the Environment* (pp. 257–270). Wallingford: CABI.

Jos, P.H. (1988) Moral autonomy and the modern organisation. *Polity* 21, 321–343.

Kant, I. (1785/1988) *Grounding for the Metaphysics of Morals* (J.W. Ellington, trans.) Indianapolis, IN: Hackett Publishing.

Kant, I. (1785/2001) *Fundamental Principles of the Metaphysics of Morals* (A.W. Wood, trans.) New York: The Modern Library.

Karwacki, J. and Boyd, C. (1995) Ethics and ecotourism. *A European Review* 4, 225–232.

Klonoski, R.J. (2003) Unapplied ethics: On the need for classical philosophy in professional ethics education. *Teaching Business Ethics* 7, 21–35.

Knowles, T., Macmillan, S., Palmer, J., Grabowski, P. and Hashimoto, A. (1999) The development of environmental initiatives in tourism: Responses from the London hotel sector. *International Journal of Tourism Research* 1, 255–265.

Kohlberg, L. (1969) Stage and sequence: The cognitive developmental approach to socialisation. In D.A. Goslin (ed.) *Handbook of Socialisation Theory and Research*. Chicago: Rand McNally.

Kolk, A. and van Tulder, R. (2002) *International Codes of Conduct: Trends, Sectors, Issues and Effectiveness*. Publication by the Department of Business-Society Management. Online at www.fbk.eur.nl/DPT/VG8. Accessed 15.09.04.

Krohn, B., Franklin, B. and Ahmed, Z.U. (1991) The need for developing an ethical code for the marketing of international tourism services. *Journal of Professional Services Marketing* 8 (1), 189–200.

Kropotkin, P. (1902/1972) *Mutual Aid: A Factor in Evolution*. London: Allen Lane.

Ladkin, A. and Martinez Bertramini, A. (2002) Collaborative tourism planning: A case study of Cusco, Peru. *Current Issues in Tourism* 5 (2), 71–93.

Lang, D.L. (1986) Organisational culture and commitment. *Human Resource Quarterly* 3,191–196.

Lang, D.L. and Malloy, D.C. (2006) *Leadership: The Final Cause of Good and Evil*. Leeds: Wisdom House.

Lea, J.P. (1993) Tourism development ethics in the Third World. *Annals of Tourism Research* 20, 701–715.

Leopold, A. (1949/1991) *A Sand County Almanac*. New York: Ballantine Books.

Lere, J.C. and Gaumnitz, B.R. (2003) The impact of codes of ethics on decision making: Some insights from information economics. *Journal of Business Ethics* 48, 365–379.

L'Etang, J. (1992) A Kantian approach to codes of ethics. *Journal of Business Ethics* 11, 737–744.

Lickorish, L.J. (1991) Roles of government and the private sector. In L.J. Lickorish (ed.) *Developing Tourism Destinations*. Harlow: Longman.

Little, W., Fowler, H.W. and Coulson, J. (1973) *The Shorter Oxford English Dictionary on Historical Principles* (3rd edn; p. 685) Oxford: Oxford University Press.

Long, D.G. (1977) *Bentham on Liberty: Jeremy Bentham's Idea of Liberty in Relation to his Utilitarianism*. Toronto: University of Toronto Press.

Lusseau D. (2003) Male and female bottlenose dolphins *Tursiops spp.* have different strategies to avoid interactions with tour boats in Doubtful Sound, New Zealand. *Marine Ecology Progress Series* 257, 267–274.

Lusseau, DD. (2004) The state of the scenic cruise industry in Doubtful Sound in relation to a key natural resource: Bottlenose dolphins. In C.M. Hall and S.W. Boyd (eds) *Nature-Based Tourism in Peripheral Areas: Development or Disaster?* (pp. 246–260). Clevedon: Channel View.

Malloy, D.C., Doherty, A., Douad, P. and Brace, D. (2006) An ethical and linguistic content analysis of a professional management code. *International Journal of Sport Management* 7, 1–19.

Malloy, D.C. and Fennell, D.F. (1998a) Codes of ethics and tourism: An exploratory content analysis. *Tourism Management* 19 (5), 453–461.

Malloy, D.C. and Fennell, D.A. (1998b) Ecotourism and ethics: Moral development and organisational culture. *Journal of Travel Research* 36, 49–58.

Malloy, D.C. and Hadjistavropoulos, T. (1998) A philosophical value analysis of the Canadian Code of Ethics for Psychologists. *Canadian Psychology* 39 (3), 187–193).

Malloy, D.C., Hadjistavropoulos, T., Douaud, P., Smythe, W.E. (2002) The codes of ethics of the Canadian Psychological Association and the Canadian Medical Association: Ethical orientation and functional grammar analysis. *Canadian Psychology* 43 (4), 244–253.

Mamic, I. (2004) *Implementing Codes of Conduct: How Businesses Manage Social Performance in Global Supply Chains*. Sheffield: Greenleaf.

Marcus, G. (2004) *The Birth of the Mind*. New York: Basic Books.

Marcuse, H. (1998) Some social implications of modern technology. In D. Kellner (ed.) *Technology, War and Fascism: Collected Papers of Herbert Marcuse* (pp. 39–66) Routledge: London.

Martin, G. (1998) Once again: Why should business be ethical? *Business and Professional Ethics Journal* 17 (4), 39–60.

Mason, P. (1994) A visitor code for the Arctic. *Tourism Management* 15 (2), 93–97.

Mason, P. (1997) Tourism codes of conduct in the Arctic and Sub-Arctic Region. *Journal of Sustainable Tourism* 5 (2), 151–165.

Mason, P. and Mowforth, M. (1995) Codes of conduct in tourism. *Occasional Papers in Geography* No. 1. Plymouth: Department of Geographical Sciences, University of Plymouth.

Mason, P. and Mowforth, M. (1996) Codes of conduct in tourism. *Progress in Tourism and Hospitality Research* 2 (2), 151–167.

Mayr, E. (1988) *Toward a New Philosophy of Biology: Observations of an Evolutionist*. Cambridge, MA: The Belknap Press.

McArthur, S. (1998) Embracing the future of ecotourism, sustainable tourism and the EAA in the new millennium. *Proceedings of the Sixth Annual Conference of the Ecotourism Association of Australia* (pp. 1–14). Margaret River, Western Australia, October 29 to November 1.

McDonald, G. (1999) Business ethics: Practical proposals for organisations. *Journal of Business Ethics* 19, 143–158.

McDonald, G.M. and Zepp, R.A. (1989) Business ethics: Practical proposals. *Journal of Management Development* 8 (1), 55–66.

McKercher, B. (1993) Some fundamental truths about tourism: Understanding tourism's social and environmental impacts. *Journal of Sustainable Tourism* 1 (1), 6–16.

McLain, D.L. and Keenan, J.P. (1999) Risk, information and the decision about response to wrongdoing in an organisation. *Journal of Business Ethics* 19, 255–271.

Messmer, M. (2003) Does your company have a code of ethics? *Strategic Finance* 84 (10), 13–14.

Metelka, C.J. (1990) *The Dictionary of Hospitality, Travel and Tourism* (3rd. edn). New York: Delmar.

Midgley, M. (1994) *The Ethical Primate: Humans, Freedom and Morality*. London: Routledge.

Mihalic, T. (2000) Environmental management of a tourist destination: A factor of tourism competitiveness. *Tourism Management* 21, 65–78.

Milgram, S. (1974) *Obedience to Authority*. New York: Harper and Row.

Mill, J.S. (1861/1957) *Utilitarianism*. New York: Bobbs-Merrill.

Miller, A.S. (1991) *Gaia Connections: An Introduction to Ecology, Ecoethics and Economics*. Lanham, MD: Rowman & Littlefield Publishers, Inc.

Milne, R.J. (2004) ISPORS code of ethics for researchers: Is it ethical? *Value and Health* 7 (2), 107–111.

Molander, E.A. (1987) A paradigm for design promulgation and enforcement of ethical codes. *Journal of Business Ethics* 6, 619–631.

Montoya, I.D. and Richard, A.J. (1994) A comparative study of codes of ethics in health care facilities and energy companies. *Journal of Business Ethics* 13, 713–717.

Murphy, P. (1995) Corporate ethics statements: Current status and future prospects. *Journal of Business Ethics* 14, 727–740.

Newsome, D., Moore, S.A. and Dowling, R.K. (2002) *Natural Area Tourism: Ecology, Impacts and Management*. Clevedon: Channel View Publications.

Norton, B.G. (1993) Environmental ethics and weak anthropocentrism. In S.J. Armstrong and R.G. Botzler (eds) *Environmental Ethics: Divergence and Convergence* (pp. 286–289). New York: McGraw-Hill, Inc.

Norzalita, A.A. and Norjaya, M.Y. (2004) The influence of market orientation on marketing competency and the effect of internet-marketing integration. *Asia Pacific Journal of Marketing and Logistics* 16 (1), 3.

O'Boyle, E.J. and Dawson, L.E. (1992) The American Marketing Association Code of Ethics: Instructions for marketers. *Journal of Business Ethics* 11, 921–932.

O'Halloran, R. (1991) Ethics in hospitality and tourism education: The new managers. *Hospitality and Tourism Educator* 3 (3), 33–37.

Orams, M. (2000) Tourists getting close to whales: Is it what whale-watching is all about? *Tourism Management* 21, 561–569.

Ostrom, E. (2003) Toward a behavioral theory linking trust, reciprocity and reputation. In E. Ostrom and J. Walker (eds) *Trust and Reciprocity: Interdisciplinary Lessons from Experimental Research* (pp. 19–66). Sage, New York

Parker, S. (1999) Ecotourism, environmental policy and development. In. D.L. Soden and B.S. Steel (eds) *Handbook of Global Environmental Policy and Administration* (pp. 315–345). New York: Marcel Dekker, Inc.

Parsons, E.C.M. and Woods-Ballard, A. (2003) Acceptance of voluntary whalewatching codes of conduct in West Scotland: The effectiveness of governmental versus industry-led guidelines. *Current Issues in Tourism* 6 (2), 172–182.

Payne, D. and Dimanche, F. (1996) Towards a code of conduct for the tourism industry: An ethics model. *Journal of Business Ethics* 15, 997–1007.

Payne, R.J., Twynam, G.D. and Johnston, M.E. (1999) Tourism and sustainability in Northern Ontario. In J.G. Nelson, R.W. Butler and G. Wall (eds) *Tourism and Sustainable Development: Monitoring, Planning, Decision Making: A Civic Approach* (pp. 237–266). Waterloo, Ontario: University of Waterloo, Department of Geography.

Pearce, D. (1987) *Tourism Today: A Geographical Analysis*. New York: Wiley & Sons.

Pearce, J.A. and David, F. (1987) Corporate mission statements: the bottom line. *Academy of Management Executive* 1 (2), 109–116.

Peterson, T.R. (1997) *Sharing the Earth*. Columbia, SC: University of South Carolina Press.

Piaget, J. (1948) *The Moral Judgement of the Child*. Glencoe: Free Press.

Pigram, L. (2000) Benchmarking. In J. Jafari (ed.) *Encyclopedia of Tourism* (p. 51). London: Routledge.

Pinker, S. (2002) *The Blank Slate: The Modern Denial of Human Nature*. New York: Viking.

Pinkerton, E. and Weinstein, M. (1995) *Fisheries that Work: Sustainability through Community-Based Management*. Report 219. Vancouver, BC: David Suzuki Foundation.

Pirsig, R. (1975) *Zen and the Art of Motor Cycle Maintenance: An Inquiry into Values*. New York: Bantam Books.

Plummer, R. and Fennell, D.A. (in review) Exploring co-management theory: Prospects for sociobiology and reciprocal altruism. *Journal of Environmental Management*.

Poon, A. (1993) *Tourism, Technology and Competitive Strategies*. Wallingford: CABI.

Prabhupada, A.C.B.S. (1972) *Bhagavad Gita As It Is*. Los Angeles: The Bhaktivedanta Book Trust.

Przeclawski, K. (1996) Deontology of tourism. *Progress in Tourism and Hospitality Research* 2, 239–245.

Rachels, J. (1999) *The Elements of Moral Philosophy*. New York: Random House.

Raiborn, C.A. and Payne, D. (1990) Corporate codes of conduct: A collective conscience and continuum. *Journal of Business Ethics* 9, 879–889.

Rawls, J. (1971) *A Theory of Justice*. Cambridge: Harvard University Press.

Ray, R. (2000) *Management Strategies in Athletic Training* (2nd edn). Champaign, IL: Human Kinetics.

Regan, T. (2004) *The Case for Animal Rights*. Berkeley, CA: The University of California Press.

Richter, L. (1991) Political issues in tourism policy: A forecast. In D. Hawkins and J. Ritchie (eds) *World Travel and Tourism Review* (Vol. 1; pp. 189–193). London: CABI.

Ritchie, J.R. Brent (1999) Crafting a value-driven vision for a national tourism treasure. *Tourism Management* 20, 273–282.

Rivera, J. (2004) Institutional pressures and voluntary environmental behavior in developing countries: Evidence from the Costa Rican hotel industry. *Society and Natural Resources* 17, 779–797.

Rohitratana, K. (2002) SA8000: Tool to improve quality of life. *Managerial Auditing Journal* 17, 60–64.

Rolston III, H. (1986) Is there an ecological ethic? In H. Rolston III (ed.) *Philosophy Gone Wild: Essays in Environmental Ethics* (pp. 12–29). Buffalo, NY: Prometheus Books,

Rolston III, H. (2000) The land ethic at the turn of the millennium. *Biodiversity and Conservation* 9, 1045–1058.

Roe, D., Harris, C. and de Andrade, J. (2003) Addressing poverty issues in tourism standards: A review of experience. *PPT Working Paper No. 14*. Pro-Poor Tourism.

Ross, G.F. (2003) Workstress response perceptions among potential employees: The influence of ethics and trust. *Tourism Review* 58 (1), 25–33.

Ross. W.D. (1975) The right and the good. In K.J. Struhl and P.R. Struhl (eds) *Ethics in Perspective* (pp. 100–107). New York: Random House.

Rousseau, J.J. (1762/1979) *The Social Contract*. Harmondsworth: Penguin Books.

Russ-Eft, D. and Hatcher, T. (2003) The issue of international values and beliefs: The debate for a global HRD code of ethics. *Advance in Developing Human Resources* 5 (3), 296.

Ryan, C. (2002) Equity, management, power sharing and sustainability: Issues of the 'new tourism'. *Tourism Management* 23, 17–26.

Saltzman, J. (2004) Writing a code of ethics for your business. Online at www.shakeitbooks.com/stb-ethics.Writing%20a%20Code%20of%20Ethics%20for... Accessed 15.10.04.

Sartre, J.P. (1957) *Existentialism and Human Emotions*. New York: The Winston Library.

Sasidharan, V., Sirakaya, E. and Kerstetter, D. (2002) Developing countries and tourism ecolabels. *Tourism Management* 23, 161–174.

Saul, J.R. (2001) *On Equilibrium*. Toronto: Viking.

Saul, J.R. (2005) *The Collapse of Globalism and the Reinvention of the World*. Toronto: Penguin.

Saul, J.R. (1995) *The Unconscious Civilisation*. Toronto: Anansi.

Saura, I.G. (2000) Standardisation. In J. Jafari (ed.) *Encyclopedia of Tourism* (pp. 55–56). London: Routledge.

Scarpaci, C., Dayanthi, N. and Corkeron, P.J. (2003) Compliance with regulations by 'swim-with-dolphins' operations in Port Phillip Bay, Victoria, Australia. *Environmental Management* 31 (3), 342–347.

Scott, W.G. and Hart, D.K. (1979) *Organisational America*. Boston: Houghton Mifflin.

Scottish Natural Heritage (2005) The Scottish marine wildlife watching code. Online www.marinecode.org/index.asp. Accessed 11.02.05.

Seabrook, J and Burchill, J. (1994) Keep your shirt on. *New Statesman & Society* 7, 315–320.

Senge, P.M. (1990) *The Fifth Discipline: The Art and Practice of the Learning Organisation*. New York: Doubleday.

Sethi, S.P. (2000) Gaps in research in the formulation, implementation and effectiveness measurement of international codes of ethics. In O.F. Williams (ed.) *Global Codes of Ethics: An Idea Whose Time Has Come* (pp. 117–127). Notre Dame, IN: University of Notre Dame Press,

Sharpley, R. (1996) *Tourism and Leisure in the Countryside* (2nd edn). Huntington: ELM.

Shephard, K.L. and Royston-Airey, P.C.M. (2000) Exploring the role of part-time ecotourism guides in Central Southern England. *Journal of Sustainable Tourism* 8 (4), 324–332.

Singer, P. (1981) *The Expanding Circle: Ethics and Sociobiology*. New York: Farrer, Straus & Giroux.

Sirakayal, E. and Uysal, M. (1997) Can sanctions and rewards explain conformance behaviour of tour operators with ecotourism guidelines? *Journal of Sustainable Tourism* 5 (40), 322–332.

Smith, M. and Duffy, R. (2003) *The Ethics of Tourism Development*. London: Routledge.

Smith, S.L.J. (1990) *Dictionary of Concepts in Recreation and Leisure Studies*. Greenwood Press, New York.

Splettstoesser, J. (1999) IAATO's stewardship of the Antarctic environment: A history of tour operator's concern for a vulnerable part of the world. *International Journal of Tourism Research* 2, 47–55.

Starr, W. (1983) Codes of ethics: Toward a rule-utilitarian justification. *Journal of Business Ethics* 2, 99–106.

Stark, J.C. (2002) Ethics and ecotourism: Connections and conflicts. *Philosophy & Geography* 5 (1), 101–113.

Stefanovic, I.L. (1997) A code of ethics for Short Hills Park. In A. Wellington, A. Grenbaum and W. Cragg (eds) *Canadian Issues in Environmental Ethics* (pp. 246–258). Toronto: Broadview Press,

Stevens, B. (1994) An analysis of corporate ethical code studies: 'Where do we go from here'. *Journal of Business Ethics* 13, 63–69.

Stevens, B. (1997) Hotel ethical codes: A content analysis. *International Journal of Hospitality Management* 16 (3), 261–271.

Stevens, B. and Brownell, J. (2000) Ethics: Communicating standards and influencing behavior. *Cornell Hotel and Restaurant Administration Quarterly* (April), 39–43.

Stonehouse, B. (1990) A traveller's code for Antarctic visitors. *Polar Record* 26 (156), 46–58.

Superior National Forest (1998) *Will You Accept the Wilderness Challenge?* Washington, DC: Government Printing Office.

Swenson, W. (2000) Raising the ethics bar in a shrinking world. In O.F. Williams (ed.) *Global Codes of Ethics: An Idea Whose Time Has Come* (pp. 3–12). Notre Dame, IN: University of Notre Dame Press.

Sykes, J.B. (ed.) (1974) *The Concise Oxford Dictionary of Current English* (6th edn). Oxford: Clarendon Press.

Tapper, R. (2001) Tourism and socio-economic development: UK tour operators' business approaches in the context of the new international agenda. *International Journal of Tourism Research* 3, 351–366.

Taylor, P.W. (1986) *Respect for Nature: A Theory of Environmental Ethics*. Princeton: Princeton University Press.

Tearfund (2000) *A Tearfund Guide to Tourism: Don't Forget Your Ethics*. London: Tearfund.

Tearfund (2001) *Tourism: Putting Ethics into Practice*. London: Tearfund.

Theerapappisit, P. (2003) Mekong tourism development: Capital or social mobilisation? *Tourism Recreation Research* 28 (1), 47–56.

Tinkler, H. (2005) Ethics in business: The heart of the matter. *Executive Speeches* 19(5), 14–19.

Tourism Bill of Rights and Tourist Code (1985) On WWW at http://www.world-tourism.org/protect_children/statements/wto_a.htm. Accessed 04.12.06.

TIAC (1991) *Code of Ethics and Guidelines for Sustainable Tourism*. Ottawa: Tourism Industry Association of Canada in association with the National Roundtable on the Environment and Economy.

Travel Wire News (2004) 2004 to close with 70 million more international arrivals. Online at http://www.travelwirenews.com/cgi-script/csArticles/articles/000 022/002256.htm. Accessed 09.11.04.

Tribe, J. (2002) Education for ethical tourism action. *Journal of Sustainable Tourism* 10 (4), 309–324.

Tribe, J., Font, X., Griffiths, N., Vickery, R. and Yale, K. (2000) *Environmental Management for Rural Tourism and Recreation*. London: Cassell.

Trivers, R. (1971) The evolution of reciprocal altruism. *Quarterly Review of Biology* 46, 35–57.

Tucker, L.R., Stathakopolous, V. and Patti, C.H. (1999) A multidimensional assessment of ethical codes: The professional business association perspective. *Journal of Business Ethics* 19, 287–300.

UNEP (1995) Environmental code of conduct for tourism. *Technical Report* No. 29. Paris: United Nations.

Upchurch, R.S. and Ruhland, S.K. (1995) An analysis of ethical work climate and leadership relationship in lodging operations. *Journal of Travel Research* 34 (2), 36–42.

Valentine, P.S. (1992) Nature-based tourism. In B. Weiler and C.M. Hall (eds) *Special Interest Tourism* (pp. 105–128). London: Belhaven Press.

Vallen, G. and Casado, M. (2000) Ethical principles for the hospitality curriculum. *Cornell Hotel and Restaurant Quarterly* 41 (2), 44–51.

Van Zyl, L. (2002) Virtue theory and applied ethics. *South African Journal of Philosophy* 21 (2), 133–144.

Varandani, M. (1999) Differentiating between tourism and 'sustainable' tourism. Online at www.igc.org/scdngo/csd-7/tour_spac.htm. Accessed 03.03.99.

Veatch, R.M. (2003) *The Basics of Bioethics* (2nd edn). Upper Saddle River, NJ: Prentice Hall.

Victor, B. and Cullen, J. (1988) The organisational bases of ethical work climates. *Administrative Science Quarterly* 33, 101–125.

Vinton, G. (1990) Business Ethics: Busybody or corporate conscience? *Leadership & Organisational Development Journal* 11 (3), 4–11.

Vorley, W., Roe, D. and Bass, S. (2002) *Standards and Sustainable Trade: A Sectoral Analysis for the Proposed Sustainable Trade and Innovation Centre* (STIC). London: IIED.

WDCS (2000) Whale Watching Regulations. On WWW at http://www.wdcs.org/dan/publishing.nsf/allweb/1BA1ABAB38C5C139802568DB002EAD32. Accessed 3.10.05.

WDCS (2003) WDCS and whale watching. Online at http://www.wdcs.org/dan/publishing.nsf/allweb/1AA47C5A6C6672CE802568B002ED3F0. Accessed 03.10.03.

Watson, K., Skeat, H. and Barnett, B. 1998) Tourism management in the Great Barrier Reef, Australia. *Proceedings of the International Tropical Marine Ecosystems Management Symposium* (pp. 253–258). November 26–28, Townsville, Australia,

Weaver, G.R. (1995) Does ethics code design matter? Effects of ethics code rationales and sanctions on recipients'justice perceptions and content recall. *Journal of Business Ethics* 14, 367–385.

Weber, K. (1984) *The Globe Modern Dictionary.* Toronto: Globe/Modern Curriculum Press.

Webster, N. (2002) *Webster's Third International Dictionary* (p. 152). Springfield, MA: Merriam-Webster,

Weeden, C. (2005) Ethical tourism: Is its future in niche tourism? In M. Novelli (ed.) *Niche Tourism: Contemporary Issues, Trends and Cases* (pp. 233–245). Oxford: Butterworth Heinemann.

Weeden, C. (2001) Ethical tourism: An opportunity for competitive advantage? *Journal of Vacation Marketing* 8 (2), 141–154.

Wheat, S. (1999) Ethical tourism: Tourism Concern. Online at www.mcb.co.uk/services/conferen/jan98/eit/1_wheat.html. Accessed 01.11.99.

Wheeler, M. (1994) The emergence of ethics in tourism and hospitality. *Progress in Tourism, Recreation & Hospitality Management* 6, 46–56.

Wheeler, M. (1995) Tourism marketing ethics: An introduction. *International Marketing Review* 12 (4), 38–49.

Wheeller, B. (1994) Egotourism, sustainable tourism and the environment: A symbiotic, symbolic or shambolic relationship. In A.V. Seaton (ed.) *Tourism: The State of the Art.* Chichester: John Wiley and Sons.

White, L.Jr (1971) The historic roots of our ecologic crisis. In R.M. Irving and G.B. Priddle (eds) *Crisis* (pp. 5–17) London: Macmillan and Co.

Wiley, C. (1998) Reexamining perceived ethical issues and ethics roles among employment managers. *Journal of Business Ethics* 17, 147–161.

Wiley, C. (2000) Ethical standards for human resource management professionals: A comparative analysis of five major codes. *Journal of Business Ethics* 25: 93–114.

Williams, P.A. (1993a) Can beings whose ethics evolved be ethical beings? In M.H. Nitecki and D.V. Nitecki (eds) *Evolutionary Ethics* (pp. 233–239). Albany, NY: State University of New York.

Williams, P.A. (1993b) Environmental business practice: Ethical codes for tourism. In S. Hawkes and P. Williams (eds) *The Greening of Tourism: From Principles to Practice* (pp. 81–93). Burnaby, BC: Simon Fraser University Central Duplicating.

Williamson, M. (2003) Space ethics and protection of the space environment. *Space Policy* 19, 47–52.

Wood, G. and Rimmer, M. (2003) Codes of ethics: What are they really and what should they be? *International Journal of Value-Based Management* 16, 181–195.

WTO (2002) *Voluntary Initiatives for Sustainable Tourism.* Madrid: World Tourism Organisation.

WTTC (1997) *Agenda 21 for the Travel and Tourism Industry.* London: World Travel and Tourism Council.

WTTHRC (1998) *Steps to Success: Global Good Practices in Travel and Tourism Human Resources.* Vancouver: World Travel and Tourism Human Resource Development.

WWF (1997) Linking tourism and conservation in the Arctic (Supplement). *WWF-Arctic Bulletin* No. 4. Oslo: WWF.

WWF (2000) *Tourism Certification: An Analysis of Green Globe 21 and Other Tourism Certification Programmes.* World Wildlife Fund. On WWW at www.wwf.org.uk/filelibrary/pdf/tcr.pdf. Accessed 17.06.02.

Yunis, E. (2002) Keynote presentation to workshop on Sustainable Tourism Accreditation, convened by the Rainforest Alliance at the World Ecotourism Summit, Quebec.

Index

Page numbers in *italics* indicate boxes; *g* refers to glossary; *n* refers to endnote.

181